D0945427

THICKENING
GOVERNMENT

Paul C. Light

THICKENING GOVERNMENT

Federal Hierarchy and the Diffusion of Accountability

THE BROOKINGS INSTITUTION
Washington, D.C.

THE GOVERNANCE INSTITUTE
Washington, D.C.

Library of Congress Cataloging-in-Publication Data

Light, Paul Charles.
  Thickening government : federal hierarchy and the diffusion of
accountability / Paul C. Light
    p. cm.
  Includes bibliographical references and index.
    ISBN 0-8157-5250-4 (alk. paper).—ISBN 0-8157-5249-0 (pbk. : alk.
paper)
    1. Government executives—United States. 2. Bureaucracy—
United States. I. Title.
JK723.E9L53 1995
353—dc20   94-37043
                                                 CIP

9 8 7 6 5 4 3 2 1

The paper used in this publication meets the minimum requirements
of the American National Standard for Information Sciences—Perma-
nence of Paper for Printed Library Materials, ANSI Z39.48-1984

Set in Garamond

Typeset by Monotype Composition Company, Inc.
Baltimore, Maryland

Printed by R.R. Donnelley
Harrisonburg, Virginia

The Brookings Institution

The Brookings Institution is an independent, nonprofit organization devoted to nonpartisan research, education, and publication in economics, government, foreign policy, and the social sciences generally. Its principal purposes are to aid in the development of sound public policies and to promote public understanding of issues of national importance. The Institution was founded on December 8, 1927, to merge the activities of the Institute for Government Research, founded in 1916, the Institute of Economics, founded in 1922, and the Robert Brookings Graduate School of Economics, founded in 1924.

The Institution maintains a position of neutrality on issues of public policy to safeguard the intellectual freedom of the staff. Interpretations or conclusions in Brookings publications should be understood to be solely those of the authors.

The Governance Institute

The Governance Institute, a nonprofit organization incorporated in 1986, is concerned with exploring, explaining, and easing problems associated with both the separation and division of powers in the American federal system. It is interested in how the levels and branches of government can best work with one another. It is attentive to problems within an organization or between institutions that frustrate the functioning of government. The Governance Institute is concerned as well with those professions and mediating groups that significantly affect the delivery and quality of public services. The Institute's focus is on institutional process, a nexus linking law, institutions, and policy. The Institute believes that problem solving should integrate research and discussion. This is why the Institute endeavors to work with those decisionmakers who play a role in making changes in process and policy. The Institute currently has three program areas: problems of the judiciary; problems of the administrative state; and challenges to the legal profession.

Foreword

The president of the United States has never had more help than he does today. There have never been so many layers of management between the president and the front lines of government, nor so many presidential appointees and senior executives at each layer. Paul Light labels this phenomenon "thickening." Adding more layers of management increases the height of the hierarchy, while more appointees and executives at each layer increase the width. The two add up to thickening.

Using detailed organization charts collected for every department from every administration since 1960, Light asks six basic questions about the thickening of government: How thick is government? Why did government thicken? Does thickening matter? Where does thickening start? How does thickening endure? Can thickening be stopped?

The answers suggest that it is not so much the number of political appointees and senior executives that matters to government, but the way those key officials sort out into layers of management. Each new layer increases the distance between the top and the bottom of government, adding to the potential distortion downward of information and the movement upward of ideas for improvement. The answers also suggest that the thickening did not occur suddenly. As the tables in the appendix indicate, every president since Herbert Hoover has left government thicker. There is no party of thickening, nor any single president or Congress to hold accountable. Thickening appears to be an almost inexorable product of modern public management, although one that Light argues can be controlled.

This book is Light's second joint publication with the Brookings Institution and the Governance Institute. Paul Light is professor of public affairs at the University of Minnesota's Hubert H. Humphrey Institute of Public Affairs, a senior fellow of the Governance Institute, and a visiting fellow of the Brookings Institution. He gratefully acknowledges the initial financial support and continuing intellectual feedback of the Governance Institute and its president, Robert Katzmann. In addition, the author would like to thank his colleagues who provided input at various stages of this project, including John Brandl, Stephen Hess, Patricia Ingraham, James Jernberg, Donald Kettl, Rosalyn Kleeman, Thomas Mann, the anonymous reviewers who read the manuscript in detail, and the federal officials who gave their time for interviews on the project. Leslie Bruvold, Richard Christofferson, Kirk Johnson, Shannon Swangstue, and Lisa Zellmer all contributed to the project as research assistants; Alison Rimsky and Mary Ann Noyer verified its factual content; Ingeborg Lockwood provided administrative support; Janet Mowery edited the manuscript; and Robert E. Elwood prepared the index. The author also thanks his wife, Sharon Light, and his family for their patience and support.

Funding for the book was generously provided by the Dillon Fund.

The views expressed in this book are those of the author and should not be ascribed to the persons or organizations acknowledged above, to the trustees, officers, or staff members of the Brookings Institution, or to the directors, officers, or other staff members of the Governance Institute.

BRUCE K. MAC LAURY
President, the Brookings Institution

October 1994
Washington, D.C.

Contents

Top-Level Titles Open in Government, 1992

secretary
chief of staff to the secretary
deputy chief of staff

deputy secretary
chief of staff to the deputy
  secretary
associate deputy secretary

under secretary
principal deputy under secretary
deputy under secretary
principal associate deputy under
  secretary
associate deputy under secretary
assistant deputy under secretary
associate under secretary

assistant secretary
chief of staff to the assistant
  secretary
principal deputy assistant
  secretary
deputy assistant secretary
associate deputy assistant
  secretary

deputy associate deputy assistant
  secretary
assistant general counsel/
  inspector general
deputy assistant general counsel/
  inspector general

administrator
chief of staff to the administrator
principal deputy administrator
deputy administrator
associate deputy administrator
assistant deputy administrator
associate administrator
deputy associate administrator
assistant administrator
deputy assistant administrator
associate assistant administrator

principal office director
office director
principal deputy office director
deputy office director
assistant deputy office director
associate office director
deputy associate office director

assistant office director
deputy assistant office director
principal division director
division director
deputy division director
associate division director
assistant division director

deputy assistant division
    director
sub–division director
deputy sub–division director
associate sub–division director
assistant sub–division director
branch chief

1

How Thick Is Government?

Nineteen hundred and thirty-seven was a very good year for federal hierarchy. Franklin Roosevelt's New Deal was in full swing; agencies were rising faster than skyscrapers. Federal employment grew from 600,000 in 1930 to nearly 900,000 seven years later, and the federal budget increased more than tenfold. Sixty new agencies took their place in the executive branch.

The federal hierarchy was clearly starting to thicken. New agencies and units widened government's base, while new management layers increased its height. Together, these two tightly related events pushed the hierarchy upward and outward, expanding the president's scope beyond any hint of scientific control.

Into this administrative chaos stepped a small group of scholars whose confidence in the science of management would shape the government hierarchy into the very present. Their goal was a tightly rationalized bureaucracy, led by a fully informed president. Alas, as this book suggests, their management principles may have created exactly the opposite outcome, an unwieldy, towering hierarchy in which accountability is diffuse at best and the president is sometimes the last to know. This chapter explores the history in more detail, while offering a first look at how the federal hierarchy has changed over the past fifty years.

The Principles of Administration

No scholar was more confident of the value of tight coordination than Luther Gulick, who published his *Papers on the Science of Administration* with L. Urwick in 1937.[1] The book was filled with detailed insights into the business of government, not the least of which was a new acronym,

POSDCORB, to describe the work of the executive: *P*lanning, *O*rganizing, *S*taffing, *D*irecting, *C*oordinating, *R*eporting, and *B*udgeting. ¡

The Principles, as the associated public administration scholarship of the time eventually became known, involved much more than a simple acronym, however. Gulick and his Institute of Public Administration colleagues offered a wide set of core ideas for organizing public enterprise—from authorizing executives to reorganize their agencies freely to decentralizing administration.[2] Central to rising federal hierarchy were Gulick's three basic principles of coordination.

First, Gulick argued for a unity of command. "From the earliest times," Gulick wrote, "it has been recognized that nothing but confusion arises under multiple command. 'A man cannot serve two masters . . .' The rigid adherence to the principle of unity of command may have its absurdities; these are, however, unimportant in comparison with the certainty of confusion, inefficiency, and irresponsibility which arise from the violation of the principle."[3] No matter how many agents might report from below, all had to know who was the boss.

Second, Gulick and his colleagues argued that this one master needed help, hardly a surprise given the range of duties envisioned under POSDCORB. Executives could not be expected to do everything. It is also no surprise, given Gulick's view "that the job of the President as Chief Executive is POSDCORB," that he would emphatically endorse the creation of an Executive Office of the President composed of "a group of able and informed men who will see that the President has before him all relevant facts and that all appropriate clearance is secured before decisions are made and that a decision once made is known to those who are involved."[4] In particularly large enterprises—read U.S. government—chief executives would have to delegate pieces of POSDCORB to trusted allies and units.

Third, and most important to the thickening of hierarchies, Gulick argued for a narrow span of control. A human being could supervise only so many people. This principle was not based on mistrust, however. Gulick and his colleagues made no mention of scheming subordinates. Rather, they were quite forgiving regarding the "inexorable limits of human nature." Gulick wrote:

> Just as the hand of man can span only a limited number of notes on the piano, so the mind and will of man can span but a limited number of immediate managerial contacts. . . . The limit of control is partly a matter of the limits of knowledge, but even more is it a matter of the

limits of time and energy. As a result the executive of any enterprise can personally direct only a few persons. He must depend on these to direct others, and upon them in turn to direct still others, until the last man in the organization is reached.[5]

Gulick clearly understood that spans of control would vary with the size of the organization and the nature of the task. "Where the work is diversified, qualitative, and particularly when the workers are scattered, one man can supervise only a few. This diversification, dispersion, and non-measurability is of course most evident at the very top of any organization."[6] For the precise number of subordinates, Gulick relied on research by a French management consultant, V. A. Graicunas, who concluded that six was usually the maximum:

> Generally speaking, in any department of activity the number of separate items to which the human brain can pay attention at the same time is strictly limited. In very exceptional cases, for instance, an individual can memorize groups of figures of more than six digits when read out and can repeat them accurately after a brief interval. But in the vast majority of cases the "span of attention" is limited to six digits. The same holds good of other intellectual activities.[7]

Whether driven by hubris or just plain confidence, the Principles set a bold course for the president. Follow these guidelines, they seemed to say, and all will be well. The machine would go of itself. The Principles were not without their critics, however. They prompted almost two decades of intense review and spawned an entire generation of research designed to disprove the notion that organizations could be governed by any hard and fast rules. This nearly unrelenting attack uncovered at least two potentially fatal flaws in the Principles.

The first was that the principles did not operate in isolation from each other. Some contradicted, others interacted. A narrow span of control and staff assistance for the president meant a taller rather than shorter hierarchy. The resulting mischief was central to Herbert Simon's critique of what he labeled "the proverbs of administration." "It is a fatal defect of the current principles of administration," Simon wrote in 1945, "that, like proverbs, they occur in pairs. For almost every principle one can find an equally plausible and acceptable contradictory principle. Although the two principles of the pair will lead to exactly opposite organizational recommendations, there is nothing in the theory to indicate which is the proper one to apply."[8]

Consider the contradiction between the span-of-control principle and the efficiency principle. "The dilemma is this:" Simon noted, "in a large organization with interrelations between members, a restricted span of control inevitably produces excessive red tape, for each contact between organization members must be carried upward until a common superior is found. If the organization is at all large, this will involve carrying all such matters upward through several levels of officials for decision, and then downward again in the form of orders and instruction—a cumbersome and time-consuming process."[9] As this book suggests, the contradiction appears to have been resolved in favor of span of control and likely to the detriment of administrative efficiency and the one-master rule.

The second flaw in the Principles was that Gulick and his associates seemed to view organizations as neutral tools of executive direction, things to be controlled through simple command and control. Gulick did realize that, "next to the church, government organizations are in all civilizations the most vigorous embodiments of immortality." Yet, after noting that government's monopoly status protects it from the "purifying influence of competition," Gulick reached the conclusion that this immortality shows "the ultimate elasticity of governmental institutions." After all, governments would not endure if they did not somehow "mend their ways and their policies so that they may survive."[10] It was an exceedingly hopeful assumption.

Alas, as Herbert Kaufman would later find in asking, "Are government organizations immortal?," government agencies, and the bureaucratic structures within them, are remarkably interested in long life. "They are not helpless, passive pawns in the game of politics as it affects their lives;" wrote Kaufman, "they are active, energetic, persistent participants." Their leaders become quickly attached to the cause, even if they were brought to the job with a mandate to end the life of their organization. "Once aroused, they have a large arsenal of weapons to employ in their agencies' defense. They cultivate their allies and the mass media. Covertly and openly, they attack and try to embarrass their adversaries. They strike bargains to appease the foes they cannot overcome. If this sounds like warfare, it is—at least a type of warfare, a struggle for organizational existence."[11]

Every agency born will not survive, a point well illustrated by the demise of the alphabet agencies established in the 1930s to combat the

Great Depression. Nevertheless, Kaufman's research shows an actuarial balance in favor of long life. Tracing 175 government organizations from 1923 to 1973, Kaufman found that 148, or 85 percent, were still alive at the end of the fifty-year period. Some had fallen to a lesser bureaucratic rank; others had moved from their original departmental orbit to float elsewhere in the executive branch. Despite the occasional deaths, "The chances that an organization in the 1923 sample would be not only alive in 1973 but in virtually the same status were quite good; 109 of the original 175 (over 62 percent, or better than three out of five) were in this situation."[12] Alongside these impressive survival rates, government celebrated the birth of 246 new units, an average of five a year, a rate roughly double that in the 1874–1923 era.

These birth and survival rates raise troubling questions about the ultimate shape of the federal hierarchy. "For example," Kaufman muses, "suppose the number of units in a sample comparable to this one in [the year] 2023 bears the same ratio to the 1973 population that the 1973 population bears to the 1923 group. The 2023 organizational sample would then consist of 887 units, including 333 survivors from 1973 and 554 created in the five decades following."[13] Although there is a great deal of chance associated with the survival of any organization, a point made explicit in Kaufman's later work, the general trend appears inexorable.[14] Indeed, Kaufman writes of "a 'built-in' thrust that encourages and assists the ever finer division of labor in organizations."

> Collectively, if this hypothesis is valid, these insignificant changes could transform administrative structures without anyone ever having made a single, major, deliberate decision to alter them. Much of the growth observed in this study seems to have occurred this way. It may have been hastened or slowed by a favorable or hostile presidential administration or perhaps by other chance factors. . . . The driving force, however, is inherent and unremitting.[15]

Gulick's Principles are likely only an expression of this driving force, for concerns about hierarchy have existed for thousands of years. Public administration scholar Marshall Dimock found evidence of thickening in ancient Egypt—a papyrus from a Roman officer to the district governor of Middle Egypt complaining about the number of persons who "have invented titles for themselves, such as comptroller, secretary, or superintendent, whereby they procure no advantage to the Treasury but [to] swallow up the profits. It has therefore become necessary for me to send you instructions to arrange a single superintendent of good standing to be chosen for each estate on the responsibility of the local municipal council, and to abolish all remaining offices, though the superintendent elected shall have power to choose two, or at most three, assistants."[16] Administrative efficiency, unity of command, staff assistance—all were present in 288 A.D.

Whatever their origins, Gulick's Principles have survived. "Abstract doctrine has been enshrined in practice," Kaufman wrote in 1978, after publishing *Are Government Organizations Immortal?*

> Staff assistance for executives resulted not only in the Executive Office of the President, which was created in 1939 and experienced very rapid growth almost continuously from that time on, but in corresponding multiplication of deputy secretaries, under secretaries, assistant secretaries; assistants and deputies to all these new lieutenants; and staff units (legal counsel, public relations, congressional relations, personnel, administrative management, housekeeping services, budgeting, policy planning, and others) in virtually all the departments.[17]

Indeed, the interaction between span of control and staff assistance goes some way toward explaining the proliferation of hierarchy documented in this book.

Yet the irony in the Principles is not that they survived. Public administration scholar Dwight Waldo predicted three decades ago that the classical theory underpinning the principles "will be around a long, long time."[18] Rather, the irony is that the original assumptions underpinning the principles may no longer hold. If, in fact, supervisors can handle more than a handful of subordinates at one time, and if they can process much more information than once thought humanly possible, then perhaps the thickening of government, and the diffusion of accountability that goes with it, is no longer needed. If so, the burden of proof would fall to those who defend the thickening in spite of the information distortion, administrative inertia, disunity of command, and the like, that appear to be associated with increased distance between the top and bottom of organizations. Is tight supervision truly worth the cost?

The Changing Shape of Government

Measuring the height and width of the hierarchy, which together create the thickening discussed in this book, is a daunting task. Because no department keeps detailed organization charts covering all employees top to bottom, no one knows how many layers of management really exist or the true span of control at different levels of the departments.

The traditional surrogate is to divide the number of managerial employees into the number of nonmanagerial employees. The higher this span-of-control ratio, the flatter the organization.[19] Alas, span-of-control ratios reveal little about the height or width of a hierarchy or about the actual layer-by-layer distance between the top and bottom of government.

The only sure method for tracking the changing shape of government is to draw the organization charts from scratch using federal telephone books, lists of presidential appointee "plums," government organization manuals, and congressional documents, all of which were used to construct the core tables in the appendix. The 126 charts drawn for this book—one for every department of government that existed in 1935, in 1952, and at the end of every four-year administration since 1960—clearly reveal a thickening government. (Because the organization charts were assembled from imperfect sources, readers are urged to read the appendix for needed explanations and caveats. The numbers used below are best viewed as illustrations of the trends, not absolute proof.)

Thickening at the Top

There is no question that today the federal government has more leaders than ever. As the core tables show, the total number of senior executives and presidential appointees grew from 451 in 1960 to 2,393 in 1992, a 430 percent increase. The president is the "one true master" of a very large empire, indeed.

However, it is not just the sheer number of leaders that matters. More important may be how those leaders sort into layer upon layer of management. The top of the federal government contains senior management layers that simply did not exist thirty years ago. In 1960, there were seventeen layers of management at the very top of government, of which eight existed in at least half or more of the departments. By 1992, there were thirty-two layers, of which seventeen existed in at least half the departments (see table 1-1).

It is important to note that these thirty-two layers do not stack neatly one on top of the other to compose a unified chain of command, however. Some layers come into play on some issues and not on others. Nor do all of the layers exist in every department. Some only exist in a

TABLE 1-1. *The Layering of Government, Selected Years, 1960–92*

Measure	1960	1972	1980	1992
Layers open I–IV	12	13	15	21
Layers institutionalized[a] I–IV	5	7	8	12
Layers open V	5	8	10	11
Layers institutionalized V	3	5	4	5
Layers open I–V	17	21	25	32
Layers institutionalized I–V	8	12	12	17

SOURCE: See appendix.
a. A layer is considered institutionalized if it is found in half or more of the departments.

single department—only the Defense Department has assistant deputy under secretaries; the Energy Department, the only principal associate deputy under secretary. Others are still spreading outward—only six departments had associate deputy secretaries in 1992; only four had chiefs of staff to assistant secretaries. Of the thirty-two layers open, seventeen can be called common to almost all the departments.

Only five of the thirty-two layers are automatically subject to presidential appointment and Senate confirmation: secretary, deputy secretary, under secretary, assistant secretary, and administrator. Almost all the rest have come into being under presidential or departmental orders. This is not to suggest that the title creep is accidental, for departments pay great attention to the latest fashion in bureaucratic nomenclature. Rather, presidents and departments are mostly free to establish titles as they wish, as is Congress.

Unless an old layer is stripped out along the way—a rare occurrence, indeed—each new layer obviously increases distance between the top and bottom of government. Each one also begins to attract more occupants over time. More layers of leaders; more leaders at each layer. Between 1960 and 1992, the number of department secretaries increased from 10 to 14, the number of deputy secretaries from 6 to 21, under secretaries from 14 to 32, deputy under secretaries from just 9 to 52, assistant secretaries from 81 to 212, deputy assistant secretaries from 77 to 507, administrators from 90 to 128, and deputy administrators from 52 to 190 (see table 1-2).

As this sediment has thickened over the decades, presidents have grown increasingly distant from the front lines of government, and the front lines from them. Clinton faced a more complicated hierarchy than

TABLE 1-2. *The Widening of Government, Selected Years, 1960–92*

Measure	1960	1972	1980	1992
Occupants. Executive levels I–IV	249	475	928	1,626
Occupants. Executive level V	202	370	651	767
Total occupants I–V	451	845	1,579	2,393

SOURCE: See appendix.

any president in history, one in which reaching down to Gulick's every "last man in the organization" could be nearly impossible.

Individual layers do disappear from time to time over the years but almost always return an administration or two down the line. The largest number of departments to adopt a new layer at one time is eight, recorded in 1976 at the associate administrator rank, following a drop of four at the same rank just four years earlier.

The next largest number of departments to adopt a new layer is five, found at three different points in the thirty-year history: at the associate deputy assistant secretary layer in 1960, and at the chief of staff to the secretary layer and deputy secretary layer in 1988. Otherwise, the diffusion occurs one or two departments at a time. Similarly, the largest number of departments to drop a title at one time is three, recorded in 1992 when three departments abolished their under secretary posts when the layer was elevated to deputy secretary rank. Historical trends suggest that those under secretaries will soon be back.

The core tables contain two other patterns worth noting. The first is the growth of the assistant secretary compartment, which contains all assistant secretaries and their associated deputies, associates, and so forth. The compartment grew from just 43 occupants and two layers in 1935 to 1,439 and eight layers a half century later. This growth is particularly impressive when compared with that of the administrator compartment just below. The two compartments were roughly equal in 1960: there were 87 assistant secretaries and 119 associated titles, what this book calls title-riders versus 90 administrators and 112 title-riders. Seven presidents later, the administrator compartment was only half as large as the assistant secretary compartment: 128 administrators and 639 title-riders versus 212 assistant secretaries and 1,227 derivatives of one kind or another.

Although the administrator compartment still accounted for a rather sizable number of layers—eleven in 1992—Presidents Ronald Reagan and George Bush were mostly successful in imposing a twelve-year diet on new administrator titles. The assistant secretary compartment grew 77 percent during the Reagan and Bush years; the administrator compartment only 18 percent. It is too early to tell whether the weight will return under a Democrat or two.

The second pattern is the accelerated thickening of all offices since 1976. This could be a lagging effect of Johnson's Great Society or a consequence of Nixon's effort to create an administrative presidency run by a growing number of handpicked political aides. It could also be a product of the 1978 Civil Service Reform Act, which gave the president a greater say in overseeing the newly created Senior Executive Service (SES), composed of the most senior career officers in government.

Looking at 1988–92, public administration scholars Patricia Ingraham, Elliot Eisenberg, and James Thompson report that SES appointees increased about 22 percent, up 1,400 positions over the four years: "Three quarters of this increase occurred during the Bush Administration, when the total number of SES appointees increased from 7,057 in 1988 to 8,130 at the end of 1992, an increase of 1,073 appointees."[20] These senior appointees had to go someplace.

The acceleration could also be a consequence of some underlying thrust. Just as Kaufman argues that the birth of new agencies may be geometric, so too might the expansion of the management ranks below. Each assistant secretary in 1960 accounted for just 1.4 title-riders; each assistant secretary in 1992 accounted for 5.8. The compartments surrounding the top jobs are clearly flooding upward, giving pause to those who believe that downsizing the middle levels of government will somehow eliminate what Kaufman calls the underlying "incessant, uncontrived division and subdivision" of labor that generates thickening.[21]

Ultimately, these core numbers confirm Hugh Heclo's earlier research in *A Government of Strangers*. Using an imaginary time traveler as his storyteller, Heclo writes of "organizational abundance":

> If he could find his old offices, the time-traveling clerk would discover not only a larger number of people but, more important, people organized into more layers higher in the department and divided into more specialized divisions with each layer. . . . Whereas in all likelihood the bureau clerk's chief reported to a department head who had at most one or two ad hoc assistants, today there is a luxuriance of intermediating organizational layers—assistant secretaries and depu-

ties, specialized staff assistants, and what in Washington jargon are termed "shops" for management analysis, policy evaluation, automatic data processing, auditing, budgeting, and many more activities.[22]

As Heclo suggests, the thickening of government is not caused solely by new departments, a point that will be examined in further detail in chapter 4. The number of occupants in the top jobs at the Department of Agriculture increased from 81 in 1960 to 242 in 1992, at the Commerce Department from 29 to 217, at the Defense Department from 85 to 287, at the Interior Department from 50 to 160, at the Justice Department from 49 to 175, at the Labor Department from 23 to 115, at the State Department from 50 to 154, and at the Treasury Department from 46 to 219. And, even though the Education Department was divided from the Department of Health, Education, and Welfare in 1978, the old shell of HEW still increased from 27 in 1960 to 339 thirty years later. The average executive hierarchy looks very different today as a result of the growth (see table 1-3).[23]

Thickening also requires far more than hungry appointees looking for better plums.[24] It often requires a kind of building material. Some of the expansion recorded in the core tables involved whole agencies converted or merged into cabinet departments—for example, the Federal Aviation Administration's merger into the new Department of Transportation. Some involved internal units that rose steadily within their existing departments—the core tables are filled with deputy secretaries who were once under secretaries, under secretaries who were once assistant secretaries, and assistant secretaries who were once administrators. Others involved pieces of the secretary's office that were pushed downward into the hierarchy—for example, the offices of congressional or intergovernmental affairs that were made into assistant secretaryships in the 1970s and 1980s. Still others involved what appeared to be entirely new units that never existed before—for example, the offices of Inspector General, which were actually created by consolidating a rather eclectic collection of lower-level audit and investigatory offices into a single unit at the assistant secretary level.

Of some importance to the expansion of departmental hierarchies, therefore, is a steady supply of elevation fodder. At the federal level, that supply appears to be nearly inexhaustible. From 1960 to the present, for example, the number of independent agencies counted by the *U.S. Government Manual* rose from fifty-three to fifty-nine. This growth

TABLE 1-3. *Number of Occupants in the Average Department Hierarchy, Selected Years, 1960–92* [a]

Layer (Primary Title)	1960	1972	1980	1992
Secretary	1	1	1	1
Chief of staff	. . .	. . .	. . .	1
Deputy secretaries	. . .	. . .	1	2
Associate deputy secretaries	. . .	. . .	. . .	. . . [f]
Under secretaries	2	2	2	2
Deputy under secretaries	. . .	3	3	4
Associate deputy under secretaries	. . .	. . .	. . .	. . . [g]
Assistant secretaries [b]	9	10	12	15
Chief of staff to assistant secretaries	. . .	. . .	. . .	. . . [h]
Principal deputy assistant secretaries	. . .	. . .	. . .	5
Deputy assistant secretaries [c]	8	14	28	36
Associate deputy assistant secretaries [d]	2	5	7	18
Deputy associate deputy assistant secretaries [e]	. . .	. . .	. . .	9
Assistant general counsels/inspectors general	. . .	5	10	15
Deputy assistant general counsels/ inspectors general	. . .	. . .	. . .	4
Administrators	9	10	9	9
Principal deputy administrators	. . .	1	. . .	. . .
Deputy administrators	5	9	11	14
Assistant deputy administrators	. . .	. . .	. . .	. . . [i]
Associate administrators	. . .	4	5	8
Deputy associate administrators	. . .	. . .	. . .	. . . [j]
Assistant administrators	6	9	11	11
Deputy assistant administrators	. . .	. . .	. . .	5

SOURCE: Coding of *Federal Yellow Book*, Monitor Publishing. Italics indicate the primary title in a compartment. Ellipses indicate that a layer has not yet been created or does not exist in at least half the departments in that year.
   a. Layers must exist in at least half the departments to be included.
   b. Includes general counsel and inspector general.
   c. Includes deputy inspector general and deputy general counsel.
   d. Includes associate assistant secretary, associate inspector general, and associate general counsel.
   e. Includes deputy associate general counsel.
   f. Six departments had the title.
   g. Six departments had the title.
   h. Five departments had the title.
   i. Four departments had the title.
   j. Six departments had the title.

happened despite the elevation of a half dozen independent agencies to cabinet rank through the establishment of the Departments of Housing and Urban Development (HUD), Transportation, Energy, and Veterans Affairs.

At the bottom line, whether in the number of independent agencies, new departments, small offices to push down, or old offices to split or raise up, there is little reason to expect anything other than growth. Each new layer or position may be created for the most rational reasons.

Yet something else is going on, something almost inevitable, that "built-in thrust" Kaufman highlighted. It appears worth attacking but likely will not be dented with just one pass and not just at the middle-management level.

Thickening at the Middle

This book is primarily about upper-level thickening, where histories are clearer and impacts are usually greater. Nevertheless, thickening has occurred in the middle too, where the number of managers and supervisors continues to grow.

Unfortunately, it is nearly impossible to draw detailed organization charts covering the 165,000 managers that now work in the middle of government. The best one can do is chart the growth among a smaller number of titles toward the top of the middle at one or two points in time. Those charts—one each for every departmental office listed in the 1980 and 1992 *Federal Yellow Book* telephone directories—suggest that the office director compartment also thickened over the years (see table 1-4).

Office directors, division chiefs, bureau heads, and their assistants added an additional twenty layers and over 13,000 occupants to the departmental hierarchy in 1992. The most growth occurred at the office director title itself, where the number of directors jumped 58 percent. However, because the total number of layers has remained steady at twenty, the average office structure has grown much wider but not taller (see table 1-5).

Once again, not all of the layers exist in all of the departments. Of the twenty, nine can be called common to almost all. Adding the assorted layers together—from the secretary on down to the branch chief—the federal hierarchy now has fifty-two layers open for occupancy.

Even fifty-two may be a bit of an undercount, however. After all, most under secretaries, assistant secretaries, and administrators have office directors, division directors, bureau chiefs, and so forth, of their own. The total number of layers open for occupancy may actually be closer to a hundred than fifty. And that is just at the very top. Exit Washington for the federal regional offices, and the thickness increases further. Exit the regional offices for the field and district units, where federal services are actually delivered, and the thickness grows almost beyond comprehension.

TABLE 1-4. *The Thickening of Office Compartments,*
1980 and 1992

	1980		1992	
Layer	Departments	Occupants	Departments	Occupants
Principal office director	. . .	. . .	1	17
Office director	13	1,090	14	1,721
Principal deputy office director	2	3	3	13
Deputy office director	13	493	14	640
Associate deputy office director	2	2	. . .	. . .
Assistant deputy office director	2	7	1	4
Associate office director	10	170	8	108
Deputy associate office director	2	25	5	18
Assistant associate office director	1	2	. . .	. . .
Assistant office director	11	240	11	138
Deputy assistant office director	5	20	3	14
Sub office director	1	12	. . .	. . .
Principal division director	. . .	. . .	1	1
Division director	13	3,555	14	4,494
Deputy division director	12	343	14	541
Associate division director	5	52	8	66
Assistant division director	9	315	9	260
Deputy assistant division director	1	4	1	8
Sub–division director	7	501	6	409
Deputy sub-division director	4	20	4	97
Associate sub-division director	. . .	. . .	2	26
Assistant sub-division director	2	6	1	8
Branch chief	13	4,169	14	4,532
Total	20	11,029	20	13,115

SOURCE: See table 1-3.

Together, the growing height and width of the senior hierarchy, from secretaries on down to branch chiefs, may have changed the very shape of government. In the 1950s, the federal government looked like a relatively flat bureaucratic pyramid, with few senior executives, a somewhat larger number of middle managers, and a very large number of front-line employees. By the 1970s, it was beginning to look like a circus tent, with a growing corps of senior political and career executives, a sizable "bulge" of middle managers and professionals, and a shrinking number of front-line employees.

Through the 1980s and 1990s, it was moving toward a pentagon, with even more political and career executives at the top, and almost

TABLE 1-5. *Number of Occupants in the Average Office Hierarchy, 1980 and 1992* [a]

Measure	1980	1992
Office director	84	123
Deputy office director	38	46
Associate office director	13	8
Assistant office director	18	13
Division director	273	321
Deputy division director	26	39
Associate division director	. . .	5
Assistant division director	35	19
Sub–division director	39	. . .
Branch chief	321	324

SOURCE: See table 1-3.

equal numbers of many middle-level and front-line employees. In 1983 there was one employee at the middle for every 1.6 on the front line. By 1992 the ratio was moving down toward one-to-one.

If current trends continue, the federal hierarchy may eventually resemble a circle, with very few employees at the bottom, hordes of managers, supervisors, and technical analysts of one kind or another at the middle, and a vast coterie of political and career executives at the top. The rest of the traditional bureaucratic pyramid will still exist, of course, not filled in by federal employees, but by those who work for the increasing number of contractors, nonprofits, and state and local agencies that deliver services once provided above.

It is important to note that the causes of middle-level thickening may be very different from those shaping upper-level thickening. Although both appear to be shaped by Gulick's span-of-control principle, middle-level thickening also responds to at least two other factors that have less play at the top.

The most familiar culprit is the growing pay gap between public and private salaries. Informal efforts to close this gap through promotions may produce more middle-level managers than might otherwise be expected—adding supervisory duties to a nonsupervisory job is the easiest way to justify a promotion and the pay that goes with it.[25] The Congressional Budget Office argued in 1984, for example, that "the gradual increase in average grade commenced at the same time annual pay adjustments below comparability became more frequent. To some extent, rapid promotions and related grade increases represent the system's ability to accommodate the pressures associated with current pay constraints."[26] It is an argument used by the Rand Corporation to explain Defense Department grade creep in the 1970s,[27] and by President Ronald Reagan's Private Sector Survey on Cost Control (which came to be known as the Grace commission after its chairman, J. Peter Grace) to justify a battle of the bulge in the 1980s.[28] It is also a pattern implied in Vice President Al Gore's 1993 National Performance Review, which recommended a rough doubling of the government-wide span of control from 1:7 to 1:15.[29]

The second cause is occupational. There is substantial evidence that middle-level thickening is caused in large measure by the changing nature of federal employment—that is, by an evolving mix of jobs that favors professional, hence more highly paid, employees over blue-collar and clerical workers. Between 1954 and 1961, for example, government added 1,800 lawyers, 45,000 engineers, 16,000 accountants and budget analysts, 12,000 scientists, 5,800 educators, 22,000 business and industrial specialists, 4,000 social scientists, and 20,000 transportation specialists (including air traffic controllers); at the same time, government eliminated 75,000 lower-level jobs, including 2,000 messengers, 14,000 typists, and 10,000 clerical jobs. Grade levels increased as a result.[30]

It is nearly impossible to untangle these two competing factors. However, the best available evidence suggests that pay is not quite the dominant force once imagined. According to public administration scholars Samantha Durst, Patricia Patterson, and John Ramsden, the pay gap does contribute to the rising middle level but is far outweighed by the changing mix of jobs. Increasing the number of professionals in government—whether scientists, engineers, or contract managers—pulls average grade upward. "Since increases in grade which are attributable to increases in job responsibilities or qualifications do not threaten the consistency or equity of the pay system across departments," conclude Durst and her coauthors, "they may be regarded as legitimate and not as grade 'inflation.'"[31]

One factor that does not explain much of the rising middle is the increasing use of outside contractors to perform work once done by government employees. Despite recent concerns about the emergence of a "hollow government" composed mostly of managers and contract officers, the level of contracting out comes in a poor third in the analysis by Durst and her colleagues.

Public administration scholars have known for some time, of course, that the strategies and tactics of the federal government have changed.[32] Federal contracting grew from roughly $100 billion in 1980 to $170 billion ten years later, while unfunded mandates requiring state and local government to act have exploded. Less is being done by the federal government "in-house"; more is being delegated either downward to state and local government through mandates or outward to private firms and nonprofit agencies through contracts.

Yet hollow government may be more a consequence of the thickening hierarchy than a cause. It is possible that the rising tide of middle- and upper-level federal managers may create less and less capacity to produce the desired outcomes in-house, thereby increasing the pressure to mandate down to the states or contract out to the private and nonprofit sector.

Obviously, the federal government would be mandating and contracting even if every last middle manager and senior appointee were fired—estimates suggest that contractors outnumber federal civil servants by as much as 4 to 1, while state and local government employees outnumber federal by almost 9 to 1. Yet the thickening of government detailed above has occurred in every department—in those that do a great deal of mandating down (Education and Health and Human Services) or contracting out (Defense and Energy) and in those that do very little (Labor, State, and Veterans Affairs).

Moreover, the federal contracting corps, while likely expanding, is hardly the largest occupational category in the federal service—there are almost twice as many doctors, nurses, and health professionals in the veterans' hospital system alone. Of the roughly 660,000 federal employees identified by the Gore reinventors engaged in one kind of "control" function or another in 1993, just over 10 percent were in contract management (acquisition), another 10 percent in accounting and auditing, 5 percent in personnel, 2 percent in budget, almost 30 percent in headquarters management, and 42 percent in more traditional management posts running front-line programs such as air traffic control, social security, and the national forest and park systems.[33]

Finally, although the absolute amount of mandating and contracting has clearly grown, their relative size in relation to other federal activities is not startling. In 1949–51, for example, defense and nondefense purchases accounted for 7.5 percent of gross domestic product; by 1990 the number was up just 0.1 percent to 7.6. Although the percentage devoted to state and local government grants-in-aid jumped from 0.8 percent to 2.1 percent during the forty-year period, the figure was actually a 1.3 percent drop from the record 1980 level.[34]

Even if hollowing-out does not quite fit with the expanding federal hierarchy—the thickening began long before scholars began to note the hollowing phenomenon—it most certainly raises questions about the continued merits of thickening.[35] What is the proper ratio of federal contract officers to outside contractors? How many contracts is too many for each federal officer to handle? Does the thickening of government hierarchy parallel or provoke the thickening of contractor organizations? Can the government span of control be expanded through the use of evaluation or other outcome measurement? The world has changed since Gulick rationalized his span-of-control principle; providing direction to the very last person in the organization may not require the same tight control he once imagined.

Growth Industries

However interesting the middle-level thickening, or however attractive the potential savings from further battles of the bulge, the more important thickening may be at the top, where policy gets made, guidance is sent, and information is interpreted. As chapter 3 shows, it is also where a surprisingly large number of the layers reside that might theoretically get in the way of front-line employees.

Not surprisingly, much of the continued thickening at the top of government occurs for the same reasons new agencies are created. "Agencies come into existence," Kaufman argues, "in response to demands for service from politically mobilized segments of society, both inside and outside the government." These duties get assigned to new agencies rather than old for the same reasons that they are created in the first place: "distrust of the existing bodies and a strategy of assuring emphasis on a program by making it the exclusive concern of a separate body."[36]

As for clusters of growth that occur in administrations not noted for a commitment to activism, Kaufman argues that "factors other than the personal qualities and political outlook of the chief executive, such as swings in economic conditions, aggravation of international tension, or achievement of international accord, spawn new agencies." It is entirely possible that the growth curve continues well beyond the boundaries of the administration that began the work. Yet Kaufman concludes that there may be something far less rational at work, a process driven by a host of understandable but entirely haphazard events. "It is a kind of 'spontaneous creation' of new units," Kaufman puzzles, "spontaneous in the sense that it is governed by the internal dynamics of organizational life rather than by calculations and overall plan."[37] The core tables may demonstrate the same pattern. A new layer gets created for the most ordinary of reasons—the need for equal footing in a high-level international negotiation, for example, or the passage of a new program—but spreads quickly across the departments as they compete for equal status.

One way to appreciate this somewhat random process is to examine three growth industries: (1) title-riders, who attach themselves to formal presidential appointee titles, (2) chiefs of staff, and (3) general counsels and inspectors general. The first positions in each industry started with the very best of intentions, but they multiplied and diffused steadily through the executive branch nonetheless.

Title Riders

The first growth industry involves attaching modifiers to the statutory originals, secretary, deputy secretary, under secretary, assistant secretary, and administrator. After all, title-riding cannot occur without existing titles. Over time, this growth industry has produced at least five basic modifiers that can be attached to any existing title, either separately or pieced together, in a nearly infinite number of combinations: deputy, associate, assistant, senior, and principal.

Title-riding occurs in the compartments built around every presidential advise-and-consent appointee except the secretary: a first associate deputy secretary was created in 1960, and the number grew to twenty-one by 1992; the first deputy under secretary was created in 1952, and there were fifty-two by 1992; the first assistant deputy under secretary was created in 1968, and there were eleven by 1992; the first, and as of 1992 only, principal associate deputy under secretary (at Energy) and the first, and as of 1992 also only, associate under secretary (at Commerce) were created in 1988. Title-riding is particularly heavy in the assistant secretary and administrator compartments: after the first principal deputy assistant secretary appeared in 1960, there were 76 by 1992; 12 deputy assistant secretaries in 1952 grew to 507 by 1992; one principal deputy administrator in 1964 grew to 9 by 1992; the first deputy administrators appeared in the late 1940s, and there are 190 or more today. From deputy associates to assistants, deputy assistants to associate assistants, the combinations keep coming.

Consider the rising number of principal deputy assistant secretaries. First established in the Department of Defense in the 1950s, the title had a perfectly rational beginning. The number of deputy assistant secretaries was growing faster than the ability of political assistant secretaries to keep up with the workload. Moreover, no one was in charge when the assistant secretary was out. The creation of the principal title seemed a reasonable solution to a rational organizational problem and is easily justified by span-of-control theories.

Once established, the principal deputy title caught on in other departments and began percolating upward by attaching itself to other titles. It is now best viewed as another in the growing list of alter-ego layers. "The alter-ego phenomenon permeates government," one assistant secretary remarked during the course of an interview for this book. "Every director, manager, and political appointee has an alter-ego deputy who is essentially duplicative and expendable. It's almost as if we need redundancy in case someone is down the hall in the bathroom. And every time we appoint a new principal anything, it slows down the process because more people must be consulted and memos have to cross more desktops. The value added is practically zilch."[38]

Alter-ego deputies actually have a distinguished place in public administration theory and were first endorsed in 1949 by the Commission on the Organization of the Executive Branch of Government (the so-called Hoover commission), chaired by Herbert Hoover. These first alter egos were to be called under secretaries.[39] According to the Hoover task force report on departmental management:

> The Under Secretary should be regarded as the alter ego of the Secretary, responsible both for major policy decisions and for administrative direction of the department.
>
> The external demands upon a Secretary are such that he needs a strong person to give continuing attention to internal problems. At the same time the Under Secretary must be so nearly an extension of the Secretary's own personality that the two are regarded practically as one. The relations between the Under Secretary and the Secretary must be based first of all upon complete mutual confidence. The Secretary can then rely upon the Under Secretary to carry much of his political and administrative burden.[40]

Because of this intense personal relationship, the Hoover Commission believed that "the post of Under Secretary cannot be filled by a career Government employee as a matter of general requirement." And because the under secretary's role was to focus mostly on internal management, he or she "should be a kind of chief of staff directing both top management assistants and the subordinate operating officials."[41] That these under secretaries might eventually be supplanted by deputy secretaries was never considered. Neither, for that matter, was the possibility that under secretaries might eventually have principal deputies of their own to ride herd on deputy under secretaries and associate deputy under secretaries, or that secretaries might eventually appoint their own chiefs of staff who would, in turn, start appointing their own deputy chiefs of staff. So much for Gulick's unity-of-command ideal. As staff assistance grew, so too did the number of principals competing to lead.

Chiefs of Staff

The second growth industry involves the title chief of staff. Although chiefs of staff have existed in the armed services for two hundred years, this phenomenon is very different. Created by Reagan's first secretary of health and human services in 1981, the title spread to three other departments by 1984, to two more by 1988, and to five more by 1992. During the same period, two deputy secretaries picked up the title for their offices, as did assistant secretaries in four departments.

What makes the position particularly interesting is that it was apparently created in response to an ever-tightening White House appointment process. The more the Reagan process tried to control who got what jobs, the more secretaries sought some device to get their trusted aides into senior positions. If that meant creating de facto deputy secretaries called chiefs of staff, so be it.

Presidents face ample incentives to control the appointment process, a point well made by political scientist Terry Moe: "The appointment power is simple, readily available, and enormously flexible. It assumes no sophisticated institutional designs and little ability to predict the future, and it is incremental in the extreme: in principle, each appointment is a separate action."[42] Yet what the White House joins together, secretaries appear quite willing to tear asunder through chiefs of staff.

There is some question whether chiefs of staff should be counted as a management layer at all, however. If all that the chiefs of staff do is monitor traffic, keep the appointments schedule, supervise the executive secretariat, handle protocol, guard the gate, and so forth, there is no superior-subordinate relationship to define as "in line." This position description has existed in the departments from the beginning of organizational time, whether called aide-de-camp, special assistant, confidential secretary, or chief of staff.

What makes the 1980s different is the rise of the chief of staff as chief operating officer. At HHS, for example, the chief of staff appears to have started out in a rather traditional head-of-staff role well out of any line responsibilities. As tensions increased between the secretary, Richard Schweiker, and his White House-dictated under secretary, the chief of staff began to take on a far different role. By 1986 the chief of staff had the following duties and responsibilities:

> Reviews recommendations for actions on official matters to be brought to the Secretary's attention. Insures that all points of view and all program interests are developed for consideration. Acts as a principal policy advisor to the Secretary on issues which require the most careful analysis. Is responsible for determining and evaluating the issues presented, in the light of established policies and operations, using appropriate sources of information, within and outside the Department. Carries out special assignments on matters of special concern to the Secretary involving a wide variety of matters incidental to the operation of the Department. Develops facts, makes recommendations and/or reports results.[43]

Further down the list, the chief of staff "participates with the Assistant Secretaries in monitoring policy development and policy implementation activities of interest to the Secretary"; "directs special studies and work groups on major departmental policy and staff issues assigned by the Secretary or Under Secretary"; "represents the Secretary in discussions with Agency Heads and other members of the Department in conveying the Secretary's point of view, desired emphasis and goals"; and "represents the Secretary in discussions and negotiations of matters involving Department programs, and operation with key officials at the White House, the Office of Management and Budget, other government agencies and the Congress. Makes commitments in accordance with the Secretary's wishes."[44]

As such, the position was a new layer between the secretary and deputy secretary, provoking some uncertainty about who was second in command. Although the deputy secretary was appointed by the president, confirmed by the Senate, and paid at executive level II, the chief of staff was likely to be the secretary's true alter ego. What mattered most was that the chief of staff was picked by the secretary, *not* confirmed by the Senate, and subject entirely to the secretary's control.

The resulting confusion eventually prompted the General Accounting Office (GAO) to complain about a "de facto situation of two principal deputies in the department—one, the Under Secretary, whose position is specified by law; the other, the chief of staff, holding powerful influence by virtue of his relationship with the Secretary."[45] One (the under secretary) is also subject to Senate confirmation; the other is a noncareer member of the SES, subject to the secretary's approval. As GAO concluded:

> The chief of staff has weakened the effectiveness of the HHS leadership team for two reasons. First, the chief of staff has become involved in a variety of departmental affairs, thereby confusing the assigned roles and responsibilities within the Department. Second, the chief of staff has decreased the accessibility of other departmental leaders to the Secretary, thereby diminishing (1) their opportunity to further their understanding of the Secretary's goals, which affects their success in achieving these goals, and (2) their ability to report back about potential problems.[46]

Again, so much for Gulick's unity-of-command principle.

Health and Human Services is not alone in having a strong chief of staff. The Veterans Administration chief of staff had such a strong role that the Senate Governmental Affairs Committee elected to warn the new department not to use the position to supervise the deputy secretary.[47] Although the job description varies from department to department, the growing use of chiefs of staff as alter-ego deputies is worth following as a harbinger of future thickening down through the hierarchy.

Lawyers and Inspectors

The third thickening industry involves the positions of general counsel (GC) and inspector general (IG). General counsels were a stable fixture of department organizations by the early 1900s and had a sophisticated office structure well before 1976, when the first modern IG was created. The history of both offices is one of widening (more staff), followed by layering, followed by more widening. It has never been quite clear which came first, the height or the width.

Start with the government's lawyers. As the government's legal agenda thickened in the 1950s and 1960s after the enactment of the Administrative Procedures Act in 1946, the GCs began adding layers to disperse the workload among a growing staff. Most of the offices had a deputy GC by the early 1960s, and most had an assistant GC or two. As the government's regulatory activity increased, so too did its legal staff.

Still, the GC organization charts remained relatively flat until the late 1970s, after the enactment of a host of statutes designed to open up government to greater scrutiny—the Freedom of Information Act, Government in the Sunshine Act, Government Ethics Act, and Budget and Impoundment Control Act. The rough doubling of legal staffs during the period prompted an associated rise in hierarchy. During the 1970s, for example, Commerce added a deputy GC, two associate GCs, a half dozen assistant GCs, and five deputy assistant GCs; HHS added three deputies, one associate, another half dozen assistants, and nine deputy assistants; Interior added two deputy solicitors, five associates, two deputy associates, and twenty-one assistants.

The new layers diffused outward during the Reagan-Bush administrations, attracting more and more occupants, culminating in roughly five times as many GCs in 1992 as in 1960. Commerce dropped the associate GC title in 1992 but in fact grew deeper by creating a host of "bureau counsels" and "division counsels," who do not show up as title-riders per se but who clearly thicken the organization; HHS followed Commerce's lead, adding new chief counsel and associate chief counsel titles and a principal deputy GC title as well.

This growth can be explained by a variety of factors, including the parallel thickening of the Washington legal establishment, the rising tide of litigation against government, and the onslaught of new ethics rules and regulatory review, all topped by growing legislative complexity. A cursory review of the *Federal Register* shows the connection—the number of pages jumped from just over 5,307 in 1940 to a peak of 87,012 in 1980. Yet even as these external pressures explain much of the widening, layering remains a mystery. Moreover, as the number of pages in the *Federal Register* dropped to a low of 47,418 in 1986, the GC offices continued to expand.[48] What goes up with expanding workload does not necessarily come down once the pressure is off.

This same upward pressure may explain the rise of the IG offices too. The first modern IG office was created by the secretary's order at the Agriculture Department after Billie Sol Estes was caught stealing from the department's grain storage and crop subsidy programs in the early 1960s. Modified to give the IG greater independence, the first statutory IG was created at HEW in 1976, expanded to Energy in 1978, to eleven other departments and agencies in 1978, to Education in 1979, and to virtually every corner of the federal government by 1992.[49]

The IG offices were amalgams of existing audit and investigation offices within the department—thereby reducing the size of the office director compartment as they rose to the assistant secretary level. By statute, the department IG offices were to contain a presidential IG and at least two assistant IGs, one for audit, the other for investigation. Otherwise, their bureaucratic structure was left entirely up to the IG—one of several protections against interference from the president or secretary.

The IG offices flourished during Reagan's war on fraud, waste, and abuse. The more the IGs could demonstrate in what became a "body-count" war on waste, the more they won in resources and staff. The offices expanded by 23 percent from 1980 to 1986 alone, growing wider with new units—evaluation and inspection, administration—and taller with new assistants, associates, and deputies. The offices went from relatively flat organizations in the late 1970s to increasingly elegant hierarchies.

Consider the HHS Office of Inspector General (OIG) as a case in point. In 1980 the four-year-old office had two major units—investigations and audit and systems—plus a deputy IG, which had been mandated by the 1976 statute (see table 1-6).[50] Along with the two assistant IGs required by statute, the office had a third for health care and system review, a senior assistant IG, and an executive assistant IG.

By 1983 the OIG had expanded to five units—audit, management and policy, health financing and integrity, investigations, and program inspections—still led by an IG and a deputy but now with four assistant IGs and a growing rack of deputy assistants. The IG's legislative liaison officer, a single name in the 1980 organization chart, had by then become head of a small office reporting directly to the IG.

The OIG actually looked flatter in 1986—the health integrity and administration units were gone from the superstructure. But in reality, the office had thickened further. Numerous units had been drawn together into formally labeled units and divisions that began to resemble small agencies.

The thickening continued into the 1990s. By 1993 the office had added a principal deputy IG, bumped the assistant IGs to deputy rank, and created eleven assistant IGs in their place (see table 1-7). None of the changes required legislation, and all were fully permissible under the IG's authority to organize the office without secretarial interference. Having outgrown its space in the new Hubert H. Humphrey Building due to its growing staff, the entire OIG moved back across the street to the building that once housed the entire HHS headquarters. The fact that the IG decided to take the same suite the department secretary had

TABLE 1-6. *The Office of Inspector General, Department of Health and Human Services, 1980*

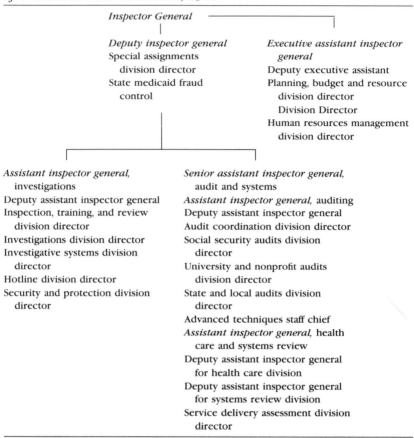

Inspector General

Deputy inspector general
Special assignments
  division director
State medicaid fraud
  control

Executive assistant inspector
  general
Deputy executive assistant
Planning, budget and resource
  division director
Division Director
Human resources management
  division director

Assistant inspector general,
  investigations
Deputy assistant inspector general
Inspection, training, and review
  division director
Investigations division director
Investigative systems division
  director
Hotline division director
Security and protection division
  director

Senior assistant inspector general,
  audit and systems
Assistant inspector general, auditing
Deputy assistant inspector general
Audit coordination division director
Social security audits division
  director
University and nonprofit audits
  division director
State and local audits division
  director
Advanced techniques staff chief
Assistant inspector general, health
  care and systems review
Deputy assistant inspector general
  for health care division
Deputy assistant inspector general
  for systems review division
Service delivery assessment division
  director

SOURCE: 1980 *Federal Yellow Book*, Monitor Publishing, 1980.

once occupied was not lost on those who marveled at the OIG's emerging departmentlike structure.

The HHS OIG is not an isolated case. All of the OIGs grew during the 1980s, and not in some random fashion either. They grew taller and wider by enhancing their independence from the departments they were required to audit and investigate. Along the way, many of the IGs created their own offices of personnel and legal counsel and freed themselves from regulations that burdened most other federal managers.

TABLE 1-7. *The Office of Inspector General, Department of Health and Human Services, 1993*

Inspector general

Principal deputy inspector general

Deputy inspector general

Assistant inspector general, management and policy

Executive secretariat

Deputy inspector general, Office of Evaluation and Inspections
- Assistant inspector general
- Policy and oversight division director
- Program evaluation division director

Deputy inspector general, Office of Audit Services
- Assistant inspector general, accounting and financial management
  - Financial systems audit director
- Assistant inspector general, audit policy and oversight
  - Audit planning and execution director
- Assistant inspector general, health care financing audits
  - Financial and systems audits director
  - Programs and operations audits director
- Assistant inspector general, human family and department services audits
  - Departmental management audits director
  - HDS and FSA audits director
- Assistant inspector general, public health service audits
  - Health research, regulation, and management director
  - Health resources, service delivery, and financial director
- Assistant inspector general, social security audits
  - Financial and compliance audits director
  - Program and operations audits director

Deputy Inspector General, Office of Investigations
- Assistant inspector general, civil and administrative remedies
  - Health care sanctions staff director
- Assistant inspector general, criminal investigations
  - Investigative operations branch chief
  - Program operations branch chief
- Assistant inspector general, investigation policy and oversight
  - Internal support operations director
  - Computer techniques staff director
  - Policy coordination and instructions staff director
  - State fraud branch chief

SOURCE: 1993 Federal Yellow Book, Monitor Leadership Directories, Inc, 1993.

The IGs merely wanted what every other government manager wanted: out of the cumbersome, rule-bound personnel system; out of the endless paperwork; out of the inflexible regulations and oversight; out of the clutches of the classification analysts in their departments. . . . But by breaking free of the burdens that most managers faced and making their organizations more efficient, the IGs lost some measure of sympathy for those they oversaw because they became less sensitive to the colossal problems of managing in a tightly regulated environment and less understanding of the shortcuts some managers had to take to get their jobs done.[51]

Inside the Assistant Secretary Compartment

These growth industries come together most visibly in the assistant secretary compartment. Looking at the percentages of occupants who are general counsels, inspectors general, and staff or line assistant secretaries, one sees that the ratios have been surprisingly stable (see table 1-8). There appears to be some underlying equilibrium at work.

Line occupants started out with 59 percent of the assistant secretary space, fell a bit in 1964 (possibly an artifact of problems in the Plum Book numbers), and hit their high in 1972. The peak appears to be easily explained by full implementation of the Great Society, which spilled over into the first Nixon term. However, as the Great Society settled in, the number of staff subunits began to rise as well, either to help those line units do their work or to provide greater departmental control and information about what was happening below.

This staff assistant secretary growth was followed in short order by the remarkable expansion of the IG offices, again a pattern likely explained by the Great Society. Indeed, waste in medicare and medicaid prompted the two congressional investigations leading to the statutory creation of the HEW inspector general, which in turn spawned the rest of the crop. The first investigation was led by Senator Frank Moss, Democrat of Utah, alleging $1.8 billion in kickbacks, fraudulent billings, unnecessary care, and inflated costs in medicaid; the second was led by Representative L. H. Fountain, Democrat of North Carolina, and targeted glaring audit and investigation weaknesses in HEW.

The IGs clearly affected the distribution of capacity across the compartment. The IGs occupied 7 percent of the space by 1980, 10 percent in 1984, and their presence has remained stable ever since.

TABLE 1-8. *General Counsel and Inspector General Offices within the Assistant Secretary Compartment, 1960–92*

Year		GC Office	IG Office	Staff assistant secretaries[a]	Line assistant secretaries	Total
1960	Total staff	52	4	28	121	205
	Percentage growth	25	2	14	59	
1964	Total staff	58	8	63	151	280
	Percentage growth	21	3	23	54	
1968	Total staff	78	8	47	204	337
	Percentage growth	23	2	14	61	
1972	Total staff	79	11	56	244	388
	Percentage growth	20	3	14	63	
1976	Total staff	134	14	105	309	562
	Percentage growth	24	2	19	55	
1980	Total staff	188	54[b]	151	422	815
	Percentage growth	23	7	19	52	
1984	Total staff	230	102[b]	118	527	977
	Percentage growth	24	10	12	54	
1988	Total staff	209	107[b]	147	600	1,063
	Percentage growth	20	10	14	56	
1992	Total staff	251	144	196	848	1,439
	Percentage growth	17	10	14	59	

SOURCE: See appendix.
a. Here, "staff" is defined as those units that facilitate the activities of "line," or service delivery, units.
b. Includes inspectors general at Executive Level V and nonstatutory inspectors general at Justice and Treasury.

However, it seems evident that much of that space was cut from the GCs and staff assistant secretaries as the line assistant secretaries began a twelve-year buildup in capacity. Although every corner of the compartment grew, the IGs clearly thickened the fastest, while the increase in GCs began to slow down.

Together, the figures suggest three patterns. First is the undeniable thickening of the IG subcompartment and its likely impact on the GC share—after all, included in the IG growth were their own new offices of legal counsel. Second is the stability of the line subcompartment, with a possible exception during the Ford and Carter years, when its share fell sharply against a rising tide of monitors and helpers, only to make a comeback by 1992.[52] Third is the slight rise in the staff subcompartment during the Nixon, Ford, and Carter years, a likely product of new evaluation and intergovernmental relations units throughout government coupled with the movement of congressional liaison officers out of direct secretarial orbit into formal assistant secretary appointments. Together, these patterns suggest a kind of internal competition that may lead to thickening over time, a form of bureaucratic "keeping up with the Joneses" that raises the cost of whatever services government eventually delivers.

Conclusion

The first step in deciding whether thickening is bad is to ask why thickening occurs in the first place. If it grows because layers are what managers produce, then a one-time mowing of the kind envisioned by doubling the government's span of control will not suffice—the layers will grow back. If it occurs because presidents define leadership by the number of appointees at their disposal, a one-time mowing will not work either— the quest for leadership will continue. And if it occurs because some hidden mechanism diffuses layers ever outward through the agencies, the challenge is to find it, make it visible, and control the effect.

The core tables suggest that the thickening of government was not accidental—the growth seems predictable, even unrelenting. In fact, thickening appears to be the logical consequence of a number of perfectly understandable events. New positions are almost always created with the best of intentions—to enhance accountability, improve coordination, underscore a priority. Once created, they tend to spread outward, in part because the price of thickening is so low.

Chapter 2 explores the "why" of thickening in greater detail. Although thickening can be traced all the way back to Thomas Jefferson's conclusion that few presidential appointees die and none resign, the modern era began in earnest in 1937 when Roosevelt's Committee on Administrative Management, chaired by Louis Brownlow, used the Principles to create an agenda for thickening that was carried forward over the next three decades. The notion that more leaders equals more leadership was more formally endorsed by the 1949 Hoover commission and implemented under President Dwight Eisenhower, who might be labeled "the hidden-hand thickener." From then on, an orthodoxy of thickening was in control.

Chapter 3 explores the "so what" of thickening. The chapter begins with a discussion of the diffusion of accountability that comes with ever thicker hierarchy—the information distortion, the inertia, the uncertainties about who is in charge. The chapter then turns to three ways to measure the possible consequences of thickening: (1) spans of control, which measure the ratios of managers to nonmanagers; (2) ladders, which measure the distance between the top and bottom of government by examining real jobs; and (3) the change in the mix of political appointees and career civil servants, which suggests the potential confusion caused by vacancies at the top.

Chapter 4 begins the search for solutions by looking for the roots of thickening. There are plenty of possibilities. New departments or old? The inner cabinet or the outer? Democrats or Republicans? Presidents or Congress? One set of answers comes from the basic organization charts that were used to create the core tables. Old departments, for example, were more often the source of innovation in layering than new departments over the past thirty years. A second set of answers emerges from a detailed review of statutory changes in Title 5 of the *U.S. Code*, where all executive level positions are recorded. Analysis of the 199 changes in code over the past three decades reveals a number of patterns, not the least of which is Congress's increasing role in shaping the formal hierarchy.

Chapter 5 continues the search by asking how thickening manages to endure over time. The answer involves at least two subquestions. The first is why individual positions come into being in the first place. There have been at least eight different justifications for new posts in government—from the need to do something, anything, about a department's morale to the quest for visibility for a new congressional initiatives—all of which seemed perfectly reasonable in context. In turn, these individual events appear closely linked to budget and size, two traditional explanations of organizational growth. The second subquestion is why those positions spread to other departments. Bluntly asked, Is there some inexorable force that leads other departments to adopt the latest innovations in thickening? The answer appears to be yes, in part because of parallel layering in the White House and on Capitol Hill, in part because of a simple desire by organizations within the same environment to look alike.

Chapter 6 asks what can be done about thickening. The first set of recommendations deals with reducing the thickening that now exists—for example, by eliminating all but two alter-ego deputies in government, the vice president of the United States and the deputy secretaries of departments; and the second set focuses on keeping the thickening from growing back—for example, by forcing tighter central clearance of any new layers of management. The book concludes with a discussion of the implications of thickening for the leadership of government.

2

Why Did Government Thicken?

If 1937 was a good year for hierarchy, 1993 was just the opposite. The attack on big government has rarely been more visible. Standing on the White House lawn, side by side with the president, framed by a pair of bright yellow forklifts stacked high with federal regulations, Vice President Al Gore presented the final report of his National Performance Review. It was titled *From Red Tape to Results: Creating a Government That Works Better and Costs Less*.

Framed by "a vision of a government that works for people, cleared of useless bureaucracy and waste and freed from red tape and senseless rules," the report singled out industrial-age bureaucracies as "the root problem" in the crusade to reinvent government.[1] The report was an affront to the Principles:

> From the 1930s through the 1960s, we built large, top-down, central-ized bureaucracies to do the public's business. They were patterned after the corporate structures of the age: hierarchical bureaucracies in which tasks were broken into simple parts, each the responsibility of a different layer of employees, each defined by specific rules and regulations. With their rigid preoccupation with standard operating procedure, their vertical chains of command, and their standardized services, these bureaucracies were steady—but slow and cumbersome. And in today's world of rapid change, lightning-quick information technologies, tough global competition, and demanding customers, large, top-down bureaucracies—public or private—don't work very well.[2]

If one word appears almost as often as "reinventing," it is "streamlining." And if one recommendation stands above all others, it is doubling the government's span of control. The rationale is tied to images of industrial-age bureaucracy: "Too many rules have created too many layers of supervisors and controllers who, however well-intentioned, wind up 'managing' simple *tasks* into complex *processes*. They waste workers' time and squander the taxpayers' money."[3] Almost everything in the report flows from this attack on hierarchy. Fewer managers means fewer rules; fewer rules means more time; more time allows agencies to listen to customers and react to the market forces unleashed by competition.

The doubling was to be driven by the elimination of 252,000 federal jobs—a cut Congress eventually upped to 272,900. Compared with the sophisticated mathematics underpinning Gulick's span-of-control principle, the Gore numbers were rather soft. According to Robert Stone, senior project director of the Gore review:

> We made a head count government-wide of supervisors, budget specialists, financial specialists, procurement specialists, personnel specialists, and headquarters people, plus regional offices. The total count was . . . 670,000. We said, "This is twice as big as it ought to be."
>
> But if you cut that group in half, you have to substitute for them—for example, groups that measure progress, that set goals. So you can't just cut 335,000. The judgment was that maybe a quarter of what you cut you ought to put back to perform these other functions. So half of the control and micromanagement force is 335,0000, a quarter of the 335,000 is about 85,000 or 83,000. That leaves you at about 252,000. That's roughly the arithmetic.[4]

In short, the 1:15 span-of-control number was mostly the product of a staff-cutting exercise. Unlike Gulick, who argued his 1:6 principle on the basis of the direct and theoretical relationships caused by an increasing span of control, the Gore team justified 1:15 because that is how the numbers added up.

Moreover, as chapter 1 shows, middle managers are not the only ones who get in the way. The distance between the top of the hierarchy and the first middle manager has also grown steadily over the past thirty years. It may not matter to front-line employees whether the layers are in the executive suite or at the bureau level. A layer is a layer is a layer.

More to the point of this chapter, the thickening of government hierarchy is much more deeply rooted in statute and practice than most reinventors imagine, and much more resistant to short-term diets than most believe. Yet Gulick's Principles survived in part because presidents could use them for political, not administrative, goals. Whereas Gulick and his colleagues endorsed narrow spans of control because of the innate limits of leaders, more recent presidents have increasingly justified thickening because they want tighter control of bureaucrats they do not trust. This shifting philosophy is all part of a history of thickening that, if ignored, will likely undermine the ultimate success of any efforts at reform.

Lessons of History

The Clinton administration was hardly the first to propose sweeping management reform. The notion of holding government accountable for results can be traced back to Lyndon Johnson's Planning, Programming, Budgeting System twenty-five years ago; the pledge to empower front-line employees can actually be found in Richard Nixon's justification for a new Office of Management and Budget in the early 1970s; the support for market mechanisms can be traced to Ronald Reagan's privatization initiatives in the early 1980s; and the effort to streamline personnel policy began with George Bush's Office of Personnel Management scarcely two years before the Gore reinventors began work. There is rarely anything new under the sun, including government management reform.

There are three lessons in this long history. The first is that, contrary to conventional wisdom, most reforms eventually find their way into law or practice, perhaps not immediately but usually over the long haul. According to one accounting, of the 273 recommendations in the first Hoover commission report in 1949, 196, or 72 percent, were adopted; of the 314 in the second Hoover report in 1955, exactly 200 and one-half, or 64 percent, were adopted.[5] One of those recommendations—the creation of the Senior Executive Service—took two decades to pass.

Ironically, it is quite reasonable to argue that the problem with government management is not that there has been too little reform over the years, but too much; not that too many commission reports are allowed to gather dust on long-lost library shelves, but that too many poorly formed ideas pass into statute. As a result, government lurches from one reform philosophy to another, trying new idea after new idea, without ever dredging out the old reforms and the hierarchy that comes with them.

Over the past fifty years, there have been at least six different streams of reform designed to fix what ails government: (1) scientific management, which generates narrow spans of control and unity of command; (2) government in the sunshine, which seeks greater public involvement through disclosure and access; (3) the war on waste, which emphasizes tight internal policing of government spending; (4) results management, which focuses on defining outcomes and creating incentives for performance; (5) competition, which stresses market pressure; and (6) liberation management, which puts its trust in front-line employees and their customers to make government better.[6]

All six streams are still active; all six produce new legislation or executive regulation every year. The problem, of course, is that all six are not compatible with each other. The war on waste conflicts with liberation management, a fact noted in the Gore report recommendation to reorient the federal Inspectors General; scientific management contradicts with government in the sunshine. Yet, contradictory or not, the reforms keep coming.

A second lesson of history is that today's problems with bureaucracy may have more to do with organizational age than with management systems. Those "industrial-age" bureaucracies of the 1930s and 1940s did not somehow journey into the present unaffected by time and reform. In fact, many of the New Deal bureaucracies that receive so much scorn today had the decentralized, self-directing nature praised in *Reinventing Government*. They were young, energetic organizations, clearly focused on their mission. It was precisely their independence and messy organizational structure that provoked a backlash against decentralization in the 1950s.

It is tough to keep a flat, lean shape over time. Aging has its advantages, of course, not the least of which are greater wisdom and expertise. But as organizational scholar Anthony Downs argues, aging also has high costs. An organization's officers may shift their focus from pursuing the original ideals to ensuring survival, even as the original founders are driven out by ossification. For Downs, the problem is bureaucratic self-interest:

As a bureau ages, its officials become more willing to modify the bureau's original formal goals in order to further the survival and growth of its administrative machinery. This shift of emphasis is encouraged by the creation of career commitments among a bureau's more senior officials (in terms of service). The longer they have worked for the bureau, the more they wish to avoid the costs of finding a new job, losing rank and seniority, and fitting themselves into a new informal structure. Hence they would rather alter the bureau's formal goals than admit that their jobs should be abolished because the original goals have been attained or are no longer important.[7]

This tendency to protect one's future creates what Downs calls the Law of Increasing Conservatism: *"All organizations tend to become more conservative as they get older, unless they experience periods of very rapid growth or internal turnover."*[8] As rules and administrative structure pile up like so much sediment at the mouth of a river, and age slows the current, government agencies may lose their passion, cast adrift from the mission that set them on their original course. If the primary problem with contemporary government is one of age, not design, reformers should think more broadly about finding a fountain of youth, or at least protecting their new reforms from the natural consequences of aging.

A third lesson of history is that the underlying justification for thickening has changed over the years. The original span-of-control principle was justified by the frailties of leaders—recall Gulick's notion that the "hand of man can span only a limited number of notes on the piano."[9] By the 1950s, however, the span-of-control principle was starting to be justified by the frailties, even outright sabotage, of subordinates—presidents and their staffs began to complain of their inability to influence unwieldy bureaucracy, of disloyalty in the civil service, of cabinet secretaries being "captured" by their departments. Narrow spans of control were increasingly unforgiving of public employees.

The question was less and less how to provide the best leadership and more how to protect the president against the self-serving behavior of bureaucrats. It is not surprising, for example, that the Gore report did not mention political appointees except in a tiny recommendation in the appendix dealing with the need for orientation. Even though the report carried a hopeful tone toward the career civil service, it concluded nonetheless that the basic problem in government is at the middle or bottom, not the top. By not including even one political appointee in the 272,900 cut, the report implicitly accepted the "orthodoxy" of thickening that sees more leaders as equal to stronger leadership.

The Orthodoxy of Thickening

If title-riding is a basic event in the thickening of organizations, George Washington bears at least some responsibility for the current shape of government. After all, he not only named the first department secretaries but also appointed the first assistant postmaster general in 1789 and the second two years later.[10] Washington and the federalists were so effective at patronage that a frustrated Thomas Jefferson asked in 1801, "If a due participation of office is a matter of right, how are vacancies to be obtained? Those by death are few; by resignation, none."[11]

Once in office, however, Jefferson resisted the thickening temptation, as did the seven presidents who followed. No new assistant secretaries were added to government until Zachary Taylor added one at Treasury in 1849. From then on, the numbers accelerated steadily, with the addition of an assistant secretary at the State Department in 1853, an assistant attorney general in 1859, assistant secretaries at the War and Navy departments in 1861, an assistant secretary at the Interior Department in 1862, and a second assistant secretary at State in 1866. The numbers continued to grow slowly until 1909, when the first under secretary appeared at State, a new layer that spread to Treasury in 1921 and to Agriculture in 1934.

Brownlow's Spark

This rich history notwithstanding, the modern era of thickening began in earnest with Franklin Roosevelt's 1937 Brownlow committee.[12] It was this three-member committee—consisting of the practical politician Brownlow, political theorist and Chicago politician Charles Merriam, and Gulick as the principal administrative theoretician—that formally articulated leadership in raw numbers of executives, managers, and supervisors of the president's own choosing. The definition is easy to find in the final report, which starts with one famous sentence: "The President needs help."[13]

For the Brownlow committee, decentralization was the root problem of the New Deal administrative chaos—the committee likely would have rejected the Gore proposals for empowering front-line employees.[14] Instead, the committee believed that "managerial direction and control of all departments and agencies of the Executive Branch . . . should be centered in the President; that while he now has popular responsibility for this direction . . . he is not equipped with adequate legal authority or administrative machinery to enable him to exercise it."[15]

One proposed remedy was to create an Executive Office of the President (EOP), which would serve as a fulcrum for administrative leadership. Another was to strengthen the accounting and financial management systems governing the federal budget. Still another was to expand the merit system "upward, outward, and downward." Yet another was to reorganize the independent agencies into twelve powerful departments, all reporting directly to a single master, the president. Gulick's philosophy can be found everywhere in the report.

It would be a mistake to characterize the Brownlow report as just about the EOP, though. It was but one of many items on the agenda. However, almost everything but the EOP was lost in the controversy surrounding legislative passage. Although most of the Brownlow plan passed in the House of Representatives in late 1937, the reforms got caught in the uproar surrounding Roosevelt's Supreme Court-packing proposal. Suddenly the Brownlow plan looked to some senators like a plan for dictatorship. According to political scientist James Morone, the firestorm against the plan, which included some 330,000 telegrams, was so great that Roosevelt was forced to issue the following statement:

A. I have no inclination to be a dictator.

B. I have none of the qualifications that would make me a successful dictator.

C. I have too much historical background . . . to make me desire any form of dictatorship . . . in the United States of America.[16]

The EOP was all that survived the bitter exchange. Acting under reorganization authority enacted after the legislative struggle, Roosevelt created the office in 1939. Built around the Bureau of the Budget, the Central Statistical Board, and the National Resources Planning Committee as its foundation, the EOP also included six presidential assistants who were to serve entirely at the president's pleasure.[17]

The search for presidential help had just begun, however. It continued almost immediately with an effort to strengthen presidential control of the departments. What Brownlow and Roosevelt left unfinished, Herbert Hoover and his Commission on the Organization of the Executive Branch of Government would continue in 1949.

Hoover's Design

The executive branch hierarchy did not grow dramatically between 1935 and 1952 (see appendix tables). The first deputy secretaries showed up in the period, as did twelve new deputy assistant secretaries. Although the number of under secretaries inched up from three to seven, and assistant secretaries went up by eight, a jump of twenty-five total occupants is the lowest total recorded. It is the 1952–60 period that shows the most impressive growth, jumping by 168 occupants and 207 percent.

The most important accelerator for that growth was the first Hoover commission, which created a new orthodoxy of public administration. As political scientists Harold Seidman and Robert Gilmour write:

> The commission's report on "General Management of the Executive Branch" represents the most categorical formulation of the orthodox or class organization doctrine derived largely from business administration and identified with the scientific management movement during the early decades of this century. . . . Government organization is seen primarily as a technological problem calling for "scientific" analysis and the application of fundamental organizational principles: a single rather than a collegiate executive; limited span of control; unity of command (a person cannot serve two masters); a clear distinction between line and staff; and authority commensurate with responsibility.[18]

This orthodoxy flows from Hoover's simple indictment of the sprawling executive branch in 1947. The first three Hoover commission findings would fit easily into the Gore report:

> *First Finding.* The executive branch is not organized into a workable number of major departments and agencies which the President can effectively direct, but is cut up into a large number of agencies, which divide responsibility and which are too great in number for effective direction from the top.
> *Second Finding.* The line of command and supervision from the President down through his department heads to every employee, and the line of responsibility from each employee of the executive branch up to the President, has been weakened, or actually broken, in many places and in many ways.
> *Third Finding.* The President and the heads of departments lack the tools to frame programs and policies to supervise their execution.[19]

Whatever its future parallels with the Gore task force, the Hoover commission adopted an entirely different cure, one of centralization, limited spans of control, and more hierarchy. Those were the prevailing principles of administration. There was nothing yet in the literature on alternatives to hierarchy, virtual organizations, self-managed teams, or total quality management. "Flawed and imperfect as they may be, the orthodox 'principles' remain the only simple, readily understood, and comprehensive set of guidelines available to the president and Congress for resolving problems of executive branch structure," write Seidman and Gilmour. "Individual members of Congress can relate them to their own experience within the Congress or in outside organizations. They have the virtue of clarity, a virtue often scorned by the newer orthodoxies . . . who tend to write for each other in an arcane language that is unintelligible to the lay public." [20]

Regardless of the pertinence of these principles today, the Hoover commission applied them to sketch a basic organization chart that fueled three decades of government thickening. Striving to end the chaos caused by the "gigantic and sudden growth of the executive branch," the commission made five recommendations on the general management of government: (1) the agencies of government should be grouped into departments by major purposes; (2) bureaus within departments should also be grouped by major purposes; (3) the heads of those departments should have full operating responsibility through "a clear line of authority reaching down through every step of the organization"; (4) there should be more decentralization of operating services such as accounting, budgeting, and personnel; and (5) secretaries should have adequate staff assistance at the top. [21]

It was the simultaneous centralization of agencies into departments, coupled with the decentralization of operating functions, what the commission itself labeled "decentralization under centralized control," that created the commission's "Proposed Typical Organization of a Federal Agency." Arguing that some of the then existing departments of government were larger than the whole government just twenty years earlier, and concluding that some had "far less management staff than industrial enterprises half the size," the commission recommended a ten-layer hierarchy, of which only the top three would be appointed by the president and confirmed by the Senate.

The chart on the facing page was clearly designed to strengthen departmental secretaries on behalf of the president. Paraphrasing John Millett, coauthor of a key task-force report on departmental structure, the secretary needs help too: "It is a truism today that no top administrator can fulfill his basic responsibilities without help. . . . Management practices and personnel which may have been adequate 100 years ago,

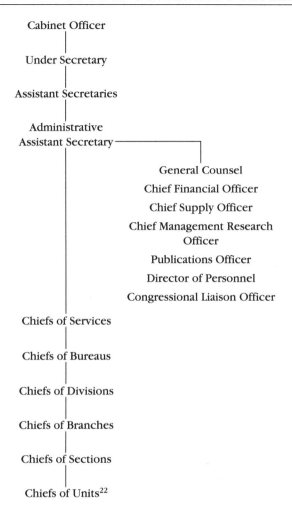

Cabinet Officer

Under Secretary

Assistant Secretaries

Administrative
Assistant Secretary

General Counsel

Chief Financial Officer

Chief Supply Officer

Chief Management Research
Officer

Publications Officer

Director of Personnel

Congressional Liaison Officer

Chiefs of Services

Chiefs of Bureaus

Chiefs of Divisions

Chiefs of Branches

Chiefs of Sections

Chiefs of Units[22]

or even 50 years ago, when the political role of the department head was probably more important than his administrative role, are most unlikely to be adequate now. Our departments are big enterprises; their management requires large-scale effort."[23]

Hence the commission's two innovations in departmental structure. First was the administrative assistant secretary, "who might be appointed solely for administrative duties of a housekeeping and management nature and who would give continuity in top management." This ASA, as it was abbreviated, would be appointed from the career civil service at a lower pay grade than the rest of the assistant secretaries but would have enormous supervisory influence as a kind of chief facilitating officer in the departments.[24] According to Alan Dean, a long-time administrative assistant secretary (ASA) at Transportation,

> The Hoover Commission deliberately avoided a detailed prescription of what should be considered "duties of a housekeeping and management nature" in keeping with its philosophy that the heads of departments should be given substantial freedom in the organization and administration of their agencies. As the new positions were created, most came to exercise oversight over such administrative functions as personnel management, the budget, accounting and financial systems design and operation, management analysis, procurement and contracting and miscellaneous functions relating to space, transportation, travel regulations, printing, building security, mail distribution, and paper work management.[25]

Second was the effort to centralize and coordinate all staff advice under the ASA. The commission apparently viewed the general counsel's office as primarily administrative, a departure from still current views of the GC as an intimate secretarial adviser. Whether GCs would have been content reporting through a level V career assistant secretary is still not known. The recommendation was never followed. However, the concept of legal advice coming through a career officer was certainly a novel idea and would have been a clear demotion of the general counsel.

Despite its elegant designs, the Hoover commission began breaching its own ideal organization chart almost immediately.[26] The commission's charts for Interior, its proposed department of social security and education, and Treasury gave the ASA supervisory responsibility over all "staff services" *except* for those of the general counsel and solicitor. In all three departments, the Hoover reports clearly recommended both in writing and in associated charts that the GC not be placed under the ASA. The text describing the new structure of Labor also put the GC outside the ASA reporting chain. In the meantime, the chart for the Department of Defense did not provide for an ASA at all, or, for that matter, for any of the staff services listed in the "typical organization" chart.

The commission's chart for State also breached the model, permitting at least four violations of the standard chart: (1) two deputy under secretaries, one for administration, the other for "substance"; (2) two political assistant secretaries, one for public affairs and the other for congressional relations, merely codifying existing practice but breaching the model nonetheless; (3) the State Department's legal adviser as a "senior official of rank equivalent to that of Assistant Secretary"; and (4) two additional positions, planning adviser and special assistant for intelligence, both at the assistant secretary rank.[27]

Hoover seemed to be creating a hoped-for organization chart for most departments, while sanctioning the violations already in place at State, Interior, and Treasury, three of the oldest departments in government. Taking on State and Treasury would likely have proven futile. Yet in approving the status quo in those departments, the commission failed to recognize one of the underlying mechanisms of thickening. Those positions would spread across government as other departments sought to keep up with the Joneses.

More important, there was no guarantee the new positions would actually improve management. According to Seidman and Gilmour, they generally failed, leaving "a vacuum within the departmental management systems that has never been satisfactorily filled. This vacuum cannot be filled merely by multiplying the number of staff advisers to the secretary. . . . As one secretary expressed it, what he needed were 'people to do the job,' not more people to tell him how someone else should do the job."[28]

Hidden-Hand Thickening

The first Hoover commission approved of some thickening as a rational extension of presidential authority, but Dwight David Eisenhower brought the whole process to full flame. By itself, the first Hoover commission recommended just twenty-one new positions (including those in the proposed department of social security and education): one secretary; two under secretaries; two deputy under secretaries; ten assistant secretaries, including two in the new department of social security and education; and six ASAs.[29]

Even if one counts the inevitable title-riding that would come with those twenty-one posts, the first Hoover commission cannot be held accountable for the dramatic increases that quickly followed. Between 1952 and 1960, government added one secretary, three deputy secretaries, two associate deputy secretaries (both at Justice), eight under secretaries, one principal deputy under secretary (at Treasury), eight deputy under secretaries, forty-two assistant secretaries, one principal deputy assistant secretary (at State, labeled a senior deputy assistant secretary), sixty-six deputy assistant secretaries, sixteen associate deputy assistant secretaries, four deputy associate assistant secretaries, and sixteen assistant GCs, for a total of 168 positions. During the same period, government also created five new layers of hierarchy—associate deputy secretary, principal deputy under secretary, principal deputy assistant secretary, deputy associate assistant secretary, and assistant GC. Whatever the Brownlow and Hoover contributions to the orthodoxy of thickening, Eisenhower was the first modern president to apply the orthodoxy across the executive branch. Consider the White House first, where Eisenhower's expansion eventually prompted political scientist John Hart to write of "Eisenhower and the swelling of the presidency." Eisenhower's organizational innovations were impressive. He created the first chief of staff (labeled assistant to the president), the first special assistant to the president for national security, a congressional liaison office, the ongoing President's Advisory Committee for Governmental Organization (PACGO), weekly meetings with the Republican leadership, and a cabinet secretariat to coordinate weekly meetings with the cabinet.

Moreover, using discretionary funds buried in the White House budget—most important, the Special Projects Fund, created in 1955— Eisenhower was able to cover the costs of a large number of "hidden" staff. "The first appropriation under the Special Projects Fund in 1956 was $1,250,000, a sum that was equivalent to two-thirds of the regular White House Office staff appropriation at the time," writes Hart as he muses about possible connections to Watergate. "Richard Nixon may not have been the only President of the United States to make substantial additions to the White House staff during his term of office and, . . . given his previous eight years as Eisenhower's Vice President, he may well have learnt some lessons about expanding the presidential staff from Eisenhower himself."[30]

Consider the executive departments next, where Eisenhower's military training colored his philosophy of executive management, not just in terms of hierarchy but of the subtle play of bureaucratic politics. It is a point well made by Fred Greenstein in *The Hidden-Hand Presidency*. Starting from the conclusion that "Eisenhower ran organizations by deliberately making simultaneous use of both formal and informal organization," Greenstein argues that:

Eisenhower's binocular perspective on leadership accounts for the universal recognition of his prowess as an organizer during his pre-White House years. From his West Point graduation in 1915, through World War II to NATO, his assignments either required organizational management or gave him vantage points from which to view and reflect on the problems of guiding large-scale collective endeavors. With this preparation he proved superlative as wartime supreme commander, a role that demanded supervision of the largest invasion force ever assembled; alliance management; mediation among fractious personalities; and maintenance of the morale of fellow leaders, troops, and the civilians on the home front. Ironically, for a man whose presidency gave the contemporary impression of reflecting narrow, militarily derived formalism, he was universally recognized in his military capacities (even by critics of his skill as a soldier) as outstandingly gifted in "political generalship"—that is, management of the personal (and by this token informal) component of leadership.[31]

This does not mean, however, that Eisenhower ignored organization. Rather, Eisenhower gave his secretaries great discretion as part of his general view of delegation. "As long as Eisenhower had established general guidelines within which departments were to operate," writes Greenstein, "he was prepared to leave many specifics to the department secretary. More than one former cabinet member was surprised at how much leeway Eisenhower gave him, but he remembers that Eisenhower told him, in effect, 'You'll be hearing from me if I disapprove of your actions.' "[32]

This discretion included freedom to select subcabinet officers.[33] Eisenhower even created the civil service Schedule C mechanism, in March 1954, to give secretaries freedom to appoint "positions of a confidential or policy determining character" without regard to merit. Although widely criticized by Democrats at the time as a new spoils system, the schedule was a logical extension of presidential leadership. As civil service historian and political scientist Paul Van Riper wrote at the time, "That the move was stimulated by the concern of a new administration to enable its top political executives quickly to bring around them a few persons of their own choosing without going through the strict and often time-consuming merit system procedures, fanned controversy but did not make the step any less rational."[34]

The schedule also provided an appointment device by which secretaries could thicken the tops of their departments. Because of counting problems, it is not clear just how many Schedule Cs there were under Eisenhower. The minimum, in 1954, appears to have been 868, the maximum as high as 1,128. The number may not matter much, however, given that many of Eisenhower's Schedule Cs were engaged in lower-level, nonmanagerial activities. Both the number and type of activity changed over time. By the end of the 1980s, the 1,700 Schedule Cs were very much involved in higher-level policy and managerial activities.[35]

Moreover, the new schedule was but one of Eisenhower's several initiatives to win greater presidential control of the civil service, whether in pursuit of better management or of patronage. As Van Riper notes, "As if it were not enough for many civil servants to face unemployment as a result of economy cuts and reorganizations, there was a renascence of spoils systems tactics during the first two years of the new regime. From a Republican point of view, the whole civil service was suspect. The campaign of 1952 had been based upon an assumption of widespread corruption and disloyalty, and Republican leaders felt that a general housecleaning was imperative." Perhaps the most important of the initiatives was the so-called Willis Directive, if only because Vice President Richard Nixon may have again learned important lessons about governing. Issued in the form of two mimeographed booklets in May 1954 by Charles Willis, an aide to the president's chief of staff, Sherman Adams, the program was designed to centralize the presidential appointments process. According to Van Riper, "The new program provided for a special assistant in each department and agency to control vacancies in both the higher competitive and political posts by reporting them to the Republican National Committee. The Committee was to be given time to recommend candidates with satisfactory political clearances." He concludes, "The secretiveness surrounding the plan and the uncertainty of its application gave the impression—probably a correct one—that this was a thinly veiled raid on the federal service."[36] Similar complaints were raised two decades later in the aftermath of Watergate.

This is not to argue that Eisenhower was the first president to expand the government hierarchy or politicize the career civil service. The Truman administration, for example, may have forced the first conversion of a level V career administrative assistant secretary to a level IV presidential appointment. "This politicizing action resulted from an effort to place a non-career public relations officer in the career ASA post at the end of the Truman administration," writes Alan Dean. "This transparent misuse of a career position led to a predictable action on the part of the new Eisenhower Administration to remove the unqualified incumbent by abolishing his position. This precedent was not forgotten when in 1969 the Nixon Administration launched its assault on career ASAs."[37]

Yet Eisenhower's greater contribution to the thickening of government was in a new rationale for tight spans of control based on distrust of the civil service. If hardly the first president to worry about patronage, Eisenhower was motivated by a now familiar worry about fealty. The career civil service was not to be trusted, in part because so many got their jobs during twenty years of Democratic rule.

Part of this colder climate reflected changing times—the New Deal was over, government employment was shrinking from its Korean War high, Congress was in high panic over communists in government. Congress began asking tough questions about employee levels and enacted what appears to be the first effort to "thin" the hierarchy: an amendment sponsored by Mississippi Democrat Jamie Whitten to require the Civil Service Commission to review all new positions "created or placed in a higher grade" and "abolish all such positions which are found to be unnecessary."[38]

Congress also gave Wisconsin Republican senator Joseph McCarthy the running room for a devastating series of hearings on civil service disloyalty. Although McCarthy eventually overstepped his authority and was censured by the Senate, Van Riper argues that "the damage had been done. For two years almost no influential member of the administration had effectively supported the federal service against constant and vitriolic attacks."[39] Obviously, the "Red Scare" had started before Eisenhower; otherwise, Nixon would never have been able to make his anti-communist reputation that won him the vice presidency. But the lack of support from the Eisenhower administration left the civil service defensive, and a residue of distrust still lingers in public opinion today.

Into the Present

Led by a new orthodoxy, instructed by Eisenhower's less trusting model, and armed with the new Schedule C, the thickening of government accelerated into the current era. The underlying hope was simple: more leaders salted into more layers would enhance presidential leadership. Every president since Eisenhower has followed the lead, each one appointing more leaders, yet each one perhaps feeling more frustrated by the lack of leadership. And every president since Eisenhower has had his own commission or advisory group to support the effort.

Johnson

Lyndon Johnson actually had two sources of support for thickening, although neither likely saw itself as such. The first was the Task Force on Government Reorganization, chaired by Harvard scholar Don Price in 1964, which recommended five new departments: transportation, education, housing and community development, economic development, and natural resources. Drawing upon the lessons of past reform efforts, the Price task force argued that most "important programs require the cooperation of two or more departments and agencies and such teamwork requires, among other things, (a) the use of Presidential staff agencies, and (b) a system for higher personnel that assures responsiveness to new policy and program objectives."[40] The evolving justification for narrow spans of control is obvious. Civil servants will not respond otherwise.

Johnson also had his 1965 Task Force on Government Organization, chaired by industrialist Ben Heineman, which eschewed new departments in favor of greater coordination. If a task force on reorganization did not work, perhaps one on organization might. Instead of reorganizing competing units into new departments, the Heineman team recommended a new White House office of coordination running parallel to the budget office, "to reflect the President's perspective, concerns, and desires in program areas requiring cooperation between two or more Federal agencies, and State and local governments."[41] That, plus a new office for program development in the Bureau of the Budget, would give the president the ability to mediate and settle arguments, ensure cooperation, and develop a fully integrated domestic social policy program.

In the meantime, the president was to "require *Cabinet Secretaries to expand, develop, and use* high-calibre staff assistance for the tasks of *program planning, review, budgeting and coordinated field management* to enable department heads to unify and to discharge their program management responsibilities effectively." Although the unpublished report also argued for continued efforts to reduce "through merger and realignment—*the number of departments substantially in the grip of parochial interests* (Labor, Commerce, Interior, and Agriculture), *and resist proposals to create additional departments* likely to be dominated by narrow, specialized interests or professional clienteles (Health or Education)," the task force put its faith more directly on directing cabinet secretaries "*to unify operations in the field under strengthened departmental regional executives of higher rank and calibre* who owe clear allegiance to department heads and the President."[42] Thus, whether Johnson wanted to invoke the reorganization theory of Price or the coordinating philosophy of Heineman, he had ample support for thickening.

Nixon

Richard Nixon had a similar embarrassment of theoretical support for centralization, starting with his Advisory Council on Executive Organization, chaired by the president of Litton Industries, Roy Ash. Reporting in 1970, the Ash council offered the widest reform package since the first Hoover commission. It weighed in on White House structure to recommend an office of management and budget in place of the old Bureau of the Budget, as well as a domestic policy council, both successfully implemented under reorganization authority. It also proposed four new superdepartments—natural resources, human resources, economic affairs, and community development—none of which were ever created. As political scientist Peri Arnold summarizes Nixon's motives:

> Like his predecessors, Richard Nixon sought to increase the presidential influence over the executive branch and consequently over the implementation of public policy. At the same time, as many Nixon watchers have noted, President Nixon sought an organizational arrangement in domestic administration that would enhance his power without demanding his time. His political agenda demanded redirection in domestic policy and its management, but his own interests lay in foreign policy. Thus President Nixon sought a domestic organizational system that would locate organizational responsibility such that his staff could act for him, becoming assistant presidents within limited contexts.[43]

Nixon's belief in a strong presidential presence in the departments is revealed in his draft organizational charts for the four superdepartments. According to his message to Congress conveying the reforms, each of the new departments was to have a deputy secretary and two under secretaries, plus a Senate-confirmed "high-level administrator who would be responsible for effectively managing a particular group of related activities." As Nixon explained:

> It is my philosophy that we should give clear assignments to able leaders—and then be sure that they are equipped to carry them out. As a part of the same effort, we should do all we can to give the best new management tools to those who run the new departments. There

is no better time to introduce needed procedural changes *within* departments than a time of structural change *among* departments.[44]

Of particular note in this early initiative was Nixon's forgiving tone toward the career service. The problem with government, he believed, was not in poorly motivated people at all, but in the systems that serve them. Toward giving civil servants better leadership, Nixon also proposed a reform of the federal field structure: "Each Department, for example, would appoint a series of Regional Directors who would represent the Secretary with respect to all Department activities in the field. Planning, coordination and the resolution of conflicts could thus be more readily achieved without Washington's involvement, since there would be a 'Secretarial presence' at the regional level."[45]

Because a growing number of departments already had deputy secretaries or their equivalents, and several already had multiple under secretaries, Nixon's proposals would have meant little net change in the total number of political occupants. So noted, Nixon's proposal represented a sharp increase in formal layering—the new program administrators and field directors would have added to, not replaced, existing layers.

Yet if the Ash council represented a more hopeful view of the civil service, Nixon had Fred Malek, an associate director at the new Office of Management and Budget (OMB), to reinforce the more negative approach to political layering. Whether Malek actually wrote the document in 1972 that came to be known as the Malek Manual is in some question—Malek denies authorship. That the manual was inspired by a desire to control a hostile career civil service is not in doubt—it is even evident in the cover page, a xeroxed copy of the *Federal Personnel Manual* with handwritten inserts retitling it the "Federal Political Personnel Manual." The cover page also included a cynical dedication to the U. S. Civil Service Commission.

Most of the 113-page manual consists of detailed advice to secretaries on how to create an office of political personnel, complete with four branches—recruitment, research and development, agency liaison, and program area liaison. The message to secretaries was absolutely clear: "You cannot achieve management, policy or program control unless you have established political control," and the function of the political personnel office was "to insure placement in all key positions of substantively qualified and politically reliable officials with a minimum burden on line managers in achieving that goal."[46]

Although notable for its sophisticated organization chart, such offices have existed in most departments for years, usually run by a special assistant. The much greater problem with the manual is its advice to secretaries on how to deal with recalcitrant civil servants. After noting that the Nixon administration had inherited a legacy of "disloyalty and obstruction at high levels while those incumbents rest comfortably on career civil service status," and cautioning that such "disloyalty and insimpatico with the Administration, unfortunately, are not grounds for the removal or suspension of an employee," the manual goes forward with a series of techniques for neutralizing such subordinates, offering four strategies.[47]

The first strategy involves getting rid of the offending employee, whether through the "frontal assault"—"You simply call an individual in and tell him he is no longer wanted"; the "transfer technique"—"By carefully researching the background of the proposed employee-victim, one can always establish that geographical part of the country and/or organizational unit to which the employee would rather resign than obey and accept transfer orders"; or the "special assignment technique (the traveling salesman)"—"especially useful for the family man and those who do not enjoy traveling." Although likely destructive to agency morale, none of these techniques would thicken the organization. Not so for the other three.

The second strategy involves layering, illustrated in the manual by simple example. At step one:

> Let us assume you have two branches whose chiefs are GS-14s and report directly to your deputy, who is a GS-15, who in turn reports to you (you are a GS-16). The object is to remove from critical responsibilities your deputy and the two GS-14 branch chiefs. . . . A slot saving can be realized if you have any vacancies within your office no matter what type of job they were previously utilized for, such as secretarial vacancies. (Remember your ceiling does not address itself to how you are going to use your positions. Don't ever let the bureaucrats tell you it is automatically such-and-such slot. By budget adjustment you can use existing vacancies to create any new positions and functions you desire.)

At step two:

> Utilizing vacant positions, or new positions, and acquiring the appropriate budget adjustment, you get your position upgraded to a GS-17

NEA [noncareer executive assignment, or political]. You then create a new position of Deputy Office Director, at a noncareer GS-16. Because that position is noncareer, your former deputy has no rights to it.

At step three:

> To make sure that the reorganization does not result in a reduction of status for your former deputy, you appoint him as a GS-15 Special Assistant to yourself so that he retains both his grade and his direct reporting relationship. You then create two Staff Assistant positions for your Branch Chiefs reporting to your new Special Assistant. They also retain their GS-14 grades. You upgrade the Branch Chief positions to GS-15 and create two Deputy Branch Chief positions at GS-14.

At step four:

> To your new deputy position, the two upgraded branch chief positions and the two new deputy branch chief positions you then effect the appointment of persons of unquestioned loyalty. You have thus layered into the organization into key positions your own people, still isolating your road-blocks into powerless make-shift positions. In all likelihood the three will probably end up resigning out of disgust or boredom.[48]

If this layering approach does not work, the manual recommends the "bypass layering technique," in which the career officers remain in their jobs but are routinely bypassed by layering in "your own people to the deputy branch chief positions. From then on all business is conducted between the deputy branch chiefs, your deputy and yourself."[49]

The third strategy consists of a more elegant technique, "shifting responsibilities and isolation," in which exiting organizations are completely bypassed through "parallel organization to one already in existence, and giving that new organization most of the real authorities previously vested in the old organization it parallels." Using none other than Franklin Roosevelt as its example, the manual warns that the technique is expensive in dollars and personnel but ultimately one that seeks "to isolate and bypass an entire organization [that becomes] so hopeless that there is an immediate desire to deal with nobody in the organization at all."[50]

The final strategy, "wholesale isolation and disposition of undesirable employee-victims," involves creating a new activity of glamour and visibility but of no real consequence. This "new activity technique" is "designed to provide a single barrel into which you can dump a large number of widely located bad apples." Create a model unit, an innovation lab, a special secretary's office. "By carefully looking at the personnel jacket of your selected employee-victims, you can easily design an organization chart for the project that would create positions to which these employee-victims can be transferred that meet the necessary job description requirements, offer promotional opportunities in grade, and by having the project report directly into the Secretary's office provide for promotions in status."[51] The only thing missing is impact.

It is not clear just how often these strategies were used. After all, the manual was published just months before the Watergate break-in and its resulting paralysis. The manual does argue that the techniques were learned from the Kennedy and Johnson administrations and that they fit with Eisenhower's Willis directive. Moreover, the techniques have more than a ring of truth to those involved in presidential personnel and might explain some of the increases in the core numbers during Nixon's abbreviated second term. At the very minimum, the manual provided a widely circulated inventory of techniques for future administrations and stands as a source of some support for those presidential aides who sought more help through layering.[52] Moreover, the memo fit closely with other, more public initiatives, particularly the effort to convert the Hoover commission's administrative assistant secretaries from career appointments to political.[53]

Carter

In a very real sense, Jimmy Carter derived his support for thickening from Brownlow and Hoover. His reorganization project, directed by deputy OMB director Harrison Wellford, drew heavily on the past, even while maintaining it would adopt a "bottom-up rather than a top-down approach . . . in contrast to previous reorganization efforts which have tried to impose structural reorganization from the top, guided by abstract management principles, not by study of programs."[54]

Thus, of the project's eleven goals, Arnold concludes that six "are statements conveying the traditional or orthodox verities of reorganization at a general level—for example, 'ensuring maximum efficiency and economy in government operations,' increasing the efficacy of government's planning and coordinating activities, 'reducing fragmentation, overlap, and unnecessary paperwork,' and 'giving managers the authority necessary to do the job and then holding them accountable.' "[55] Indeed, the project's greatest contribution may have come in rescuing Brownlow's earlier proposal for a central office of personnel and Hoover's more detailed proposal for a senior executive service (SES).

The creation of the SES was a major step forward in efforts at presidential control of the bureaucracy. Under the 1978 Civil Service Reform Act, the president would direct a corps of roughly 6,000–7,000 senior executives, of which up to 10 percent would be selected on a noncareer, noncompetitive basis. Most of the career senior executives were already in government in the General Schedule supergrades 16– 18. In return for giving up their GS positions and accepting greater mobility at the president's direction, these future career SESers would get a host of potential benefits, not the least of which were the right to compete for $10,000 or $20,000 yearly bonuses and access to sabbaticals.

The goal was to create a cadre of talented executives, political and career, ready to do anything and go anywhere on behalf of the president. As Mackenzie argues, *collective responsiveness* may have been the most important principle of the SES reform package:

> It is hardly a coincidence that efforts to distinguish a top managerial corps within the career service have always stemmed either from the initiative of American presidents or from study groups organized to improve the quality of presidential management. . . . That is precisely why presidents have expended so much political capital on these proposals over the years. The responsiveness of career executives to presidents and their appointees is fundamental to the success of an administration. But without an appropriate administrative structure and the necessary management tools, that kind of responsiveness is hard to secure and maintain.[56]

Responsiveness is not necessarily a force for thickening, however, particularly if it comes from moving executives from post to post. "Practitioners and students of public administration have long bemoaned the tradition of American public service in which career employees spend all or most of their work lives in the confines of one agency," Mackenzie notes. "Neither scope of ability nor breadth of perspective is well served by that habit, and every effort to create a senior career service has sought to break it."[57] Members of the new SES were to be encouraged to move across government, changing jobs as needed. And if encouragement failed, presidents would have constrained authority to order reassignment.

The problem for the thickening of government is that the mobility provisions never took hold. Even as the SES grew from roughly 7,000 members in 1980 to just over 8,100 in 1992, mobility declined.[58] According to political scientist Toni Marzotto, both interagency and intra-agency mobility declined—interagency moves dropped from 134 (just 2 percent of the SES in 1980) to 58 (1 percent in 1992); intra-agency moves dropped from 1,016 (15 percent of the SES in 1980) to 922 (11 percent in 1992). She concludes, "This lack of movement is some evidence that the SES may be a haven for home grown agency technocrats rather than the 'go anywhere, lead anything' generalist managers imagined in the original reform"[59]

Coupled with the fact that more than 80 percent of the candidates for initial SES appointment come from within the same agency, the lack of mobility supports Marzotto's belief that "agencies tend to hire home-grown technocrats rather than generalists."[60] With the numbers and specialization rising, the career SES may have become a powerful force for thickening. If one becomes a member only through increasing experience, which is measured by progression through a series of specific job titles, the SES creates momentum for creation of those jobs.

Reagan

Unlike his predecessors, Ronald Reagan entered the presidency with little or no concern for the theoretical issues of organization. He learned from the failures of past administrations to win sweeping reform and chose instead to focus on building the most centralized presidential management system in history. As political scientists Charles Levine and Peter Benda write:

The Reagan administration received three legacies from the Carter experience: (1) some lessons about what *not* to do; (2) some lessons about what *to* do; and (3) some mechanisms for better controlling the executive branch. In the first category, Reagan administration strategists concluded that President Reagan should not be drawn into the political quagmire that surrounds large-scale executive branch reorganization efforts. Unlike Carter, who entered the reorganization process with only vague notions of "streamlining" the executive branch, President Reagan had a vision for changing government that minimized the value of redesigning the formal administrative structure of the executive branch.[61]

This lack of traditional reorganization orthodoxy was evident in Reagan's 1987 decision to support the elevation of the Veterans Administration to cabinet status, a decision that seemed at odds with his earlier promises to eliminate the Departments of Education and Energy. Having been strongly encouraged to oppose the proposal by a host of senior advisers, he nevertheless opted to give veterans a present.[62]

This is not to argue that Reagan had no philosophy of management. His personnel process still stands as a model of central clearance. Starting even before his first primary victory in 1980, the process ensured that no senior appointment—be it subject to Senate confirmation, noncareer SES, or Schedule C—would be made without White House approval. That approval, according to Reagan's deputy director of presidential personnel, was based on a simple criterion: "All noncareer/political personnel were expected to have voted in the 1980 election and to have given some level of support to the Reagan/Bush campaign or to a candidate for another office who supported Reagan/Bush." The process met both of Reagan's management goals:

A president such as Ronald Reagan who comes to the federal government with a clear set of principles, goals, and expectations for his Administration, which have been forcefully enunciated over a period of years, needs some centralization of the process to insure that personnel decisions government-wide reflect his priorities. On the other hand, he wants to be able to delegate authority to his Cabinet secretaries to the maximum, permitting them the broadest possible flexibility on personnel matters.[63]

The results were impressive. According to research by political scientists Joel Aberbach and Bert Rockman, Reagan recruited more Republicans and conservatives than any president in recent history. Ninety-three percent of Reagan's political appointees and 40 percent of his senior career civil servants identified themselves as Republicans, in contrast to 66 percent of Nixon's politicals and only 17 percent of his senior careerists. At the same time, 72 percent of Reagan's political appointees and 47 percent of his careerists opposed an active role of government in the economy, in contrast to just 19 percent and 13 percent respectively under Nixon.[64]

Moreover, Reagan was able to repoliticize the deputy assistant secretary layer. By converting many of Carter's career DASers back into political appointees, he regained a significant measure of political leverage, again building on Nixon's earlier teachings. Recall that Nixon was able to push the proportion of political DAS appointees from a 66 percent share back up to 72 percent, even as the total political and career mix fell from 66 percent to 62 percent.

Just because an administration is more Republican or conservative does not necessarily mean it will be a thicker administration, and neither does a philosophy of central clearance dictate expansion. The thickening comes in the strategies appointees use to manage a reluctant civil service and in the reactions of cabinet officers who want senior staff of their own choosing—for example, chiefs of staff. It comes when one administration's political appointees are "careered-in"—that is, converted from political status to career, creating a new layer to be layered over again.

The ultimate strategy is simple: Not only should political appointees go deeper into the agencies, particularly into the line operating units; they should also be given greater control of the central staff agencies. That is exactly what happened. Between 1980 and 1986, for example, the number of total employees at the Office of Personnel Management fell from 8,280 to 5,929, a 30 percent cut that was nearly doubled in the career SES, which dropped from 71 to 36. At the same time, the number of noncareer SES went from 5 to 11, and the number of Schedule Cs from 7 to 13.[65]

In theory, the cut should have created opportunities for de-layering. In practice, OPM remained just as tall, albeit thinner here and there. One reason, according to Patricia Ingraham, was the kind of "bypass layering" recommended in the Nixon manual.[66] Moreover, the "shift in share" across government between political and career SES was hardly large enough to make a difference in organizational structure. From 1980 to 1986, noncareer SES and Schedule C employees increased by roughly 300, while the number career SESers fell by almost the same amount. Moreover, even when agencies lost large numbers of personnel— for example, OPM, Education, and HUD—they did not get flatter. It was a kind of fad diet, in which the weight loss is real but usually transitory.

These strategies can be traced to Nixon's theory of public management, a point made by Aberbach. "The Watergate scandal kept Nixon from fully carrying out his experiment in control, but his efforts were not forgotten. In fact, E. Pendleton James, who was in charge of Ronald Reagan's preinaugural talent search and then became assistant to the president for personnel, had worked under Fred Malek, Nixon's personnel chief." Having first learned some of the techniques of presidential control from Eisenhower, Nixon was now the model for Reagan. "The Nixon experience, then, was more than just a historical aberration," concludes Aberbach. "It was a school for many who followed; its lessons were assimilated and applied with telling effect in the Reagan period."[67] Memories of Gulick's rationale were long gone by now. This was not about helping public leaders assimilate knowledge or keep track of decisions; it was about not having career civil servants make decisions in the first place.

Bush

By the time George Bush took office, grand notions of reorganization were effectively dead. Bush created no commissions, task forces, or reorganization projects. He gave his cabinet remarkable leeway in making their subcabinet appointments, and in doing so relaxed the White House clearance system. He also disposed of long overdue pay reform, approving pay raises for the SES and civil service pay add-ons in high-cost localities. And he presided over a large SES expansion—up from 6,702 in 1986 to 8,130 by October 1992.

Even with the pay increases and cabinet freedom, the thickening continued. Once in place, the chiefs of staff continued to spread, even if they were no longer needed as de facto deputy secretaries. "It is impossible to walk the cat back," one senior executive remarked in the course of an interview for this book. "It becomes a status thing. 'We're not going to be the first department to get rid of this.' "[68] Moreover, those 1,500 new SESers had to go someplace, and many filled the new and wider layers.

One problem for Bush was that he had little or no interest in the structure of government. He sent a signal early that any assembly would do in the domestic agencies. In one of his first acts as president, he chose not to trigger a congressionally authorized "third Hoover commission," as it was known among some of its sponsors.

The commission had been created under the Department of Veterans Affairs Act in 1988 as price for the elevation of VA to cabinet status and perhaps to tweak the Reagan White House for having supported its elevation in the first place. The Senate's original proposal for a national commission on executive organization and management focused on five goals, several of which were explicitly designed to inoculate the legislative process against a backlog of other elevation proposals. The commission was to study the criteria by which the president and Congress could evaluate future proposals for structural changes in the federal government; it was also to ask whether the number and organizational structure of each executive department was appropriate to ensure effective functioning of the executive branch.[69]

To win House support for the commission, the Senate subsequently agreed to a triggering mechanism by which the president would have sixty days after inauguration to accept or reject the commission. Rejecting the commission was simple: all the president had to do was not act. This is precisely what Bush did. Bush's new director of OMB, Richard Darman, either did not want to spend the $1.5 million or did not want a congressionally authorized commission, with a majority of congressionally appointed members, poking about the executive branch, or both. In fact, according to Senate staffers, the commission was rejected more for a lack of any interest in executive organization than for any other reason.

Conclusion

That this third Hoover commission died aborning confirms what Arnold has already written about White House reorganization planning: "The plain fact is that no modern president has fully managed the executive branch. . . . It becomes clear that the managerial conception of the presidency is untenable. It places impossible obligations on presidents. It also raises public expectations about presidential performance that cannot be met. The managerial presidency then becomes a trap, offering increased capacity and influence to presidents but creating even greater expectations about presidential performance."[70] When they do take on grand reform, as Gore did in 1993 by proposing a merger of the Drug Enforcement Administration and the FBI, and by proposing to create a quasi-public corporation in place of the Federal Aviation Administration, they are quickly reminded why government organizations so often prove immortal—the proposals were instantly rejected by Congress.

Ultimately, Gulick's Principles still hold. The underlying rationales may have changed with the times—from a more hopeful view of political and career executives mostly pulling together to a more troubling sense that careerists cannot be trusted; from the notion that leaders need help to the belief that civil servants are self-aggrandizing. This bifurcation of Gulick's rationale ultimately allowed presidents to continue the thickening of their political corps, even as they decried the middle-level bulge.

Regardless of the rationale, however, thickening continued. Sparked by Brownlow, designed by Hoover, and given new impetus by Eisenhower, the layering and widening of government has survived repeated efforts to make government work better and in fact has been an unintended by-product of virtually every reform commission or task force since Gulick first put pen to paper. One president adds a layer of help, only to be followed by another who layers over. Since layers almost never disappear, the constant struggle to gain control of the executive branch produces an onslaught of leaders but no guarantee of leadership. The question is whether this thickening makes any difference. If not, perhaps the growing hierarchy is tolerable, albeit modestly expensive, a living testament to Gulick's prescience. Chapter 3 suggests otherwise.

3

Does Thickening Matter?

This is a tough time for bureaucracy. Once hailed for its efficiency, it is now reviled for its cost; once celebrated for its standardization, it is now attacked for its hierarchy.[1] It has become the enemy of all things good in management. "We are being strangled by bloated staffs, made up of carping experts and filling too many layers on the organizational chart," writes management guru Tom Peters. "Today's structures were designed for controlling turn-of-the-century mass-production operations under stable conditions with primitive technologies. They have become perverse, action-destroying devices, completely at odds with current competitive needs."[2]

Peters's nostrum is simple: five layers, maximum, top to bottom, the same number the Catholic Church uses to manage 800 million members. And even this five-layer limit should apply only to "very complex organizations such as multi-dimensional firms." For everyone else, *three layers—supervisor (with the job redefined to deal with a span of control no smaller than one supervisor for twenty-five to seventy-five people), department head, and unit boss—should be tops for any single facility, such as a plant or operations or distribution center."[3]*

In the near term Congress and the president are buying Peters's flattening argument because of simple politics—getting rid of 272,900 federal employees cannot hurt back home, nor can pushing federal employment below the 2 million mark for the first time in decades.[4] The federal hierarchy will surely get thinner at all levels as a result. Whether it will remain thin for long is a very different question, however. Fad diets usually do not work any better for government than they do for people.

Moreover, early implementation of the cuts suggests that government is not going to get much shorter from the cuts. The number of occupants per layer will clearly decline, but not the absolute number of layers itself. Merely reclassifying supervisors as "team leaders" to make them count as nonsupervisors is not exactly what Tom Peters had in mind.

The Diffusion of Accountability

One reason the thinning of government may not hold is that the case against thickening is weakly grounded in both theory and measurement. Notwithstanding best-selling books on the need for private sector flattening, public administration scholars have yet to prove a cause-and-effect relationship between almost any aspect of thickening and decreased productivity, efficiency, or effectiveness. This chapter provides a first effort to make the case.

The popular argument against thickening sounds just right—the notion that bureaucrats get in the way, that they impose needless rules to justify their existence, that they are doing jobs not really worth doing. But saying it does not make it true. Lacking a strong critique based on hard measurement, the old principles will hold, as will the old politics of distrust. As Dwight Waldo argued thirty years ago, "a social theory widely held by the actors has a self-confirming tendency and the classical theory now is deeply ingrained in our culture." [5]

Consider the notion that thickening costs money. "Billions of dollars in precious tax revenues are squandered annually to support a federal management structure that is excessively bloated and that is unavailable to perform 'front line production' work," the president of the American Federation of Government Employees wrote Gore in 1992. "These needless layers upon layers of management are not benign. They significantly delay work product getting out timely and they micromanage to justify their existence thereby ultimately creating customer (public) dissatisfaction. The related pay and classification problems have contributed to this 'pyramiding' of supervisors upon supervisors to justify grade levels." [6]

Even if some of these "needless" layers serve a purpose—after all, front-line workers can inform basic government policy, particularly as it relates to more efficient operation, but cannot make policy from scratch—there is money in the control structure, as the Gore report makes clear:

Counting all personnel, budget, procurement, accounting, auditing, and headquarters staff, plus supervisory personnel in field offices, there are roughly 700,000 federal employees whose job it is to manage, control, check up on or audit others. *This is one third of all federal civilian employees.*

Not counting the suffocating impact these management control structures have on line managers and workers, they consume $35 billion a year in salary and benefits alone. *If Congress enacts the management reforms outlined in this report*, we will dramatically cut the cost of these structures.[7]

Such personnel savings often prove elusive, however. Even before the very first of the Gore cuts were implemented, Congress was looking for ways to spend the savings. The dollars eventually went toward 100,000 new police officers to battle crime in America's cities.[8] Moreover, the fixed personnel costs of hierarchy are actually quite low. The elevation of the Veterans Administration to cabinet status in 1988, for example, cost less than $50,000 in additional personnel costs for senior executives. Pay compression at the top of the hierarchy meant that each "bump" in position from one grade to another cost approximately $8,000, hardly an overwhelming taxpayer burden. The far greater expense in the VA elevation was for new signs at the several hundred VA offices and hospitals around the country and reams of new stationery. Even with a substantial pay raise in 1989, creating a department secretary still costs only $13,300 more than a deputy secretary; an under secretary only $7,200 more than an assistant secretary; and assistant secretary only $7,300 more than an administrator. The budgetary price of thickening is remarkably cheap, indeed.

The fact is that the true cost of thickening may not be in dollars at all. Neither is reform likely to be well argued on the basis of dollar savings. As John DiIulio, Gerald Garvey, and Donald Kettl argue:

It is tempting to promise that management reforms will produce major savings and reduce the budget deficit. Improved performance is in fact likely to produce budget savings, but only as a by-product. . . . Making cost savings the driving force of a performance review can detract from quality. And mingling management issues with budget questions typically increases the suspicion of government employees who have seen previous performance reforms degenerate into witch hunts to cut their salaries and criticize their work.[9]

The true cost of thickening appears to be in the diffusion of accountability that comes in nearly infinite numbers of decision points throughout government. Almost by definition, thickening increases the number of actors in any decision, thereby raising the costs of both creating and implementing presidential policy. If public leadership can be characterized as a two-person "game" in which a principal (the leader) must convince an agent (the subordinate) to act as the principal desires, thickening increases the number of games a president must play en route to a final policy resolution, thereby diffusing accountability for any given decision.[10]

In the 1930s, the president merely had to win a "game" with a secretary, who had to then win a game with an assistant secretary, who had to win a game with an administrator. The president was out of headquarters in relatively short order. Today the president must win with a secretary, who must win with a chief of staff, who must win with two deputy secretaries, who must win with two under secretaries, who must win with four deputy under secretaries—and on and on down the line to Gulick's now mythical last person in the organization. Since in each game there is the potential for defeat, the risk of flawed implementation increases with each player added. Even if every player in the chain is equally able and loyal, the negotiating scenario is mind-boggling. Factoring in the high turnover rates in these positions merely complicates the equation for the president.

In turn, the link between thickening and the diffusion of accountability may express itself in at least seven associated costs: (1) information distortion may mean that no one unit or individual can be held accountable for poor analysis or misinformation; (2) administrative inertia may mean that no one can be held responsible for a lack of action; (3) disunity of command may mean that no one actor can be held culpable for decisions made on someone else's watch, particularly as those watches become shorter and shorter; (4) the growing gap between responsibility and authority may mean that no one can be held liable when problems do not get solved; the obstacles to (5) innovation and (6) employee involvement may mean that no one can be blamed for a lack of risk taking or creativity; and (7) tension between strategies to improve entry-level recruitment and efforts to improve senior-level retention may mean that no one can be held answerable for the slow decline in government's human capital. Added to the hollowing out of government discussed in chapter 1, the thickening of government may mean that no one anywhere in government is accountable for what goes right or wrong.

Information Distortion

The original span-of-control principle was based on a series of tightly argued assumptions about human capacity. Individuals could handle only so much information, organizations could tolerate only so many interactions. Narrowing the span of control, however, automatically produces increased distance between top and bottom, creating potential distortions in information.[11] According to Anthony Downs, every official inside organizations has at least four biases:

1. Each official tends to distort the information he passes upward to his superiors in the hierarchy. . . .

2. Each official tends to exhibit biased attitudes toward certain of the specific policies and alternative actions that his position normally requires him to deal with. . . .

3. Each official will vary the degree to which he complies with directives from his superiors, depending upon whether those directives favor or oppose his own interest. . . .

4. Each official will vary the degree to which he seeks out additional responsibilities and accepts risks in the performance of his duties, depending on his own particular goals.[12]

Downs builds these biases into a simple hypothesis regarding information distortion in hierarchies. Since "condensation of information is an essential part of the bureau's communication process," and since "the quality of information finally received by A—that is, its substantive content—will probably be very different from that originally put into the communications system at the lowest level," distortion is inevitable and will grow with each connection added to the chain. Downs uses a seven-level hierarchy to illustrate the problem:

Let us assume that each screening destroys a certain fraction of the true meaning of the information from A's point of view. If this fraction is 10 percent, by the time the information passes through all six filters, only about 53 per cent of it will express the true state of the environment as A would have observed it himself. If we assume another 5 per cent distortion due to errors of transmission and poorer quality of personnel at lower levels, then the fraction of truth reaching A will be only about 38 per cent. Under such conditions, the leakage of information caused by frictions in the communications system is enormous. It may be so large that the majority of information A receives is not really information at all from his point of view, but noise—error introduced into the signals he receives by the operation of the signalling apparatus.[13]

It is an illustration well worth remembering later in this chapter in examining the true distance between the top and bottom of government. If Clinton's secretary of transportation had wanted information in 1993 from the front lines of air traffic control about ways to improve the system, and he lost but 5 percent to biases and transmission error at each screen, his fraction of truth would have been but 5 percent.

Administrative Inertia

Closely related to distortion is the lost agility that may come with tightly rationalized chains of command and formal rules for downward, upward, and side-to-side communication. The harder the organization strives to combat distortions through redundancy and multiple channels, the more it violates Gulick's one master principle and the more vulnerable it becomes to the vagaries of promotion policies.

Sociologist Theodore Reed makes just this argument in an analysis of the State Department's organizational structure. Noting first that the tenure of foreign service officers (FSOs) is extremely stable, Reed suggests that closed hiring systems and aging can create a significant "organizational lag," based in part on the amount of time needed to process information upward and in part on the inability of groups within the organization to adapt to new trends. In a sense, organizations can be damned if they do, damned if they don't. They can break intellectual bottlenecks by promoting particularly responsive individuals into new positions, but by doing so they further increase the potential for delays.[14]

This problem can occur across the government. Since promotion rules remain tight and career paths to the top quite narrow, *when* a given individual enters the system may be as important to eventual rank as *what* that individual knows or *how* that individual performs. Having been brought up in one era, trained largely in one agency, and promoted largely on seniority, some senior managers may be unable to interpret new information. This tendency was one reason Congress created the Senior Executive Service under the 1978 Civil Service Reform Act. Members of the now 8,000-member SES were to be flexible generalists, ready to move to a new post at a moment's notice.

In fact, SESers rarely move on. They reach the SES through well-established career ladders and are almost always selected on the basis of their most recent employment. They usually grow up in a single agency and rarely leave. As political scientist Toni Marzotto shows, only 1 percent of SESers move between agencies in any given year.[15] Despite efforts to encourage more movement, the rates of both interagency and intra-agency movement have been relatively flat from the beginning. This does not mean stay-at-home SESers are less motivated than their more mobile peers. However, home-grown SESers may place a greater value on internal promotion and title-riding opportunities than they might in the generalist ideal. The result may be agencies that are less flexible, in part because their most senior managers are so closely tied to existing hierarchy for future rewards.

Disunity of Command

In an ideal world, unity of command would be perfectly compatible with narrow spans of control. Appointees and senior executives would be selected during the transition, nominated immediately after inauguration, and confirmed as soon as the Senate could act. In reality, time delays have reduced the appointment process to glacial speed. The result is a disunity of command. Departments constantly operate with vacancies in the senior appointive positions.

The problems of presidential appointments need not be repeated in full here. Suffice it to quote political scientist G. Calvin Mackenzie:

> The modern presidential appointment process barely resembles its constitutional design or intent. In fact, it differs dramatically from the way presidents made appointments as recently as the late 1940s. There are more jobs to fill than ever before, and many of them have complex and technical duties. The appointment process is much more formal and structured. It takes longer, often many months longer, to fill an appointive position than it did just a few decades ago. And the process is more visible and consistently contentious than ever.[16]

According to Mackenzie, delays in both nominating and confirming the president's initial appointees have grown steadily over the past three decades: from 2.4 months under Kennedy to 3.4 under Nixon, 4.6 under Carter, 5.3 under Reagan, 8.1 under Bush, and 8.5 under Clinton. (Mackenzie's data may be particularly generous toward Clinton. Completing his analysis in January 1994, Mackenzie assumed that empty Clinton posts would be filled by the end of the thirteenth month.) It is now safe

TABLE 3-1. *Time to Confirmation by Executive Position, 1960–92*

Layer	Months from inauguration to confirmation					
	Kennedy 1960	Nixon 1968	Carter 1972	Reagan 1980	Bush 1988	Clinton 1992
Secretary	1.0	1.0	1.0	1.1	2.1	1.1
Deputy secretary	1.0	1.4	2.7	2.2	5.2	5.5
Under secretary	1.8	2.5	5.6	5.0	8.5	7.9
Assistant secretary/administrator[a]	2.8	3.8	4.7	5.9	8.9	9.2
Total	2.4	3.4	4.6	5.3	8.1	8.5

SOURCE: Data provided by G. Calvin Mackenzie.

a. Most of Mackenzie's data were at the assistant secretary level but did include occasional administrator (Executive Level V) posts.

to say that Clinton's appointment process was the slowest in history, in part because of turnover in the White House personnel office itself (Clinton had three personnel directors in the first year alone), in part because of an expanding number of appointments to be made, in part because of the administration's commitment to diversity, in part because the Clinton campaign did very little pre-election transition planning (unlike Reagan in 1980), and in part because of the financial disclosure and clearance process that increased the delays under Reagan and Bush.

These delays do not fall evenly on the five executive compartments, however. Clinton was almost as fast as Kennedy in filling his cabinet secretary posts; but he lost time further down the hierarchy (see table 3-1).

The table clearly shows the lower-level delays, with the largest increase at the assistant secretary and administrator level. It is impossible to know whether thickening itself causes delays. Certainly the White House personnel office has more to do today than in 1960—more positions, more rules. Moreover, anecdotal evidence from interviews with White House personnel directors after Clinton took office suggest that it may be more difficult to "sell" an assistant secretary post today— that is, being assistant secretary may be less attractive when the post is buried six or seven layers below the secretary than when it was the number two or three job.[17] In turn, the Senate may take longer on these now less prestigious posts, relegating them to the back of the line. Agencies end up not quite headless—after all, the secretaries are in on time—but rather "neckless." The connections between top and middle are undoubtedly strained by the delays.

The threat to unity of command is complicated by what Mackenzie calls "epidemic" turnover rates. New appointees started leaving the

Clinton administration *before* all of the appointees were even in place. As Mackenzie notes:

> The average appointee now stays on the job for only slightly longer than 2 years; almost a third have a tenure shorter than 18 months. Given the political and substantive complexity of the jobs they hold, this high turnover among presidential appointees directly and deeply affects the quality of the leadership and management they provide to the presidents they serve. Teams of administrators are constantly changing and readjusting to new members. Persistence in pursuit of policy objectives is increasingly rare as administrative agendas and priorities change almost constantly.[18]

The resulting decapitation of agencies often leaves career executives without direction, direction that they both need and want. As I have argued elsewhere, the sheer number of appointees coupled with the vacancy rates "makes it almost impossible to build the connections central to positive working relationships between appointees and careerists. The more layers, the more time it takes to forge positive relationships. The thickening leads to a curious problem: appointees eventually come to see their civil servants as competent and responsive, but the realization may come too late to be of much value in promoting cooperation."[19]

The Gap between Authority and Responsibility

One of the central tenets of the Gore report is to give government customers "a voice and a choice," which in turn means giving front-line employees the authority to solve problems for which they are now responsible.[20] As the number of senior executives expands and turnover of political appointees continues, however, granting that authority becomes increasingly difficult. A voice into a front line buried thirty or more layers from the top will barely be heard.

The success of federal toll-free telephone response lines in actually solving "customer" problems may be illustrative. As public management scholars Jane Fountain, Linda Kabolian, and Steven Kelman note, a lack of information may be a far more important problem in government 800-number service than the more familiar lack of equipment and systems. "Whereas no private sector respondents report that they fail to receive either enough help and equipment or enough information to accomplish their task," the authors write of their interviews with 800-number operators in both sectors, "more than half the public sector respondents note inadequacies in logistical support. . . . Many public sector over-the-telephone operators reported in interviews that they hear of changes in regulations or procedures through the newspaper or from callers before they receive the information through formal channels."[21]

More significant, a large percentage of public operators believe that doing a good job will not make very much difference in how their organization treats them. They are more afraid than private sector operators to take risks with their organizations and to raise concerns with management, and they are much less likely to say that management does a good job communicating the organization's goals and expectations. They are much more likely to say that they will not be rewarded for a job well done. These are not all problems of thickening. There are many causes, not the least of which is the ambiguity that makes it difficult even to formulate goals, let alone communicate them downward to the front line. But thickening clearly contributes to an imbalance between authority and responsibility.

Obstacles to Innovation

Increasing the distance between the top and bottom of organizations simultaneously creates obstacles to innovation—raising the number of checkpoints for ideas going up, siphoning off resources going down—and barriers to employee involvement. Concentration of decisionmaking at the top (what organization scholars call centralization), growing internal regulation (formalization), and layering (vertical integration) all discourage what the Gore report calls a culture of risk taking.

Consider innovation first. Basic to the risk taking envisioned by the Gore reinventors is the notion that the front line is the source of most innovation. Everyone knows the truth, the Gore report tells its readers: "Management too often is happily unaware of what occurs at the front desk or in the field. In fact, it's the people who work closest to problems who know the most about solving them."[22] The implication is that if management were to free workers from onerous rules and invite their ideas, innovation would follow naturally.

Here, what matters most is the distance an idea must travel before it reaches a champion who can supply the resources and political support needed to bring it to fruition against inevitable bureaucratic resistance.

Size is not the issue—indeed, research suggests that larger organizations are more innovative precisely because they are big enough to deploy resources to new ideas. Big agencies can be just as innovative as small ones—it is not the total number of employees or executives that matters but how they sort out.[23]

In theory, thickening could affect nearly every step of the innovation process. It shapes the organization's ability to cultivate ideas from the bottom, move those ideas forward into the research and development phase, and implement those ideas once they are proven. "No single organization form is inherently more conducive to innovation than the next: each can either stimulate or retard innovation," write organization scholars Michael Tushman and Mark Nadler. "Whatever the basic form chosen, organizations must develop formal internal linking mechanisms, which are important vehicles for creativity and innovation. These links—bridges connecting disparate functions—encourage collaboration and problem solving throughout the organization."[24] Yet, these links appear much more difficult to cultivate and sustain in thick settings, particularly in government where the links often involve short-term political appointees whose high vacancy rates can frustrate champions of even the most compelling idea.

Barriers to Involvement

Besides being an obstacle to innovation, thickening also works against employee involvement, another of the Gore ideals. "Effective, entrepreneurial governments transform their cultures by decentralizing authority," the report argues. "They empower those who work on the front lines to make more of their own decisions and solve more of their own problems. They embrace labor-management cooperation, provide training and other tools employees need to be effective, and humanize the workplace."[25] The Gore report unabashedly defends front-line workers against the "bureaucrats" above, but reserves the word for middle managers exclusively, again leaving political appointees out of the equation. The problem is that many of these senior-level positions were created precisely to *dis*empower the front line, to keep federal employees from making any decisions at all.

The evidence on employee involvement does suggest some potential gains from the strategy. As economists David Levine and Laura D'Andrea Tyson (now chair of Clinton's Council of Economic Advisers) concluded in 1989, "Participation *usually* leads to small, short-run improvements in performance and *sometimes* leads to significant, long-lasting improvements in performance. There is usually a positive, often small, effect of participation on productivity, sometimes a zero or statistically insignificant effect, and almost never a negative effect."[26]

Where positive effects exist, they seem to be enhanced by employee ownership—for example, by employee stock ownership plans (ESOPs) or gain sharing in which both employees and owners benefit. Alan Blinder (also a future member of the Council of Economic Advisers) answered the question, "Can American industry raise productivity by changing the way it pays its employees?," in an unexpected way: "It appears that changing the way workers are *treated* may boost productivity more than changing the way they are *paid*, although profit sharing or employee stock ownership combined with worker participation may be the best system of all."[27] American public administration has yet to imagine a way of simulating the effects of ownership or profit sharing in government agencies, though perhaps it could be achieved through some form of unit or agencywide performance bonus plan.

Whether the strategy involves some form of ersatz ownership or mere suggestion boxes, though, thickening is likely to undermine the success of most efforts at employee involvement. When involvement programs have failed in the Fortune 1,000—from suggestion boxes to quality circles, employee participation groups, labor-management committees (endorsed by the Gore report), job redesign, or self-managed teams— the problem is often one of an autocratic management style combined with a taller, rather than flatter, structure.[28] Thinning the organization will not automatically produce employee involvement. Autocratic executives and managers exist in even the flattest organizations. At a minimum, however, such behaviors will be more visible and therefore more accountable in flatter, not thicker, organizations.

Recruitment or Retention

Ultimately, thickening of government may mean that strategies to enhance entry-level recruitment can no longer coexist with strategies to encourage employee retention. Recruitment and retention have been linked for so long that thinking of the two as potential adversaries may be quite difficult indeed. The 1989 National Commission on the Public Service, for example, which was chaired by former Federal Reserve Board chairman Paul Volcker, had a single task force that combined recruitment and retention and considered many of its recommendations on pay and promotion to be equally valid for both entry-level and senior-level employees.[29]

Unfortunately, the things that the "best and brightest" entry-level employees value most in a federal job may be in sharp conflict with retaining senior executives. In fact, according to a Volcker commission survey of 1988 college honor society graduates, "The public service is not perceived as a place where talented people can get ahead. Few of the top graduates feel the federal government can offer good pay and recognition for performance. Fewer still say a federal job can be challenging and intellectually stimulating. Public service is too often seen as a career of last resort."[30] Among the survey findings were the following problems indirectly linked to thickening:

—More than 70 percent said the federal government does not offer a good chance for responsibility early on in one's career.

—Eighty-six percent said a federal job would not allow them to use their abilities to the fullest.

—Roughly half said that most federal jobs are routine and monotonous.

—Eighty percent said federal civil servants do not have the power and opportunity to influence government outcomes.[31]

Most troubling perhaps, less than 3 percent felt that talented individuals had a chance of ever ending up in one of the top federal jobs. These are, of course, merely perceptions about what federal employment is like. Yet to the extent that these perceptions weaken interest in federal careers, thickening takes its toll again. Moreover, given the distances between top and bottom described below, the perceptions may be disturbingly close to reality.

Three Measures of Consequence

Not every act of thickening produces dire consequences. In fact, some thickening is both reasonable and necessary—one person's stifling bureaucracy may be another's administrative fairness; one person's obstacle may be another's due process. For public administration scholars such as Charles Goodsell, bureaucracy is a glass half full:

For a fundamental feature of bureaucracy is that it continually performs millions of tiny acts of individual service, such as approving applications, delivering the mail, and answering complaints. Because this ongoing mass of routine achievement is not in itself noteworthy or even capable of intellectual grasp, it operates silently, almost out of sight. The occasional breakdowns, the unusual scandals, the individual instances where a true injustice is done, are what come to our attention and color our overall judgment. The water glass of bureaucracy is quite full, and we have difficulty realizing it.[32]

Nevertheless, thickening does appear to have measurable consequences for how government works, consequences that can be measured in three ways: First, in spans of control, where ideas, participation, and ultimately accountability are diffused; second, in the distance between the top and bottom, where guidance takes longer to flow down the chain of command and ideas longer to rise up; and third, in the crowding of the secretary's suite, where growing numbers produce disunity of command. The question for scholars and presidents alike is how much diffusion of accountability to tolerate en route to cherished goals such as merit, fairness, and consistency.

Spans of Control

Span of control is one of the most familiar measures of organizational structure, perhaps because it is so easy to calculate: divide the total number of managers into the number of nonmanagers. "Currently," according to the Gore report, "the federal government averages one manager or supervisor for every seven employees," using a ratio as its measure of strangulation simply because there is no other way to know what is going on in the hierarchy.[33]

The problem with such ratios is that spans of control vary widely from level to level in most hierarchies and are usually narrower at the top than the bottom. Thus, an aggregate ratio may hide important variance. The ratio could easily be 1:4 at the top, 1:7 at the middle, and 1:20 at the bottom, yet 1:7 overall. Or there could be a series of 1:1:1 spans of control followed by an occasional 1:20.

The Office of Personnel Management (OPM) central personnel data file contains answers to just about any question about a federal full- or part-time employee—salary, education, occupational class, age, length of service, years to retirement—but unfortunately does not keep track of how many subordinates report to the same manager. Short of building organization charts from scratch all the way down the hierarchy, there is no way to know how many layers actually exist. The ratio of supervisors to subordinates remains the best available measure of the growing bulge in government.

TABLE 3-2. *Number of Government Employees and Ratio of Supervisors to Subordinates, 1983, 1989, and 1992*

Measure	1983	1989	1992
Base numbers			
Total employment[a]	2,009,000	2,078,000	2,106,000
Total GS 1–10 employees	783,000	800,000	767,000
Total GS 11–15 employees	487,000	578,000	645,000
GS 11–15 managers	125,000	150,000	161,000
Average grade of GS 1–10 employees	8.06	8.53	8.91
Average grade of GS 11–15 employees	12.03	12.01	12.05
Ratios			
All GS 11–15 employees to all GS 1–10 employees	1:1.6	1:1.4	1:1.2
GS 11–15 managers to GS 11–15 nonmanagers	1:2.9	1:2.9	1:3.0
GS 11–15 managers to all GS 1–10 employees	1:6.3	1:5.3	1:4.8
GS 11–15 managers to all other employees	1:9.2	1:8.2	1:7.8

SOURCE: Office of Personnel Management, Agency Compliance and Evaluation Division, "Personnel Management Indicators Report," 1983, 1989, 1992.

a. Total GS 1–10 and GS 11–15 do not sum to total employment because Blue-Collar Wage System employees and Senior Executive Service employees are left out.

Table 3-2 records these ratios in 1983, 1989, and 1992 using OPM numbers—data on the total number of middle-level employees are available back to 1981 but not on the number of middle-level managers and nonmanagers. The table shows total employment, the number in General Schedule (GS) ranks 1–10, which contain most entry-level and clerical employees, and 11–15, which include most professional employees and middle-level managers. The table also includes average grades, which show more precisely where the concentrations are moving.

The raw numbers show the changing shape of government from a traditional bureaucratic pyramid (more employees at the bottom than in the middle) toward a pentagonal shape (more employees in the middle than at the bottom). This changing shape confirms the new occupational mix of federal employment and the hollowing-out phenomenon discussed earlier. Government appears to be growing less and less capable of delivering services in house. Thus, even though total federal employment inched up slightly during the Reagan and Bush years, the GS 1–10 levels were in decline. The greatest employee growth came at GS 11–15, where the number of both managers and nonmanagers increased rapidly. In fact, the GS 11–15 compartment flooded faster than managers could keep up. Professionals were being promoted or hired faster than the span of control could keep pace. As a result, the ratio inched up slightly.

The most important numbers in table 3-2 are the ratios between the various base figures. The ratio showing the relationship between GS 11–15s and 1–10s confirms the narrowing bottom of government. The GS 1–10s used to outnumber the 11–15s by six to one; now the ratio is down to just two to one. More and more of the federal government's work is being done or supervised at the middle, often through mandates and contracts.

The table shows a stable 1:3 ratio between middle managers and nonmanagers, a very narrow span of control given the higher education and skill base supposedly represented in GS 11–15 job categories. In theory, the greater the education and skills, the greater the span. In reality, professionalization does not appear to have created greater autonomy.

It is always possible, of course, that middle-level managers spend more of their time overseeing GS 1–10s than they do their fellow 11–15s. Yet the ratio of managers to all GS 1–10 employees suggests that there are simply fewer and fewer 1–10s to manage, and those that remain, by virtue of their rising average grade, are likely in need of less supervision. Again, the link to employee professionalization, here represented by average grade, does not seem to have purchased greater freedom.

Finally, the table shows a declining ratio of middle managers to nonmanagers. The changing occupational mix, coupled with the hollowing-out of government, have conspired to reduce the supervisory span for most federal managers. Together the ratios suggest that the federal government may have entered a period when it would need fewer managers, not more.

There are clear dangers in using these bulge ratios to set policy, however. One danger is that the data disguise enormous variation across departments and agencies. The number of GS 11–15s increased dramatically in some departments—State went up 169 percent from 1981 to 1992, Justice 113 percent, Treasury 61 percent, Defense 54 percent, and Veterans Affairs 40 percent; others remained steady or fell—Labor dropped 10 percent, HUD dropped 1 percent, Education was virtually unchanged, and Commerce inched up only 2 percent.

Another danger is that bulge ratios reveal little about what managers do. Some departments may need more, not fewer, managers in the mix, particularly if they are managing a large contractor work force. How many managers are enough for overseeing the government's nuclear weapons complex? How many for air traffic control?

Still another danger is that ratios do not reveal much about how managers and nonmanagers sort out, which is the most important factor in why thickening matters. Does the hierarchy widen steadily at each layer down the organization or in patterns? Should Gore target middle-level managers or just their alter-ego deputies? Table 3-3 suggests an answer by looking at executive span-of-control ratios derived from the core numbers in the appendix.

The ratios reveal two patterns. First, they suggest an equilibrium of sorts that supports a 1:4 ratio between secretaries and assistant secretaries. In 1935 that ratio was easily achieved by secretaries alone; according to the core numbers in the appendix, upon which all the spans are based, there were ten secretaries and thirty-eight assistant secretaries.

As the number of assistant secretaries grew, however, secretaries could not do the job alone. They added deputy and under secretaries as help-mates. Even as the ratio of secretary to assistant secretary rises from just 1:4 in 1935 to 1:15 in 1992, the buffer layer of deputy and under secretaries keeps the base ratio at 1:4. In turn, as the number of deputy and under secretaries itself starts to rise, chiefs of staff come into play to keep that ratio down. Even though the chief of staff position was launched to counterbalance deputy secretaries not of the secretary's own choosing, there may be something of a hidden organizational hand at work.

Second, the ratios below the secretary compartment are equal to or narrower than those above. The ratio of assistant secretaries to deputy assistant secretaries actually drops from 1:3 in 1988 to 1:2 in 1992 as the compartment swells, while the ratio of administrators to deputy administrators and administrators to assistant administrators stands steady at 1:1 throughout the 1960–92 period. As for the office director compartment, the ratios are also remarkably narrow: in 1980, office director: deputy office director, 1:1; office director : division director, 1:3; and division director : branch chief, 1:1; in 1992, office director : deputy office director, 1:0.4; office director: division director, 1:3; and division director : branch chief, 1:1.

Even acknowledging the risks in using bulge ratios, there appear to be an extraordinary number of managers managing managers. Although there are differences across departments, every organization chart shows this proliferation of 1:1:1 spans of control, which are expensive in dollars as well as in lost quality, empowerment, and innovation.

TABLE 3-3. *Executive Span-of-Control Ratios, Selected Years, 1935–92*

Year	Executive layers	Ratio
1935	Secretary : deputy and under secretary	2:1
	Secretary : assistant secretary	1:4
1952	Secretary : deputy and under secretary	1:1
	Deputy and under secretary : assistant secretary	1:5
	Secretary : assistant secretary	1:5
	Assistant secretary : deputy assistant secretary	4:1
1960	Secretary : deputy and under secretary	1:2
	Deputy and under secretary : assistant secretary	1:4
	Secretary : assistant secretary	1:9
	Assistant secretary : deputy assistant secretary	1:1
1964	Secretary : deputy and under secretary	1:2
	Deputy and under secretary : assistant secretary	1:4
	Secretary : assistant secretary	1:9
	Assistant secretary : deputy assistant secretary	1:2
1968	Secretary : deputy and under secretary	1:2
	Deputy and under secretary : assistant secretary	1:4
	Secretary : assistant secretary	1:9
	Assistant secretary : deputy assistant secretary	1:2
1972	Secretary : deputy and under secretary	1:3
	Deputy and under secretary : assistant secretary	1:3
	Secretary : assistant secretary	1:10
	Assistant secretary : deputy assistant secretary	1:2
1976	Secretary : deputy and under secretary	1:3
	Deputy and under secretary : assistant secretary	1:4
	Secretary : assistant secretary	1:11
	Assistant secretary : deputy assistant secretary	1:2
1980	Secretary : deputy and under secretary	1:3
	Deputy and under secretary : assistant secretary	1:4
	Secretary : assistant secretary	1:12
	Assistant secretary : deputy assistant secretary	1:2
1984	Secretary and chief of staff : deputy and under secretary	1:3
	Deputy and under secretary : assistant secretary	1:4
	Secretary : assistant secretary	1:13
	Assistant secretary : deputy assistant secretary	1:2
	Assistant secretary and principal deputy assistant secretary : deputy assistant secretary	1:2
1988	Secretary and chief of staff : deputy and under secretary	1:3
	Deputy and under secretary : assistant secretary	1:4
	Secretary : assistant secretary	1:14
	Assistant secretary : deputy assistant secretary	1:3
	Assistant secretary and principal deputy assistant secretary : deputy assistant secretary	1:2
1992	Secretary and chief of staff : deputy and under secretary	1:2
	Deputy and under secretary : assistant secretary	1:4
	Secretary : assistant secretary	1:15
	Assistant secretary : deputy assistant secretary	1:2
	Assistant secretary and principal deputy assistant secretary : deputy assistant secretary	1:2

SOURCES: See appendix.

TABLE 3-4. *Layers Occupied by Departments at Levels I–V, Selected Years, 1960–92*

Department	1960	1972	1980	1992
Agriculture	10	12	17	21
Commerce	8	9	16	20
Defense	10	14	17	19
Education	. . .	. . .	11	15
Energy	. . .	. . .	10[a]	16[a]
HHS/HEW	8	11	14	19
HUD	. . .	10	7[a]	9[a]
Interior	8	10	14	19
Justice	12	13	18	15
Labor	6	10	14	18
Post Office	4	. . .	. . .	. . .
State	9	10	10	13
Transportation	. . .	12	12	19
Treasury	9	13	15	18
VA	. . .	. . .	. . .	11

SOURCES: See appendix.
a. No Executive Level V offices recorded.

The ratios also suggest the potential risk in mandating a fixed 1:15 ratio across government. It is entirely possible to achieve the ratio by reclassifying existing managers as nonmanagers or by widening front-line spans through entirely mechanical supervisory practices. Using a piece-rate or quota system, which would likely undermine quality, the Social Security Administration could easily broaden the span of 800-number telephone operators to, say, a 1:80 ratio, thereby altering the overall numbers without eliminating a single alter-ego deputy. Since government has no way to keep track of layers, the ratio approach to flattening could easily result in a much thinner work force but no net decrease in the distance between the top and bottom, which is, after all, a substantial source of the diffusion of accountability.

Chains of Command

The only way currently available to estimate the true distance between top and bottom is to pick a set of front-line jobs and track the decision chains upward through the hierarchy. Departments vary greatly in the number of executive layers occupied (see table 3-4) but perhaps less so in how those layers assemble into reporting chains. The following discussion is based on the hierarchy associated with thirteen federal front-line jobs that terminate in Minnesota (presumably, front-line jobs in Minnesota do not involve radically different reporting chains from front-line jobs elsewhere in America):

—Air traffic controller (Federal Aviation Administration, Department of Transportation)

—Revenue agent (Internal Revenue Service, Department of the Treasury)

—Public housing specialist (Department of Housing and Urban Development)

—Hospital nurse (Department of Veterans Affairs)

—Immigration inspector (Immigration and Naturalization Service, Department of Justice)

—Social security claims representative (Social Security Administration, Department of Health and Human Services)

—Weather forecaster (National Oceanographic and Atmospheric Administration, Department of Commerce)

—Food inspector (Food Safety and Inspection Service, Department of Agriculture)

—Customs inspector (Customs Service, Department of the Treasury)

—Forest ranger (Forest Service, Department of Agriculture)

—Park ranger (Park Service, Department of the Interior)

—Wage and hour investigator (Employment Standards Administration, Department of Labor)

—International trade specialist (International Trade Administration, Department of Commerce)

The distance between the top of each department and the given front-line job can be measured according to four reporting chains: (1) the formal personnel reporting chain (who reported to whom for purposes of annual performance evaluations); (2) the informal reporting chain (who reported to whom for all practical purposes); (3) the policy reporting chain (who reported to whom in making policies affecting the front line); and (4) budget (who reported to whom in shaping the annual fiscal budget).[34] These chains are summarized by job in table 3-5, which measures distance as the number of steps (and resulting "stops") in the hierarchy.

The number of steps in the formal and informal reporting chains is simply equal to the number of layers, while the number of steps in the policy and budget chains includes detours down assorted branches of the hierarchy. Imagine the hierarchy as a tree. Policies and budgets travel along branches but must come back to the trunk before moving down to the next level. Making a budget, for example, often involves four or more budget units. The budget process may start with an assistant secretary for budget, move down within that office to a budget analyst, then back up before being passed down into the given administration for further fine tuning by an entirely separate budget office, before being passed even further down into a regional budget office, before being passed down to the front-line unit.

Policy chains also involve more than one unit at the same level competing to set policy—what table 3-5 calls "splits" in the hierarchy. At Commerce, for example, there appear to be sixty-nine different units responsible for setting guidelines affecting the international trade specialist answering front-line questions about U.S. trade. Because these various units may or may not be involved in any given policy decision, however, a stop at any given step in the policy chain can only be counted twice: once going down, once coming back up. This counting decision may, therefore, drastically understate the amount of potential delay in the policy process.

From a formal reporting perspective, the federal government appears relatively flat. On average, there are only nine layers from top to bottom, of which 46 percent are in the front-line unit. At the Minneapolis-St. Paul VA hospital, for example, there is not much to get in the way of the nurse:

Begin in Washington
  1. Secretary of veterans affairs
  2. Under secretary for health
  3. Deputy under secretary for health for administration and operations
  4. Associate chief medical director for operations
Exit Washington for Ann Arbor regional office
  5. Regional director
Exit Ann Arbor for Minneapolis
  6. Medical center director
  7. Chief of staff
  8. Chief nurse
  9. Nurse supervisor
  10. Nurse

These are only the people who do the personnel evaluations, however. If one adds in the informal layers, the nurse works eighteen layers down, with roughly a quarter of those layers in the hospital:

Begin in Washington
  1. Secretary
  2. Chief of staff

TABLE 3-5. *Decision Chains in Government, Selected Federal Front-Line Jobs Terminating in Minnesota, 1993*

	Chain			
Agency/Job	Formal	Informal	Policy	Budget
Air traffic controller				
Number of steps	12	19	87	84
Percentage on front line	42	26	14	12
Number of branches	. . .	. . .	5	6
Number of splits	. . .	. . .	6	. . .
Revenue agent (examinations)				
Number of steps	9	17	66	78
Percentage on front line	56	41	11	19
Number of branches	. . .	. . .	4	5
Number of splits	. . .	. . .	15	. . .
Public housing specialist				
Number of steps	6	15	71	75
Percentage on front line	66	33	7	13
Number of branches	. . .	. . .	4	5
Number of splits	. . .	. . .	6	. . .
Veterans hospital nurse				
Number of steps	10	18	41	63
Percentage on front line	50	28	22	16
Number of branches	. . .	. . .	3	4
Number of splits	. . .	. . .	1	. . .
Immigration inspector				
Number of steps	8	18	65	62
Percentage on front line	63	22	8	16
Number of branches	. . .	. . .	4	4
Number of splits	. . .	. . .	1	. . .
Social security claims representative				
Number of steps	10	16	55	61
Percentage on front line	40	25	7	7
Number of branches	. . .	. . .	3	3
Number of splits	. . .	. . .	3	. . .
Weather forecaster				
Number of steps	8	16	37	60
Percentage on front line	38	25	11	5
Number of branches	. . .	. . .	2	4
Number of splits	. . .	. . .	3	. . .

TABLE 3-5. *(Continued)*

Agency/Job	Chain			
	Formal	*Informal*	*Policy*	*Budget*
Food inspector				
Number of steps	10	17	49	58
Percentage on front line	40	29	14	12
Number of branches	. . .	. . .	5	5
Number of splits	. . .	. . .	0	. . .
Customs inspector				
Number of steps	8	16	46	57
Percentage on front line	63	31	11	14
Number of branches	. . .	. . .	3	6
Number of splits	. . .	. . .	7	. . .
Forest ranger				
Number of steps	9	16	60	55
Percentage on front line	33	19	5	6
Number of branches	. . .	. . .	5	4
Number of splits	. . .	. . .	10	. . .
Park ranger				
Number of steps	9	19	65	53
Percentage on front line	55	26	8	9
Number of branches	. . .	. . .	4	3
Number of splits	. . .	. . .	1	. . .
Wage and hour investigator				
Number of steps	9	13	48	54
Percentage on front line	33	23	6	6
Number of branches	. . .	. . .	3	3
Number of splits	. . .	. . .	6	. . .
International trade specialist				
Number of steps	8	11	70	44
Percentage on front line	25	18	3	5
Number of branches	. . .	. . .	4	4
Number of splits	. . .	. . .	69	. . .
Average				
Number of steps	9	16	58	62
Percentage on front line	46	27	10	11

SOURCES: Initial reporting chains were developed from the *Federal Yellow Book* (Monitor Leadership Directories, Inc., 1992), and checked with the thirteen district offices for further detail; additional information was supplied in interviews with nine of the thirteen directors of the offices or units which contained the thirteen front-line jobs.

3. Deputy chief of staff
4. Deputy secretary
5. Under secretary for health
6. Deputy under secretary for health
7. Deputy under secretary for health for administration and operations
8. Associate chief medical director for operations
9. Deputy associate chief medical director for operations
Exit Washington for Ann Arbor regional office
10. Regional director
11. Chief of staff
12. Associate regional director
Exit Ann Arbor for Minneapolis
13. Medical center director (Minneapolis)
14. Chief of staff
15. Chief nurse
16. Associate chief nurse
17. Nurse supervisor
18. Nurse

This research makes no claims about the value added by each of the informal layers. No doubt the chief of staff and deputy chief of staff add important input, as do the deputy secretary, deputy under secretary, deputy associate chief, and others. For the nurse, however, the question is how to provide high-quality care to the patient, not how the secretary keeps control of a growing number of assistant secretaries.

Luckily for the patient, the VA nurse has a very simple policy chain. The department sets nursing policy in Washington in the office of the associate deputy chief medical director for clinical programs. Here the nurse encounters the only split in the policy chain, between the chief of nursing service programs and environment and the chief of nursing research, mental health-behavioral sciences, and career development. Otherwise, policy runs rather smoothly downward.

Budget is more complicated, in part because it determines so much of what the VA does. Here the nurse works sixty-three steps below the top, of which only 16 percent are in the front-line unit. Although the VA hospital director has a chief fiscal officer, most of the work occurs higher up. As the number of detours suggests, that work gets done over and over and over: first in the assistant secretary and chief financial officer's budget shop in Washington (which reports to the secretary), second in the director of the medical programs' budget office also in Washington (which reports to the under secretary for health), third in the assistant regional financial manager's office in the Ann Arbor regional office (which reports to the regional director). Consider just the top of the budget chain for its complexity—the bottom of each detour, or branch, is italicized:

Begin in Washington

1.		Secretary
2.		Chief of staff
3.		Deputy chief of staff
4.		Deputy secretary
5.	15.	Assistant secretary and chief financial officer
6.	14.	Deputy assistant secretary
7.	13.	Associate deputy assistant secretary
8.	12.	Medical services director
9.	11.	*Supervising budget analyst*
10.	_↑	*Budget analyst*
16.	34.	Under secretary for health
17.	33.	Deputy under secretary for health for administration and operations
18.	32.	Associate chief medical director for resource management
19.	31.	Director, Medical Programs Budget Office
20.	30.	Deputy director, Budget Office
21.	29.	Assistant director for budget formulation
22.	28.	Director, Project Coordination and Budget Office
23.	27.	Assistant director, Project Coordination and Budget Office
24.	26.	*Supervising budget analyst*
25.	_↑	*Budget analyst*

There appears to be some relationship between the number of steps for each job and the nature of the task (see table 3-5). Jobs that involve more hazard to the public (air traffic controller, revenue agent, VA hospital nurse, and immigration inspector) or that have involved more scandal (public housing specialist) are somewhat further from the top in policy or budget than those that involve less risk (forest ranger, park ranger, international trade representative). So noted, all of the jobs, whether risky or not, have relatively little local autonomy.

The costs of this top-heavy structure, according to the assorted district managers interviewed in checking the reporting chains, are threefold.

INSULATION. Distance insulates top managers from the real world far below; it also slows the movement of guidance down from above and the movement of ideas up. "The people in the field may know more about the policy and have good suggestions as to how the policy should be implemented," said one of the managers in the high-hazard units. "But Washington has no real way of tapping into the expertise. And even if they did, it would have to be passed through so many hands that the smudging would take care of the reality check." Asked why thickening occurs, one manager answered as follows:

First, you need to get good people into the jobs. The pay won't cut it so you give them a career fast-track. Bring them in at a GS 11 instead of a 9, bump them up a grade within a year. Then you move them to Washington because that's where the action is. Once they're there, they can't get back to the field—nobody in the field wants them; they can't do anything and cost too much anyway. Never managed anyone. Then they start seeing the world differently. Lose sight of what's relevant out in the world. Creates flawed policy because the commissioner comes to rely on them rather than calling down to the field. They are just down the hall. But because those GS 13s, 14s, and 15s haven't a clue how things work out here, they put together policies that just can't work or just foul up everything.[35]

Distance is especially troublesome for implementation—distance is the enemy of clarity. "By the time an idea gets down here, it has been translated, reworked, and bureaucratized to the point where we just can't do it," remarked one of the managers. "We're still getting guidance from the mid-Bush years." The thirteen district directors were interviewed, for example, at the height of the National Performance Review, but only two mentioned any involvement in the effort, and even then the input was spotty. One who was not involved told of receiving an invitation to an agency reinventing session in St. Louis only two days in advance: "I couldn't cut a travel order in that time, didn't have the budget, and would have been seated so far away from the action that it wouldn't have made a difference one way or the other."

ACCOUNTABILITY. Distance may also weaken accountability, making it nearly impossible to know just who is responsible for any given decision. The more stops along the chain, the less likely a president is to know who to hold accountable and the more difficult it is to assign credit.

Accountability requirement may also lead to a compliance mentality, which puts its faith in enforcing rules and limiting local autonomy as a path to accountability.[36] "Two-thirds of the regional office staff is superfluous," argued one manager in a theme echoed by nearly all of his peers. "They try to find ways to make themselves more needed and more useful, but often translate into meddling. They claim credit for the good and always pass the buck when things go wrong." Moreover, these managers may create needless monitoring systems. As one of the high-hazard managers noted, "We're looking at the wrong things constantly: take out a form and make sure every box is checked properly—make a ticky mark here, a ticky mark there. But that kind of oversight isn't helping me do my job better. A lot of it is looking at whether the garbage can lids are on tight." For these front-line managers, creating more executives simply means creating more make-work. Whether headquarters and regional executives who have spent their careers supervising, disciplining, and overmanaging their employees can somehow be remade into the kind of coaching, mentoring, empowering managers admired by the Gore report remains to be seen.

Too many layers may also create an entirely unaccountable system. "It is virtually impossible to contact anyone at headquarters on any issue," one of the managers argued. "I might call with a question which needs to be answered as soon as possible, but won't get a response for two days. I just stopped calling and started making my own decisions, the problem being that no one in 'Disneyland East' knows what the hell I'm doing." As one manager put it, some local agencies might as well be flying a skull and crossbones.

The thickening may also weaken reporting relationships as the GS 14s and 15s pile up. "We are getting increased pay compression at the top," said one district head. "That means I'm a 14 and report to a 14 and have subordinates who are 14s. It creates a problem in leadership. We will be pushing the field offices up a full grade next year—clericals up from a journeyman 4 to a 5, service representatives up to 8 from 7, supervisors up from 11 to 12. Eventually, that bumping will run into the 14s already on board, and it will make a difference in how we all respond to each other."

MAKE-WORK. The one thing all thirteen managers complained most about was the make-work that flows from regional and headquarters managers who seem to have nothing better to do. One of the interviews was interrupted, for example, by a call from Washington demanding a report on this front-line unit's role in battling the devastating summer 1993 floods in the upper Midwest. As the district head reported, he had not sent a report to Washington because the office, obviously, could not add anything to the effort. It had no programs, no material, no staff to lend to the inventory some political appointee was putting together to show the press how dedicated department X truly was. The problem for the manager, apparently, was that he had also neglected to send a report on his lack of report.

Some of the anger was directed toward the regional offices: "There are too many employees within the region with nothing to do," said one. "They are twisting in the wind, dying a slow death. It'd be more humane just to shoot them." Some was meant for the presidential transition: "When Washington wants a report, we have to give it to them, even if it makes no sense. And when they don't want a report, they more than likely want a report on your last report. That's the problem with presidential transitions. New appointees want reports on what you were reporting two years ago so they don't get blind-sided." Some was directed to "number crunchers" far above. "Twenty-five percent of my time as director is spent fielding data for the front office. When a policy comes down, they want certification that we are doing it. It is mostly activity centered—how many hours did you spend on training X, how many people did you serve. I'm even expected to report when I have nothing to report."

The bottom line for all of the managers was not so much the frustration with meddling but their own resource constraints. Faced with the kinds of quality standards being pressed from Washington, coupled with the 272,900-employee cut, much of it from attrition, many saw the thickening of government as a very real threat to performance. Asked to do more and more with less, they wondered how headquarters could continue to justify its girth.

The Political-Career Mix

The concern for make-work clearly relates to the growing number of senior managers and political appointees in Washington. Here the absolute number of political appointees or senior managers is far less important than how they stack into layers of supervision or how they work together in making and implementing public policy.

As noted in chapter 2, many of the political jobs were created to enhance the president's control of government, in what political scientist Richard Nathan calls an effort to build an administrative presidency.[37] Writing in part from his personal experiences as a Nixon domestic policy adviser, Nathan chronicles the White House effort to gain control of executive branch operations—regulatory, budgetary, and grant making—through a coterie of handpicked, intensely loyal aides salted throughout government at the subpresidential level. "Getting control over these processes was the aim of the President's strategy for domestic government in his second term. Judged against the lack of legislative successes on domestic issues in the first term, there are grounds for concluding that this was a rational decision."[38]

Thus politicization, and the thickening that appears to go with it, fits the prevailing presidential incentives. According to political scientist Terry Moe, weaknesses in the institution explain the tightening of the appointments process. "By appointing individuals on the basis of loyalty, ideology, or programmatic support," writes Moe of the latter, the president "can take direct action to enhance responsiveness throughout the administration, from presidential agencies like the OMB to the most remote independent boards and commissions." Moreover, "by manipulating civil service rules, proposing minor reorganizations, and pressing for modifying legislation, he can take steps to increase the number and location of administrative positions that can be occupied by appointees."[39]

The question for the moment is whether Nixon and Reagan's strategy makes practical sense. Is the president right to pack the executive branch as deeply as possible? The National Commission on the Public Service argued that such a strategy is deceptive: "Excessive numbers of presidential appointees may actually undermine effective presidential control of the executive branch. Presidents today are further away from the top career layers of government with 3,000 appointees . . . than was Franklin Roosevelt 50 years ago with barely 200."[40] It is a classic diffusion-of-accountability argument. The issue is not numbers of appointees but how they pull together on the president's behalf.

In absolute terms the number of political executives is trivial—it is the tiniest fraction of the total federal work force. However, it is not the number that matters but how the number sorts out into layers. Consider, for example, the political layers interposed between the president and the thirteen front-line jobs described earlier (see table 3-6).

According to the table, one-third of the formal and informal chain is occupied by political appointees, one-fourth of the policy chain, and one-sixth of the budget chain. There appears to be no rhyme or reason for the differences in political penetration—why does a park ranger need more political supervision than a forest ranger? A wage and hour investigator more than a revenue examiner?

TABLE 3-6. *Political Control of Decision Chains in Government, Selected Positions, 1993*

Job[a]	Chain			
	Formal	Informal	Policy	Budget
Air traffic controller				
Number of political steps (percentage)	3(25)	7(37)	15(17)	13(16)
Revenue agent (examinations)				
Number of political steps (percentage)	2(22)	3(18)	18(27)	6(8)
Public housing specialist				
Number of political steps	2(33)	6(40)	13(18)	11(15)
Veterans hospital nurse				
Number of political steps (percentage)	2(33)	5(40)	6(18)	8(15)
Immigration inspector				
Number of political steps (percentage)	3(38)	9(50)	19(29)	13(21)
Social security claims representative				
Number of political steps (percentage)	2(20)	4(25)	13(24)	7(12)
Weather forecaster				
Number of political steps (percentage)	2(25)	5(31)	5(14)	10(17)
Food inspector				
Number of political steps (percentage)	3(30)	7(41)	10(20)	10(17)
Customs inspector				
Number of political steps (percentage)	2(30)	5(41)	5(20)	10(17)
Forest ranger				
Number of political steps (percentage)	2(22)	6(38)	8(13)	8(15)
Park ranger				
Number of political steps (percentage)	3(33)	10(48)	21(32)	19(36)
Wage and hour investigator				
Number of political steps (percentage)	4(44)	10(77)	18(38)	16(30)
International trade specialist				
Number of political steps (percentage)	4(50)	6(55)	28(40)	13(30)
Average				
Number of political steps (percentage)	3(31)	6(42)	14(24)	11(19)
Ratio of political to career steps	1:3	1:3	1:4	1:6

SOURCES: See appendix.

a. The table was created by checking each title in the thirteen job chains against the 1992 *United States Government Policy and Supporting Positions,* or "Plum Book," which records all presidential appointments. When the status of a position was unclear, it was counted as career.

Presidential appointees may be but a tiny fraction of the federal work force, but they are a rather substantial source of the layering that gets in the way of front-line employees. It is ironic, therefore, that calls for greater employee involvement and innovation so often ignore the political layering that appears to stymie risk taking. In fact, political appointees may have the greater stake in undermining innovation, particularly if the innovation happens to originate in a previous administration.

By now, moreover, it should be clear that increasing the number of executives dilutes presidential command, a fact well illustrated by the

TABLE 3-7. *Political Appointees and Career Civil Servants, Executive Levels I–IV, 1960–92*

Year, president	All executives		Deputy assistant secretaries	
	Political	Career	Political	Career
1960, Eisenhower				
Number (percentage)	221(89)	27(11)	71(92)	6(8)
1964, Kennedy-Johnson				
Number (percentage)	251(75)	84(25)	103(76)	32(24)
1968, Johnson				
Number (percentage)	297(73)	111(27)	111(73)	41(27)
1972, Nixon				
Number (percentage)	313(66)	162(34)	105(66)	54(34)
1976, Nixon-Ford				
Number (percentage)	405(62)	253(39)	178(72)	70(28)
1980, Carter[a]				
Number (percentage)	276(30)	652(70)	51(14)	313(86)
1984, Reagan				
Number (percentage)	582(51)	561(49)	245(61)	156(39)
1988, Reagan				
Number (percentage)	582(48)	639(52)	240(59)	169(41)
1992, Bush				
Number (percentage)	590(36)	1,038(64)	195(38)	312(62)

SOURCES: *United States Government Policy and Supporting Positions.*
a. The 1980 numbers are questionable because of definitional problems surrounding implementation of the newly created Senior Executive Service. The authors of the *Policy and Supporting Positions* in 1980 may not have known exactly how to classify the new positions. Any position not identified as political was coded as career. The table covers only Executive Level I–IV positions because of instability in the political and career identifications at Executive Level V.

crowding of career and political officials in the top compartments of government. Indeed, as political appointees penetrate deeper into the top five compartments, the number of careerists who lay claim to senior titles also grows. There appears to be a symbiosis—each new presidential appointee brings his or her share of deputies, assistants, and associates, many of whom are career civil servants (see table 3-7).

The growing number of career executives in the top compartments is easily one of the most curious findings in this book. After all, scholars and careerists alike have been complaining for years about the growing politicization of posts that once belonged to career civil servants.[41] The conversion of Hoover's assistant secretaries for administration (ASAs) from career civil servants to political appointees is but one case in point.

Nevertheless, table 3-7 shows a dramatic increase in the number of career executives whose job titles place them in the top four compartments. Nine out of ten senior jobs were occupied by political appointees at the end of the second Eisenhower administration; the number had fallen to just one out of three by the end of the Bush administration thirty-two years later. Except for some brief success in packing the deputy assistant secretary layer, neither Nixon nor Reagan was able to reverse the trend. The question is whether the concerns about politicization are somehow misplaced.

One answer may be in the difference between the absolute number of political appointees, which grew dramatically between 1980 and 1992, and the percentage, which actually declined from 1984 onward. There is no question that political appointees began to displace career officers or any question that they brought increasing numbers of Schedule C special assistants along with them to do much of the work once reserved for career civil servants.

Yet the political penetration was hardly equal within or across departments. The number of Schedule C appointees—a number that does not show up in the core tables for this book—increased 92 percent (from 26 to 50) at Treasury between 1980 and 1986, 82 percent (65 to 118) at Education, 30 percent (66 to 85) at Justice, 42 percent (57 to 81) at Transportation, 40 percent (83 to 116) at Agriculture, and 33 percent (51 to 68) at Interior, but actually fell by 20 percent (106 to 85) at HHS, 3 percent (128 to 124) at Commerce, and 1 percent (101 to 100) at HUD.[42] Similar variations occur across the departments in the growth of noncareer, or political, appointments to the SES. Nevertheless, all of the departments thickened to one degree or another over the 1980s, with HHS and Commerce becoming among the thickest.

Moreover, within departments, the rising number of presidential appointees has tended to concentrate in particularly sensitive units. At Commerce in 1986, for example, concentrations of Schedule Cs could be found in the International Trade Administration and the central offices surrounding the secretary and deputy secretary; only a handful at the Bureau of the Census and National Bureau of Standards; and zero at the Patents and Trademarks Office and the Office of the Chief Economist. At Justice, large concentrations could be found in the central offices and the Office of Justice Programs; only one or two at the Criminal, Civil Rights, and Criminal divisions; and zero at the Bureau of Prisons.[43] Again, all of these offices thickened to one degree or another. Bluntly put, presidents may thicken for one reason, such as responsiveness; bureaus may thicken for quite another—to stay at the same level in the executive pecking order or to defend themselves from the muscling up in central departmental offices. The net result may be the same.

These trends are somewhat different where most career civil servants meet their first political appointees: the deputy assistant secretary (DAS) layer. It is here where political appointees of one kind or another came to occupy the single largest number of jobs.[44] As above, the DAS mix can be interpreted in either percentages or absolute numbers.

In percentages, political DASers show the same general decline as the rest of the political executives but made a remarkable comeback under Reagan. Even as the bottom of the assistant secretary compartment flooded with careerists, Reagan used his centralized personnel process to rebuild a significant political share in the DAS layer. As chapter 4 suggests, Reagan may have gone to school on Nixon's earlier efforts to politicize the DAS ranks.

In absolute numbers, both Reagan and Bush increased political DASers. One out of three of their appointees came in at this rank. When principal deputy assistant secretaries are added into the totals—half of whom are political—the number rises to two out of five. This increasing number of political appointees did not, however, spoil a previously pristine career DAS layer. As the layer widened over time, it actually created more job opportunities for career than for political executives.

None of this is to argue that efforts to gain political control of the bureaucracy are misplaced. As political scientists B. Dan Wood and Richard Waterman convincingly show, presidential appointments do make a difference. Examining impacts in seven agencies—the Environmental Protection Agency, the Equal Opportunity Employment Commission, the Federal Trade Commission, the Food and Drug Administration (HHS), the National Highway Traffic Safety Administration (Transportation), the Nuclear Regulatory Commission, and the Office of Surface Mining (Interior)—Wood and Waterman conclude that political appointees can have "extraordinary influence" over agency policy: "In five of the seven programs we examined, agency outputs shifted immediately after a change in agency leadership. In four of these cases (the NRC, the EEOC, the FTC and the FDA), change followed an appointment at the beginning of a presidential administration. The direction and magnitude of these responses reflects the increased power of a chief executive in the period after a presidential election."[45]

So noted, the numbers suggest that a smaller number of presidential appointees might increase agency responsiveness even more. Presidents may be deluding themselves that the tonnage of appointments is more important than the clarity of their leadership. Just as these numbers question whether ever-expanding penetration is in the president's interest, they also question recommendations for more career-reserved top jobs as a strategy of retention. There appear to be plenty of political and career executives already. Thus, whatever the merits of politicization or more career mix yesterday, one way to increase the president's control of the executive branch today is to flatten the bureaucracy starting at the top, including both political and career posts. Doing so might actually give the president a chance to influence the front line directly.

Conclusion

This chapter has sketched a very broad case against the thickening of government, which could certainly benefit from deeper research in several areas. Consider these questions as a start:

—Is there a single appropriate span of control for government? This is one of the most vexing questions facing agencies as they struggle with the 1:15 span of control suggested by the Gore task force. How wide can a unit get without losing control or creating bottlenecks? Are there some functions that must remain narrow?

—How should government value the individual positions recorded in the decision chains presented earlier? Job audits are one place to begin. If indeed many of the alter-ego deputies in government are doing little more than making their chiefs feel more important, perhaps they should go. If, however, they fulfill key supervisory functions, particularly during frequent vacancies among their political bosses, perhaps they should stay.

—Is there "good" thickening as well as "bad," good growth in hierarchy and bad? Thickening due to increasing job complexity would, in theory, be much more acceptable to an agency (and a budget-conscious public) than thickening due to finding jobs for political allies and campaign contributors or to keep up with other departments.

—Which is more important to the thickening of government: heightening or widening? This is one of those chicken-and-egg questions that can defy analysis. Yet establishing some understanding of the relationship may help policymakers create useful guidelines for monitoring the many individual events in the thickening process.

—Is there a relationship between middle- and upper-level thickening? Although the middle-level thickening appears to be driven more by pay and job complexity, it may still trigger thickening above. And although higher-level thickening appears to be driven by an entirely different set of pressures, it may still generate thickening below. Flattening strategies that ignore one or the other may be doomed to failure.

—Are there any substitutes for hierarchy? If thickening is justified in part by desires for accountability, how might government design a system for a thinner structure? Information technology is one example of a substitute for traditional hierarchy, rendering narrow spans of control less relevant in the day-to-day operations of the front line.

Answering these and other research questions is a first step in creating a solid philosophy of thinning. Too much of the recent argument in favor of flattening has been colored by hunch, which may be what got government into its thickened state in the first place.

Until the research is done, the burden of proof on the thickening of government belongs on those who support the continued layering. What matters most to government's front-line workers—air traffic controllers, social security claims representatives, weather forecasters—is not research but the capacity to do their jobs. Asked what difference thickening makes, the air traffic controllers at Farmington Center in Minnesota had little to say about the career-political mix or spans of control in Washington. What they complained about were the lousy radar (vintage 1960), antiquated computers, and nearly constant staffing pressures that make their work so stressful. The VA hospital nurses had nothing to say about organizational design either. They complained about their pay, the lack of supplies, and a sense that needed resources were being wasted on headquarters.

In a very real sense, though, thickening is exactly what they were complaining about. It distorts front-line requests for help upward and policy clarity downward. Yet if the 272,900-employee cut is not made carefully, front-line workers will likely lose both ways. The old layers may stay in place, while front-line staffing decays further. The first step in designing an equitable flattening—one that at the very least provides more resources at Farmington Center for Minnesota frequent fliers—is to ask where thickening starts.

4

Where Does
Thickening Start?

It is tempting to believe thickening starts with middle managers buried deep in the bureaucracy—careerists with little better to do than inflate their status by promoting underqualified subordinates into higher-paying jobs. All reformers would have to do is find these wasteful bureaucrats and punish them.

The classic statement of the case against self-serving managers was made by humorist C. Northcote Parkinson. "The fact is," Parkinson wrote in 1957, "that the number of officials and the quantity of the work are not related to each other at all." Because growth is driven by two simple motives—"to multiply subordinates, not rivals," and to make work for one another so that the organization seems busy—"administrators are more or less bound to multiply." According to Parkinson's formula, any department not at war will invariably grow between "5.17 per cent and 6.56 per cent [each year], irrespective of any variation in the amount of work (if any) to be done."[1]

Parkinson steadfastly refused to define this growth as a problem. "Those who hold that this growth is essential to gain full employment are fully entitled to their opinion. Those who doubt the stability of an economy based upon reading each other's minutes are equally entitled to theirs." More to the point of the next three chapters, he also refused to offer remedies. "It is not the business of the botanist to eradicate the weeds," he noted. "Enough for him if he can tell us just how fast they grow."[2] Alas, knowing the root structure of thickening is essential to its resolution. Lacking that knowledge, Parkinson's imaginary botanist would have to be satisfied with an occasional mowing, always sure that the weeds would grow back.

In fact, thickening is rooted in many places. It can come from the top of departments, with the creation of new management layers. It can come from interest groups and the public with the pressure for new programs. It can come from either end of Pennsylvania Avenue, from a Congress that often uses thickening to demonstrate its commitment to national priorities, or from presidents in search of yet more help. It can come from the lack of a strong management focus at the Office of Management and Budget, or from back-door pay increases sanctioned by middle-level managers.

Thickening can even come from administrations that promise the opposite. Carter promised a lean and simple government, yet added two seats in his cabinet for Education and Energy and oversaw a remarkable expansion in subcabinet thickening. In fact, Carter permitted the single largest diffusion of new layers in the past three decades alongside one of the largest absolute increases in the total number of senior executives (see appendix tables).

Reagan did little better in the battle of the bulge. He too promised a thinner government, starting with abolition of Education and Energy; yet he not only permitted those departments to live but also supported elevation of the Veterans Administration to cabinet level, as well as another sweeping diffusion of layers. If Carter was one of the great thickeners of the upper levels of government, Reagan was not far behind. His administration added five new layers of senior management—from chiefs of staff to department secretaries on down to new layers of inspectors general—and witnessed a substantial rise in the absolute number of senior executives.

As for grand reorganization, presidents only rarely carry through, often abandoning their plans at the slightest hint of congressional pressure. As political scientists James March and Johan Olson argue, "Presidents, in particular, go through a cycle of enthusiasm and disappointment. Most commonly (Franklin Roosevelt and Richard Nixon are partial counterexamples), they start reorganization studies at the beginning of their terms, but by the time the studies are completed, they seem to have concluded that reorganization either will not solve their administrative problems or will not be worth the political costs." The problem may be that presidents are far less committed to reform than Congress is to protecting the status quo:

Most recent presidents have apparently considered reorganization an important part of their personal agendas, even a duty, but they have not considered it important enough to make significant political trades involving substantive legislative projects. For the most part, the political trading goes the other way. Presidents give up reorganization projects in order to secure legislative support for other things, and legislators give up opposition on other things in order to block administrative change. . . . The internal structure of an agency and its location in the departmental structure of the government are perceived by congressmen as affecting legislative influence and control and thus the capability of furthering political careers through constituency services. As a result, presidential proposals for reorganization have the consequence of providing a convenient trading chip in bargaining with Congress.[3]

The path of least political resistance for presidents is clear. Better to thicken government than pay the very high costs of thinning.

The Roots of Thickening

However tempting it is to search for the one great source of thickening in the vain hope that it can be severed, the roots are hopelessly tangled. The president cannot create statutory positions without Congress; Congress rarely creates positions without checking with interest groups; departments cannot testify without clearance from the Office of Management and Budget; OMB is an agency of the president; middle managers cannot act without approval from one or more of the above.

Thus perhaps the best an administrative botanist can do is separate the main trunks of thickening from the lesser offshoots. The following pages endeavor to do just that by separating four such tangles: new departments from old departments, the inner cabinet from the outer cabinet, Congress from the president, and Democrats from Republicans. Reformers should have a better idea where to cut, if indeed the trunks can be severed, as a result.

New Departments and Old Departments

There are several reasons why a new department might be a catalyst for new layers and subunits. Cabinet bills originate in the House and Senate government operations committees, the most likely reservoirs of state-of-the-art thinking on organizational structure.

TABLE 4-1. *Number of Occupants by Layer, 1964, 1968* [a]

Title	All departments, 1964	Housing and Urban Development, 1968	Transportation, 1968	All other departments, 1968
Secretary	1	1	1	1
Deputy secretaries	. . . [b]	. . .	. . . 1 [c]	. . . [d]
Under secretaries	2	1	4	2
Deputy under secretaries	1	1	2	1
Assistant secretaries	8	7	8	9
Principal deputy assistant secretaries	. . . [e]	1	. . .	. . . [d]
Deputy assistant secretaries	14	13	6	14
Associate deputy assistant secretaries	3	8	5	3
Assistant deputy assistant secretaries	7	. . .	4	8

SOURCES: See appendix.

a. Note that the HUD and Transportation data are from 1968 and do not necessarily represent the exact formation on day one of operation. Note also that only institutionalized layers—that is, layers that existed in at least half of all departments at the time—are shown for columns 1 and 4.

b. Three departments already had the title.

c. The administrator of the Federal Aviation Administration was paid at Executive Level II; although the under secretary was also paid at level II, the title is given precedence over pay.

d. None added the title.

e. One department already had the title.

Moreover, cabinet departments come into being through whole statute, thereby giving Congress and the president a rare opportunity to confront questions of organization design, albeit often for symbolic reasons.[4] If there is an innovative title in circulation, it is likely to show up in a cabinet bill. The Department of Veterans Affairs Act, for example, created the first statutory chief financial officer (CFO) in government, an innovation that prompted the Chief Financial Officers Act of 1990, which created CFOs in every department and agency of government.

Just because cabinet bills provide the chance to muse about hierarchy does not mean the final bills advance the cause of thickening, however. The easiest way to check the impact of new departments on thickening is to compare the organization charts of government before enactment of a new department with the charts afterward. Consider HUD and Transportation first (see table 4-1).

Nothing in the histories implicates HUD or Transportation as the source of new layers. Although HUD had a principal deputy assistant secretary by 1968, it was merely copying the already existing positions in the Department of Defense. The two new departments also stayed within normal bounds on the total number of occupants at each layer, with Transportation high on the under secretary numbers because of the Federal Highway Administration, the Urban Mass Transportation Administration, and the Federal Rail Administration, all of which resided at the under secretary rank before entering the new department.

If there was one innovation, it was the placement of the under secretary of transportation at executive level II, which is ordinarily reserved for deputy secretary positions. The reason has more to do with the politics of moving the powerful Federal Aviation Administration (FAA) into a new department than with some novel theory of executive organization. Simply put, the administrator of FAA was already at level II in 1966 when Johnson proposed the new department. Although an earlier Budget Bureau design task force had recommended a demotion to level III to keep the post at the same rank as the under secretary, Congress would not agree. Thus the decision to give the under secretary the higher pay rank.[5] Presumably, equal pay would create a certain status. With time, of course, the title caught up with the pay, creating some momentum toward creation of deputy secretaries elsewhere in government.

Indeed, new departments appear to play a critical role in building momentum for existing innovations, a role confirmed in the Departments of Education and Energy (see table 4-2).

Both of these new departments show a much more pronounced willingness than their Johnson-era predecessors to adopt the latest in informal layers as they come into being. Both accept the principal deputy assistant secretary concept, while Energy also picks up the assistant deputy assistant secretary and deputy assistant general counsel and inspector general layers. Moreover, both end up with more assistant secretaries and deputy assistant secretaries than the average in 1976 or 1980. Neither might be innovating per se, but both are taking full advantage of the opportunities to build intricate administrative infrastructures.

Of particular interest is the division of the old Department of Health, Education, and Welfare into two new departments, Health and Human Services and Education. In theory, the two new departments should not differ greatly from the one old. But for a new secretary, under secretary, and a few new assistant secretaries, Education should have been essentially unchanged. And, in theory, the new HHS should have come through the reorganization slimmer than the old HEW. In reality, both departments grew dramatically (see table 4-3).

The growth raises a variety of questions about need, particularly since neither inherited any new responsibilities in the split. As Beryl Radin

TABLE 4-2. *Number of Occupants by Layer, 1976, 1980*[a]

Layer	All departments, 1976	Education, 1980	Energy, 1980	Health and Human Services, 1980	All other departments, 1980
Secretary	1	1	1	1	1
Deputy secretaries	. . .[a]	. . .	1	. . .	2
Under secretaries	2	1	1	1	3
Deputy under secretaries	4	2	1	1	4
Assistant secretaries	11	13	15	12	12
Principal deputy assistant secretaries	. . .[b]	4	3	. . .	. . .[c]
Deputy assistant secretaries	23	36	29	32	26
Associate deputy assistant secretaries	8	9	6	4	10
Deputy associate deputy assistant secretaries	. . .[b]	. . .	2	4	. . .[a]
Assistant general counsels/ inspectors general	10	9	22	10	10
Deputy assistant general counsels/inspectors general	. . .[e]	. . .	2	12	. . .[f]

SOURCES: See appendix.
a. Five departments already had the title.
b. Three departments already had the title.
c. None added the title.
d. One department added the title.
e. One department already had the title.
f. Four departments added the title.

and Willis Hawley note in their history of the Department of Education, "The legislation creating the Department had made only marginal additions to the cluster of programs that had been housed in the Office of Education and the Office of the Assistant Secretary for Education within HEW."[6] Why, then, would Education need thirteen assistant secretaries and HHS twelve, when a total of only thirteen existed at HEW in 1976? Why sixty-eight deputy assistant secretaries in an administrative space once occupied by only twenty-five? And why would both need such a large number of assistant GCs and IGs?

The answer may simply be that both were trying to fill the space once occupied by HEW. Education may have wanted to resemble the old HEW as a way of proving its significance, HHS as a way of proving its immunity. Moreover, Education was created in response to heavy lobbying by the national education lobby, particularly the National Education Association, and therefore may have had more people it needed to reward with jobs.

TABLE 4-3. *Number of Occupants by Layer of the Department of Health, Education, and Welfare, 1976, and the Departments of Health and Human Services and Education, 1980*

Layer	Health, Education, and Welfare, 1976	Education, 1980	Health and Human Services, 1980	Education + HHS, 1980
Secretary	1	1	1	2
Deputy secretaries	...	...	...	...
Under secretaries	1	1	1	2
Deputy under secretaries	...	2	1	3
Assistant secretaries	13	13	12	25
Principal deputy assistant secretaries	1	4	1	5
Deputy assistant secretaries	25	36	32	68
Associate deputy assistant secretaries	8	9	4	13
	...	...	4	4
Assistant general counsel inspectors general	7	9	10	19
Deputy assistant general counsel/inspector general	8	...	8	8

SOURCES: See appendix.

Yet Education and HHS were merely adopting ideas in good currency. Education expanded most in the assistant secretary compartment, where it adopted all of the ideas in good currency around government: an inspector general, and one assistant secretary each for public affairs, legislation, planning and budget, and civil rights. The first Hoover Commission's image of a single assistant secretary for administration with all those functions underneath it was long dead.

Not all cabinet bills extend the hierarchy as dramatically, however. The elevation of VA to cabinet status actually came in under average in 1988 (see table 4-4), largely because of concerted Senate efforts to limit the number of political appointees. Although VA did have a chief of staff in 1988, the position had existed for several years, also as a response to the Reagan personnel process. As the Senate Governmental Affairs Committee explained its assortment of caps on the number and mix of presidential appointees:

> It is the Committee's view that the bill places presidential appointees where they belong—at the top of the agency—and establishes effective

TABLE 4-4. *Number of Occupants by Layer on Thickening, 1984, 1988*

Layer	All departments, 1988	Veterans affairs, 1992	All other departments, 1992
Secretary	1	1	1
Chiefs of staff	. . .[a]	1	1[b]
Deputy secretaries	2	1	2
Under secretaries	3	2	2
Deputy under secretaries	5	3	4
Associate deputy under secretaries	. . .[c]	. . .	3
Assistant secretaries	14	9	16
Principal deputy assistant secretaries	7	. . .	10
Deputy assistant secretaries	32	26	37
Associate deputy assistant secretaries	10	30	29
Deputy associate deputy assistant secretaries	7	9	8
Assistant general counsel/inspectors general	10	8	15
Deputy assistant general counsels/ inspectors general	3	3	5

SOURCES: See appendix.
a. Six departments already had the title.
b. Five more departments added the title.
c. Three departments already had the title.

obstacles to politicization below. . . . The issue in enacting such caps is not whether presidential and noncareer appointments are inherently positive or negative. . . . Rather, the issue is whether there is a compelling case for reducing a strong career presence at the top of VA in favor of more presidential and noncareer appointees. Given the VA's strong operational character and the need for continuity of leadership, the Committee elected to impose limits on the number of potential political appointees as a barrier to any erosion of the Department's institutional capacity and long-term vitality.[7]

Lacking these caps, VA likely would have expanded just as Education and Energy had before.

The Inner Cabinet and the Outer

The fact that new departments primarily follow existing practice leads to questions about old departments. Are there some departments that have a bigger role in creating and diffusing new layers than others? The logical answer is the inner cabinet, which contains the oldest departments of all.

The concept of inner and outer cabinets has existed for several decades.[8] According to political scientist Thomas Cronin, Defense, Justice, State, and Treasury are "vested with high-priority responsibilities that bring their occupants into close and collaborative relationships with presidents and their top staff." In contrast:

> The outer-cabinet positions deal with strongly organized and more particularistic clientele, an involvement that helps to produce an advocate or adversary relationship to the White House. . . . These departments experience heavy and often conflicting pressures from clientele groups, from congressional interests, and from state and local governments, pressures that may run contrary to presidential priorities. Whereas three of the four inner-cabinet departments preside over policies that usually, though often imprudently, are perceived to be largely nonpartisan or bipartisan—national security, foreign policy, and the economy—the domestic departments almost always are subject to intense crossfire between partisan and domestic interest groups.[9]

Political scientist Jeffrey Cohen deepens the concept considerably, however, by suggesting that the outer cabinet be divided into two subgroups based on age. His conclusions fit with Cronin's but help define the distinction between inner and outer more clearly:

> While it is clear that the traditional inner departments are privileged, not all outer departments are severely disadvantaged. Specifically, the older outer departments, those of single interests (Agriculture, Commerce, Labor, and Interior) hold special status such that their interest groups are protected to some degree from presidential desires for control. Rather than the replacement of initial appointees to these departments with "president's men," the selection of replacements continues to be dominated by interest groups. Not even the inner cabinet can boast that kind of insulation.[10]

Thus there are two reasons to suspect the inner cabinet of thickening. First, being closer to the president and run by more intimate advisers, the inner cabinet should be either subject to tighter political control or

TABLE 4-5. *The Diffusion of Layers, 1935–50*[a]

Department	Number of times a department was		
	first in creating a layer	second in creating a layer	third in creating a layer
Justice	6	2	2
State	6	0	1
HEW/HHS	4	1	3
Defense	3	5	4
Treasury	3	3	3
Commerce	2	4	2
Labor	2	4	1
Transportation	1	3	3
Agriculture	1	3	2
Energy	1	2	1
Interior	1	1	3
Education	0	1	2
Post Office	0	1	1
HUD	0	0	2
VA	0	0	0

SOURCES: See appendix.

a. No effort was made to determine precisely which department had a given layer first. If two (or more) departments created a layer in the same year, both (or all) receive credit for creating it first.

more creative in finding senior posts for highly credentialed presidential friends. Second, the outer cabinet, being more dominated by interest groups (Education, Labor, and VA, for example) or a long-term career perspective (Agriculture, Transportation), should be either less accepting of political control or more fully insulated against interference.

It is impossible to determine here which is the real motive. Nevertheless, one way to further the investigation is to look at the origins of each of the new layers (see the core tables), asking who had the position first, second, and third (see table 4-5). The chief of staff to the secretary showed up first at HHS and Labor (they created the position in the same year), spread to Transportation and Treasury (tied for second), to Commerce, Defense, Education, and Justice (tied for third), and out to Agriculture, Energy, HUD, Interior, and VA in 1992. The deputy secretary post showed up at Defense and Justice first, the Post Office Department second, Treasury and State third.

The table shows the prominent role of the inner cabinet in inventing new layers, both formal and informal. It is important to recognize that this research does not ask whether these new posts are useful or examine the circumstances that might justify the posts. All the table shows is that the four inner departments are more likely than most to invent new layers. There are, of course, some commonalities of the inner cabinet that might explain the trend.

Consider, for example, the Justice Department's role in presidential policy. Cronin writes:

> The Justice Department traditionally serves as the president's attorney and law office, a special obligation that brings about continuous and close professional relations between White House domestic policy lawyers and Justice Department lawyers. The White House depends heavily and constantly on the department's lawyers for counsel on civil rights developments, presidential veto procedures, tax prosecutions, antitrust controversies, routine presidential pardons, and the overseeing of regulatory agencies and for a continuous overview of the congressional judiciary committees.[11]

Although Cronin's 1975 analysis is somewhat dated—regulatory issues are now handled by the Office of Information and Regulatory Affairs in the Office of Management and Budget—Justice has long been a home for key presidential advisers. Kennedy's attorney general was, of course, his brother Bobby, while almost every president since has used the post to host a key adviser—Nixon gave it to John Mitchell, Carter to Griffin Bell, Reagan to Ed Meese. The two most notable exceptions are the two most recent presidents, Bush and Clinton, who relied more on the White House counsel for legal advice. That an attorney general would seek to penetrate the bureaucracy with multiple layers should not be surprising given the potential sensitivity of most Justice Department issues.

That a secretary of state would also add layers is not surprising either. All of the presidents covered by this study were involved to one extent or another in serious international crises. Two were forced out of office early because of foreign policy miscues (Johnson because of Vietnam, Carter because of the Iran hostage crisis), two were tainted by mistakes (Kennedy for the Bay of Pigs fiasco in Cuba, Reagan for the Iran/contra arms-for-hostages scandal), and two saw their greatest achievements in the arena (Nixon in the opening to China, Bush in the Persian Gulf War). It is no wonder that they would put trusted advisers in key posts and keep close hold. Whether they allow layering as a sign of trust or demand it as a way of exerting control, presidents or their national security advisers in the White House—most notably Henry Kissinger—have always kept the State Department in check.[12]

It is important to note that layering may also be an artifact of a department's age. Five of the least active departments listed in table 4-5 are also the newest departments—Transportation, followed by Energy, HUD, Education, and VA. These younger departments have had less time to innovate. They did not exist when the first deputy secretary was created at Justice and Defense or when the first under secretary was created at Justice, Treasury, and State. Even here, however, the effect of age appears to be conditioned by the distinction between inner and outer cabinet departments. The Interior and Post Office departments were both created before the Civil War, and the Department of Agriculture thirty years later. Yet they also fall at the bottom of the diffusion chart. Inner-cabinet members not only have more time to innovate, they also seem to have more invitation.

The four inner-cabinet members also seem to innovate, or specialize, in different executive compartments. Justice is more often the source of innovations in the deputy compartment; Treasury is more active in the under secretary compartment; State is much more productive in the assistant secretary compartment; and Defense has no concentration at all. HHS tended to specialize in the assistant secretary compartment. The innovations break down as follows:

—Justice: three in the deputy secretary compartment, two in the under, one in the assistant;

—State: two in the under secretary compartment, four in the assistant;

—HHS: one in the secretary compartment (chief of staff), three in the assistant secretary;

—Treasury: two in the under secretary compartment, one in the assistant;

—Defense: one in the deputy secretary compartment, one in the under, one in the assistant.

The State Department's focus on the assistant secretary compartment may be a simple by-product of its far-flung hierarchy. In 1992 the department had nineteen assistant secretaries, not including another three ambassadors-at-large and a chief of protocol also at level IV. There was plenty of room for one or another to innovate, and ultimately plenty of pressure. As Donald Warwick writes of an earlier effort to debureaucratize the State hierarchy:

The combination of a heavy message volume, a high degree of centralization, and tight security procedures sets the stage for the elongation of hierarchy and the proliferation of rules. Pressures for added levels of supervision build up on both the sending and the receiving ends. The complexity, uncertainty, threat, and dispersion of the international environment, interagency competition and concurrence, the threat of public criticism, and the avoidance of risk-taking at the bottom contribute to the volume of words moving through the system. Security requirements dictate that messages follow formally designated transmission channels, ultimately moving to the top. The result is a massive clogging at the upper levels.[13]

In turn, this clogging creates pressures for more senior staff, and ultimately, innovations in layering to manage the supervisory workload. As Warwick convincingly shows, even the most dedicated effort to flatten the department is doomed to failure against these centrifugal forces.

Congress and the President

It should be clear by now that Congress is hardly an insignificant offshoot in the tangle of thickening. Like the long-ignored seedling in the corner of a garden that, almost unnoticed, develops into a mature plant, Congress has emerged as a very large root indeed. Its growing role is not a surprise, however. After all, Congress has held what political scientist Francis Rourke calls "joint custody" of the executive branch from the very beginning of the republic, mandating in 1789 that the secretary of the Treasury report simultaneously to both the president and Congress. According to Rourke, there may be periods when one institution is ascendant in shaping the bureaucracy, but never an outright victory: "For both institutions the idea of total control lies in a field of dreams." Thus, as Rourke writes of Nixon and Reagan's centralization effort:

> This effort was doomed to fail. For one thing, it triggered an offsetting response in Congress in the form of a new wave of legislative micro-management. Moreover, the most successful political appointees of these presidents quickly discovered that power in Washington depended less on their obedient compliance with White House goals than it did on their ability to build strong congressional and public support by achieving a reputation for independent judgment on policy issues.[14]

There is nothing presidents can do, for example, by way of grand reorganization without Congress. Indeed, the inventory of departments-in-waiting on Capitol Hill virtually guarantees future widening in government.[15] By June 1993 members of the 103d Congress had already introduced six cabinet bills: four to elevate the Environmental Protection Agency to cabinet status, one for a department of trade, and one for a department of science and technology. Another proposal for a department of science was part of a budget-cutting bill introduced by moderate Democrats late in the first session, an idea that garnered almost enough votes for passage.

Yet these proposals merely add to a long list of previous bills, including thirty-three in the 95th Congress to create a department of education, eight in the 96th, nine in the 99th, eleven in the 100th for a department of trade, four in the 100th for a department of veterans affairs, two in the 101st for departments of social security and agriculture and rural development, and one in the 102d to create a department of arts and humanities. The rationale for each bill may have been slightly different—visibility, budget, status commensurate with that accorded by other nations—but the effect is the same, predictable growth.[16] A department of environment could well be part of the president's cabinet by the end of 1995.

Congress has ample reason to involve itself in executive hierarchy. Assume, for a first motive, that members of Congress care about reelection, and reelection only. They worry about the structure of government because it affects their electoral chances. According to political scientist Morris Fiorina, such an assumption would make Congress the "keystone of the Washington establishment." Since members get "credits" for both creating new programs and solving the problems those programs create, they cannot lose. When aggrieved constituents complain about big government, for example, the member "lends a sympathetic ear, piously denounces the evils of bureaucracy, intervenes in the latter's decisions, and rides a grateful electorate to ever more impressive electoral showings."[17] Fiorina concludes:

The popular frustration with the permanent government in Washington is partly justified, but to a considerable degree it is misplaced resentment. *Congress is the linchpin of the Washington establishment.* The bureaucracy serves as a convenient lightning rod for public frustration and a convenient whipping boy for congressmen. . . .

Congress does not just react to big government—it creates it. All of Washington prospers.[18]

Assume, for the sake of argument, a second, somewhat more generous motive—that members care about making good policy and worry about the structure of government because it affects the successful implementation of cherished goals. They would not argue for an under secretary of energy conservation as a means to getting reelected, but because rank is a way of communicating policy goals. They would not press for an assistant secretary for children and families because it sells back home, but because it creates a focal point for a policy priority. They would not delegate the making of rules and regulations, or "sublegislation," in the hope that agencies would fail and thereby generate business, but because agencies have more expertise than Congress.[19]

Assume a third motive—that individual members are motivated by a desire for institutional power. Some might argue, for example, that the Senate is a more likely source of positions because its members derive power from confirming presidential appointees. Others might argue that the House is the more likely source of positions because its members need more witnesses for hearings, a point made earlier regarding the IG expansion during the 1980s. With more subcommittees and staff to fuel, the House may have more incentive to create positions than the Senate. Still others might suggest that congressional staff, not members, are ultimately culpable for creating jobs they hope to occupy in a not-too-distant future.

Ultimately, reelection, good policy, and power may all come into play in thickening, if only because all members of Congress are not equally motivated by the same goals. Thus what might be thoughtful oversight to one member of a committee can be scandalmongering for another; what might be micromanaging interference for one member might be careful policymaking to the other. Goals change across time, policies, and individual members. What might be careful oversight to a committee chair at the beginning of a career might be digging dirt toward the end.

Whatever the mix of motives, Congress has become much more assertive in shaping the executive hierarchy over the past three decades. The activism reflects what political scientist James Sundquist calls the "resurgence of Congress" in the 1960s,[20] part of a post-Watergate rejection of the "president knows best" view of executive organization. This is not to argue that Congress, particularly the Senate, began to say no to the president's nominees. There was and still is a profound reluctance to challenge presidents on all but the most controversial of their nominees. Rather, Congress discovered executive structure in the 1970s and began to mine it.

The trend is clear in the legislative history of Title 5 of the *U.S. Code*, which lists all executive level positions in government. Between 1961 and 1992, for example, Congress and the president made 199 changes in the top four executive titles of secretary, deputy secretary, under secretary, and assistant secretary. These 199 changes provide a glimpse into the underlying dynamics of thickening. However, because the 199 changes were identified through legislative histories, not Plum Books, they should be viewed as an entirely different set of numbers from those presented in the core tables in the appendix.

The 199 changes came into being through sixty-four statutes (including the five cabinet bills) and two reorganization plans and had a variety of effects: 157 widened an existing layer within a department; 15 created an entirely new layer within a department; 41 thinned or flattened an existing layer by moving a position within a department up, down, or out of existence; and 25 changed the title of an existing position to be more specific regarding duties or responsibilities. (Because the Post Office Department was not abolished but was transformed into a quasi-public corporation, it is not counted in any of the totals. It was neither a thinning nor a flattening per se.)

Along the way, Congress and the president created 141 new government positions: 5 secretaries of departments (Transportation, HUD, Education, Energy, and Veterans Affairs), 11 deputy secretaries, 17 under secretaries, 105 assistant secretaries, and 3 administrators.[21] Of the 141 new positions, 53, or 38 percent, were created in cabinet bills, thereby becoming subject to the fullest possible scrutiny, while 88, or 62 percent, came into being through the authorization or appropriations process.

The question for the moment is where the ideas came from: Congress or the president? The answer is often revealed in the legislative record— a letter from a department secretary asking for a new position, a presidential message, a statement from a member. Because the record is clearest in cabinet bills, these positions were easily identified as presidential or congressional: four came from the president, the Department of Veterans Affairs from the Congress. Because the record is far less precise in the authorization and appropriations process, the origin is not always clear.

Although Congress and the president share a roughly equal activism over the thirty years, the two bodies have very different statutory

TABLE 4-6. *Characteristics and Consequences of Congressional and Presidential Statutes, 1961–92*

	Origin	
	Congress	*President*
Intent[a]		
Widen	67	56
Layer	0	5
Thin	8	9
Flatten	0	2
Change Title	9	5
Legislative visisbility		
Visible	39	56
Buried	34	13
Level of new positions[b]		
Secretary	1	4
Deputy secretary	1	2
Under secretary	7	7
Assistant secretary	52	39
Administrator	0	2
Vehicle for new positions[b]		
Cabinet bill	14	39
Noncabinet bill	47	15

SOURCES: Legislative histories of statutory changes.

a. The origins of 57 of the 199 changes are not discernible. Of the remaining 142 changes, Congress was the source of 73, the president 69. The total is greater than 142 because some changes are counted in more than one category.

b. A total of 141 new positions were created. The total here is less than 141 because the origins of some positions are not discernible.

preferences (see table 4-6). First, Congress is slightly more inclined to widen the government than the president—the number of changes shown is greater than 142 because some have more than one effect. Of these, 80 percent initiated by Congress widen, 10 percent thin, and 11 percent make a title change. By comparison, presidents are the only source of new layers, slightly less likely to widen, and only half as likely to be a source of title changes.

Second, Congress is more likely than presidents to make its change in less-visible vehicles, particularly appropriations bills. Whereas fifty-three of the sixty-nine presidential changes come through cabinet bills, all but fourteen of the congressional changes occur in the authorization or appropriations process. They are more difficult to spot and therefore much more difficult to stop. This tendency may be a result of the rise in omnibus legislation and continuing appropriations bills under Reagan, or a product of the declining number of bills introduced and passed by Congress during the 1980s. There may be fewer vehicles in town.

TABLE 4-7. *Origins of Statutes to Change the Executive Structure of Government, 1960–92*[a]

	Origin	
	Congress	President
Decade		
1960–68	1	21
1969–80	16	41
1981–92	56	7
President		
Kennedy	0	1
Johnson	1	20
Nixon	2	7
Ford	1	2
Carter	13	32
Reagan	38	7
Bush	18	0

SOURCE: Legislative histories of statutory changes.
a. The total is less than 199 because the origins of some proposals are not discernible.

Third, looking only at the 141 new positions, Congress tends to concentrate more than the president on the assistant secretary layer of government. Seventy-one percent of its changes involve assistant secretaries, in contrast to 56 percent for the president. Much of the difference is due to cabinet bills. Presidents were the source of four of the five cabinet bills covered here, Congress only one. Two out of every three positions by presidents come in a cabinet bill; one out of every four by Congress.

Once past these statutory tendencies, the trend toward increasing congressional involvement becomes clear (see table 4-7). Congress has become a key player in shaping the formal executive structure, even as presidents, particularly Reagan and Bush, have backed off. Congress simply did not have much of a role in creating executive structure in the 1960s. Presidents were given great discretion and had the final say on most questions of structure. Although Congress had debated questions of organization before—recall its unwillingness to demote the FAA administrator to level III when the Department of Transportation was created—it generally did so only in the context of presidential proposals. Of the twenty-two changes during the 1960s, 95 percent originated with the president, the bulk coming in the HUD and Transportation bills; of the fifty-seven during the 1970s, 72 percent came from the president.

By the mid-1970s, however, Congress was ready to engage executive structure on its own terms.[22] It was no longer willing to simply wait for presidential action; indeed, it was no longer willing even to give the president reorganization authority. Of the sixty-three changes made during the 1980s, 89 percent originated in Congress. This congressional connection reflects a remarkably solid turnaround from the 1960s— even giving all the "not discernibles" to the president, a dubious assumption at best, only cuts the percentage to 75. Thus even as Reagan strengthened White House control over executive appointments, Congress kept creating new positions. Reagan can still be blamed for much of the title-riding that occurred in the informal political ranks of government, but not for the formal thickening.

This is not to absolve Reagan and Bush of any guilt in building the executive hierarchy. Alas, nothing in the legislative record answers yet another chicken-and-egg question: Did Reagan add informal appointees in an attempt to gain control of congressionally mandated units, or did Congress add formal structure to create accountability for ad hoc concentrations of political appointees? There is no doubt, for example, that Reagan opposed a number of legislatively created positions. There is also no doubt that Reagan and Bush oversaw both an increase in the Senior Executive Service and a deepening of the political infrastructure.

Ultimately, it seems reasonable to suggest that Democratic Congresses are more comfortable leaving executive hierarchy to Democratic presidents, while taking a much more aggressive thickening role with Republican presidents. It also seems reasonable to argue that congressional involvement will not abate with the arrival of Clinton. Now that Congress has learned how to initiate change in the executive hierarchy, it will likely stay active. Lacking the dollars to create new programs, facing steep cutbacks mandated by a deficit reduction, cabinet refinishing may mark a new legislative strategy. Creating a new under secretary or assistant secretary is one way for Congress to do something about a problem, something that costs little in short-term dollars. This tendency to use hierarchy as a substitute for more tangible action is suggested in table 4-8. Specificity simply refers to whether the duties of a specific position or title are clearly designated.

Specificity is the simplest way for members of Congress to claim credit for addressing some problem. When Congress gets involved in the creation of new, noncabinet positions, it gets very specific indeed. Only eight of the forty-seven new positions created by Congress gave the president discretion to specify the occupants' duties.

Consider, for example, the under secretary of commerce for travel and tourism, a classic expression of symbolic thickening. The post was

TABLE 4-8. *The Source and Specificity of New Positions by Decade, 1960–91*[a]

	Number of positions created		
	1960–68	1969–80	1981–91
Cabinet bills			
President/specific	5	10	0
President/nonspecific	11	13	0
Congress/specific	0	0	5
Congress/nonspecific	0	0	9
Noncabinet bills			
President/specific	0	2	2
President/non-specific	5	6	0
Congress/specific	0	12	27
Congress/nonspecific	0	3	5

SOURCES: Legislative histories of statutory changes.
   a. Specificity refers to whether the duties of a new position or title are clearly specified. A total of 141 new positions were created. The total here is less than 141 because the origins of some positions are not discernible.

created in 1981 after Carter's pocket veto the year before. Concluding that "the existing extensive Federal Government involvement in tourism, recreation, and other related activities needs to be better coordinated to effectively respond to the national interest in tourism and recreation," Congress passed the bill again on October 1, 1981.[23] Although Reagan accepted the political realities of a certain veto override, the bill became law without his signature when the ten-day veto clock expired.

   The practice of specifying duties in statute involves more than this kind of political credit claiming. Restricting the president's authority to decide which duties to give to what officers is simply a sign of institutional distrust. Whether that general distrust accelerated in the 1980s because of divided control of Congress and the presidency is not clear. Political scientist David Mayhew has effectively demonstrated that divided government is not necessarily a recipe for stalemate.[24]

   What is clear is that Congress has become less and less willing to give the president discretion of any kind over the executive establishment. When the courts declared the legislative veto unconstitutional, Congress began inventing other tools, from regulatory deadlines and triggers to citizen action suits, personnel floors and ceilings, and highly detailed notice-and-wait reporting requirements. The VA, for example, still operates under a notorious requirement that Congress must be notified of any reorganization involving more than twenty-five headquarters employees or ten field-office employees at least thirty days before the change takes place.[25] Specifying the duties of executive officers is just another strategic device.

However onerous, reporting requirements and earmarks remain time-honored devices for giving Congress a say in administration. The VA notice-and-wait reorganization provision was enacted after the Reagan administration attempted to close a number of field units without any congressional consultation, while "backdoor" budget earmarks have been used by presidents for decades as levers on key votes. Clinton was not yet born when Congress created the federal helium reserve as a protected source for the War Department's dirigible fleet, but he let it stand nonetheless in order to win a key vote on his 1993 budget.

Ultimately, therefore, it is not easy to untangle the presidential roots of thickening even in cases where Congress is clearly the source of a new position. Congress and the president share an intimate relationship in which it is difficult to know which moves first.

Democrats and Republicans

Despite the Democratic party's stereotype as the party of big government, Democratic presidents are not the only source of thickening. Recall Eisenhower's role as a hidden-hand thickener and Hoover's as a key designer. Since the House has been held by the Democrats for the entire thirty-two-year period, the Senate by Democrats for all but six years, and the White House by Republicans for twenty, it may be impossible to untangle the motives, let alone cause and effect.

Consider a range of motives. Democrats can be accused of thickening in the cause of expanding government, Republicans in the search for greater control and accountability; Democrats in pursuit of the Great Society, Republicans in the war on waste; Democrats in the quest for more rational policy analysis through new assistant secretaries for evaluation and planning, Republicans in the drive for a new federalism through new assistant secretaries for intergovernmental relations.

Presidents of both parties have done their share of thickening, whatever the reasons (see table 4-9).

For starters, neither Democrats nor Republicans have a monopoly on creating or abolishing cabinet departments. From 1935 to the present, Republicans have two creations to their credit (HEW and VA); the Democrats five (Defense, Transportation, HUD, Education, and Energy). Of those seven departments, however, at least four (Defense, HEW, HUD, and Transportation) can be traced in one way or another back to

TABLE 4-9. *Democratic and Republican Contributions to the Thickening of Government, 1935–92*

	Democrats	Republicans
Departments created		
1935–92	5	2
1960–92	4	1
Departments abolished		
1935–92	2	1
1960–92	0	1
Layers invented at executive levels I–IV		
1935–92	4	13
1960–92	1	8
Layers invented at executive level V		
1960–92	7	− 1
Adoptions of new layers, executive levels I–IV		
1935–92	67	82
(average per year)	2	3
1960–92	54	61
(average per year)	5	3
Adoptions of new layers, executive level V		
1960–92	35	4
(average per year)	3	0
Assistant secretaryships created		
1935–92	54	113
(average per year)	2	4
1960–92	54	71
(average per year)	5	4
Total occupants added at executive levels I–IV		
1935–92	457	1,115
(average per year)	16	40
1960–92 only	429	950
(average per year)	36	48
Total occupants added at executive level V		
1960–92	439	126
(average per year)	37	6

SOURCES: See appendix.

the Brownlow committee or first Hoover commission. Only Education and VA can be seen as pure violations of the prevailing orthodoxy of Hoover—one each under a Republican and a Democrat.

As for thinning the cabinet, Democrats have two abolishments to their credit (War and Navy); the Republicans one (Post Office). However, none of them truly thinned government—War and Navy became Defense, and the U.S. Postal Service continues to grow as a quasi-governmental corporation. To further muddy the roots, the creation of the Department of Defense was clearly a Hoover idea; it was passed into law by a Republican Congress and signed with Truman's strong support.

Of greater interest is the layering of government, where Democrats and Republicans specialize in different compartments. Republican presidents clearly out-layer the Democrats only at executive level IV and above, where most policy gets made. Republicans may work these top compartments as a way of concentrating political advice—or "circling the wagons," befitting traditional Republican worries about the career civil service. In contrast, Democrats out-layer the Republicans at the administrator level, where most policy gets delivered. Democrats can distribute more of their energy further down, particularly given traditional Democratic characterizations of the career service as an ally.

This pattern holds in looking at the diffusion of layers to other departments. Again, Republicans are more likely to permit or encourage diffusion in the top four compartments. It is not that Republicans have acted intentionally at levels I–IV and merely failed to act at level V. They appear quite intentional about holding down the growth of the administrator compartment. Nixon cut two layers from the compartment, Reagan cut one and added one, Bush added only one.

Republican presidents not only sanction less growth in the level V ranks but have been the only presidents ever to cut the total number of level V occupants. Reagan's two terms showed a level V decline more than equal to the gains under Kennedy and Johnson, even as he witnessed a 32 percent increase in level I–IV occupants. The tendency of Republicans to centralize power upward, in part by gaining weight at the top, in part by losing it in the administrator compartment below, seems clear. Reagan's success in thinning the administrator compartment puts Bush's distaste for organization in perspective. By not watching government's intake, Bush gave back all of the cuts his Republican predecessors had made.

As for the number of assistant secretaryships, recent Republicans can trace much of the activity back to Congress (see table 4-10). Reagan might have endorsed the VA cabinet bill and signed it into law, for example, but Congress initiated the process and forced the issue at the White House with a near unanimous vote in the House.

The Republican reluctance to create formal hierarchy is evident on noncabinet bills as well, where Republican presidents sponsored only five, or 9 percent, of the fifty-six positions created during their administrations. Although some of the positions created by Congress during Reagan's

TABLE 4-10. *The Creation of New Positions, by Party*

	Democrats	Republicans
Executive level		
I (Secretary)	4	1
II (Deputy secretary)	8	3
III (Under secretary)	9	8
IV (Assistant secretary)	48	57
V (Associate deputy secretary)	2	1
Statutory vehicle		
Cabinet bill	39	14
Noncabinet bill	32	56
Statutory origins (All bills)[a]		
President	49	5
Congress	10	51
Not discernible	12	14
Statutory origins (cabinet bills only)[b]		
President	39	0
Congress	0	14
Statutory origin (Noncabinet bills only)[c]		
President	10	5
Congress	10	37
Not discernible	12	14

SOURCES: Legislative histories of statutory changes.
a. The total number of bills was 141.
b. 53 bills.
c. 88 bills.

term may have come from the Republican Senate, it still seems fair to release Republican presidents from most responsibility for the formal thickening of government. Nixon and Reagan are still culpable for informal thickening, particularly in the upper compartments, as is Eisenhower in the 1950s.

Hidden Roots of Thickening

In addition to old, inner-cabinet departments, Congress, and presidents, there are at least three hidden roots in the thickening of government: the Office of Management and Budget, federal managers themselves, and interest groups. All appear to have a stake in the thickening of government but often operate hidden from view. Each is considered here in order.

Office of Management and Budget

In theory, OMB could be a nearly impenetrable wall against expanding hierarchy, coupling budgetary levers with management oversight. In its heyday in the 1930s and 1940s as the Bureau of the Budget (BoB), it was just that. Working through its separate Division of Administrative Management, which actually had little contact with the budget side of things, the bureau played a dramatic role in both establishing and monitoring the structure of government. By the end of World War II, however, the division had begun to decline, in part eclipsed by growing interest in the budget. Through a series of reorganizations during the late 1940s and 1950s, the division was merged, broken out, and merged again with various elements of the budget and thereby slowly weakened as a source of durable oversight of administrative structure.[26]

This erosion eventually provoked yet another reorganization in 1969, starting with a name change to emphasize the importance of management. As Nixon explained his proposed office of management and budget in his message to Congress in 1969, "preparation of the budget as such will no longer be its dominant, overriding concern." Instead:

> Improvement of Government organization, information and management systems will be a major function of the Office of Management and Budget. It will maintain a continuous review of the organizational structures and management processes of the Executive Branch, and recommend needed changes. It will take the lead in developing new information systems to provide the President with the performance and other data that he needs but does not now get. When new programs are launched, it will seek to ensure that they are not simply forced into or grafted onto existing organizational structures that may not be appropriate.[27]

It never happened. The new management division had barely been in place for three years when it was reorganized again, inaugurating a practice of nearly constant turmoil as the agency reshuffled responsibilities again and again. By the 1980s the management division was in disarray. Eight different associate directors headed the division during the Reagan and Bush years, during which at least six different realignments of the operating units took place. The once proud "organization studies" unit that had spurred so much reform in the 1940s was renamed "organization and special projects" in 1981, then eliminated in 1982, as financial management and accounting reforms began to crowd out OMB concern with structure. By 1993 the management division consisted of just two units—one for government operations (personnel, evaluation, general services), the other for federal financial management. And even though Congress had elevated the associate director for management to the deputy director rank, turnover continued. Clinton's deputy director for management left the position in late 1993 to become one of the president's two deputy chiefs of staff.

Despite its promised renascence, the "M" side of OMB was decimated during the 1970s and 1980s. According to Ronald Moe, a senior specialist with the Congressional Research Service, the management side went from 224 full-time employees in 1970 to 111 in 1980 and 47 in 1988. "During the 1980s," Moe argues of this transformation from phoenix to ashes, "OMB systematically subordinated its remaining management capabilities to support its budgetary and financial management systems priorities. They believed that if they conducted enough financial management improvement projects, this would equal a management philosophy."[28]

Once a potential bulwark against government thickening, OMB had become a Maginot Line. By 1980 there was simply no one watching the executive level positions in government. Reagan's White House personnel recruiters only seemed to care about filling the top jobs, not about monitoring the expanding numbers, and OMB had no capacity to screen incoming legislation or departmental orders for new posts. Even if OMB's legislative clearance division, which is responsible for approving all bills, reports, and testimony to Congress, somehow spotted a new position being proposed in a bill being sent to Congress, no one was home to advise a response. By the end of the Bush years, it would have been more appropriate to label the agency $O_m B$.

Clinton continued the dismantling in 1994 with yet another reorganization. This time the entire management division was split up, with half the staff shuffled to the budget side of the agency. "Critics of these recommendations may say that the efforts to 'integrate' management and budget will end in merely bigger budget divisions, whose management responsibilities will be driven out by daily fire-fighting on budget issues," OMB director Leon Panetta admitted in describing the change. "We believe this criticism is based on a false premise that 'management' and 'budget' issues can be thought about separately."[29]

Whether the two sides can work together is not precisely the issue here, however. It is whether there is a sustained attention to broad management questions such as the thickness of departments. The integration of management and budget may improve management of the trees but do little for forest control. By the end of 1994 the old OMB might best be labeled just OB.

Federal Managers

Managers clearly have some say about the thickening of government, although much less so than Parkinson's Law imagines. They do make the case for middle-level promotions, and they work in agencies that have long had substantial autonomy to set their internal promotion guidelines. Position management is one area in which government has been highly *decentralized* for the better part of the last half century.

Unfortunately, the cumulative evidence suggests that managers may not have used their freedom wisely. Concerns about overgrading have existed almost from the beginning of the modern classification system created in 1949. Worries about overgrading were certainly the root of the 1952 Whitten amendment requiring departments to review annually all positions created or placed in a higher pay level, abolish all positions found to be unnecessary, and ensure that needed positions are properly classified. The amendment remained in effect until the late 1980s, when it was replaced by regulations that require essentially the same things.

One reason the amendment survived was recurring research implicating federal managers in middle-level thickening. The 1960s, for example, brought what appears to be the Civil Service Commission's (CSC) first ever study of grade inflation. Finding that the average grade had increased from roughly 5.5 in 1954 to 6.6 in 1961, the commission turned first to the changing job of government, whether expressed in new missions (such as the space program) or the rising demand for occupational specialists. This new occupational mix explained a great deal of the grade increase.

Yet according to CSC's report, "By no means is grade escalation the result *solely* of inexorable forces beyond the control of the Commission, the Bureau of the Budget, and responsible management officials of individual agencies." Instead, the commission pointed to two accidental sources of escalation. One was "diluting of higher level work to spread it thinly over many positions, by creating more organizational units than are necessary, by over-recruiting at higher levels, etc." The other, more relevant, cause in the thickening of government was the everyday management decisions that determine the classification, or level, of most positions:

> Poor judgment in decentralizing functions, distributing work, delegating authority to act, creating staff positions, deciding the number of supervisors, etc., results in more higher grades than needed.

Unwarranted job inflation resulting from poor management decisions cannot be corrected merely by classification audits—the solution lies in remedying the management deficiencies rather than in trying to tackle job evaluation judgments.[30]

The 1970s brought an even tougher critique from the General Accounting Office, Congress's watchdog agency. Noting that personnel costs had risen about 600 percent since Congress created the modern classification system in 1949, GAO reported that the average grade had now reached 7.87. After noting that agencies have a great deal of authority to organize and classify their positions as they deem necessary, GAO pointed to managers as a root cause of thickening. "Maintaining the integrity of the classification system is management's direct responsibility," GAO wrote. "But some managers want to upgrade as a means of rewarding and recruiting employees—the major resource for accomplishing Government programs. In view of the importance of classification and its dependence on management's attitude and support, we believe managers need to assume their roles more seriously and more responsibly."[31]

That managers were able to upgrade was due in part to weaknesses at CSC and the White House. Lacking a consistent evaluation system and any real power to downgrade department positions, CSC simply did not have the capacity to stop middle-level inflation. In addition, lacking strong, "emphatic" presidential support, CSC and agencies would not have the courage to reverse what GAO called a two-decade trend in management misbehavior. "People are people. Some may remain unaware of the legal requirements. Some will consciously flout the law, balancing the risk of discovery against the grade gains. Some will rationalize their actions on the grounds that higher grades will enhance mission accomplishments. Others will fragment duties to stay within the law but not within the spirit of the law."[32]

Although the report said that managers were a root cause, it is useful to note GAO's concerns about the thickening pressure from professional societies:

Some professional societies give the impression that the profession's prestige depends on the grade levels set by CSC guidelines. Employees and their representatives try to influence agencies and the Congress to upgrade certain positions. Sometimes their efforts to upgrade one group or occupation adversely affects other employees whose representatives then exert pressure on their behalf. By the nature of the classification system, the grades are balanced and interrelated among occupations. Upgrading the working level in one occupation leads to pressures to upgrade another occupation.[33]

Thus does thickening in one area of an agency yield parallel thickening elsewhere. However rational the explanation for the initial bump, it is likely to spread outward through other pressures.

The 1980s brought an onslaught of investigations from a veritable smorgasbord of agencies: GAO, the Congressional Budget Office, the Rand Corporation, and CSC's successor, the Office of Personnel Management. None of the reports was more visible than that of Reagan's 1983 Private Sector Survey on Cost Control, chaired by J. Peter Grace. As part of a massive government-wide study involving hundreds of corporate volunteers unleashed on the agencies, the Grace task force on personnel concluded that government-wide position management was so weak as to be nonexistent. By 1983 average grade had inched up to 8.4, leading Grace to conclude that the federal government had almost three times as many managers as it needed.

Again, managers were on the firing line. Notwithstanding its reputation for bureaucrat bashing, the Grace commission was mostly forgiving. Managers could not help it, the report seemed to say. Part of the problem they faced was pay. According to the Grace commission's comprehensive report:

Compensation is generally too low for entry level professional positions. The Government's ability to attract and retain professional employees, therefore, is adversely affected. To compensate for lower starting salaries, managers promote employees quickly, assigning them to higher grade levels (i.e., higher salary levels). With a GS system of only 18 grades and relatively rapid promotion, the opportunities for further advancement can be limited and career employees cluster at the upper grade levels."[34]

Part of the problem was also lack of leadership in the Executive Office of the President, including OPM. According to the final task force report:

OMB is aware that periodic assessments of position management are to be conducted by both that office and OPM. With its small workforce, OMB feels that it cannot get into these position management "details."

It feels that OPM should carry the primary responsibility in this area, but that a good job has not been done to date. OPM, on the other hand, is aware of the joint responsibility on position management, but feels that OMB has "primary" responsibility. OPM feels it does not have by law, rules, or regulations any "authority to direct corrective action." In effect, OPM makes recommendations which agencies may elect to accept or ignore.[35]

Again, lacking oversight, managers were bound to overgrade, particularly given the structure of the federal classification system. The more employees a manager supervised, the higher his or her grade and salary.[36]

The task force also cited OPM's unwillingness to grant special pay rates that might reduce the thickening pressure for hard-to-recruit positions: "Some department and agency personnel perceive this as a form of deliberate 'foot dragging' in the name of cost control. Under these conditions they often choose the option of deliberate overgrading, rather than using the appropriate 'special rates' procedures."[37] Whether described as self-promoting or compassionate, federal managers were clearly a suspect in middle-level thickening.

Interest Groups

In predicting that the executive branch will become more bureaucratic in coming decades, political scientist James Q. Wilson points directly at interest groups as the underlying force: "The groups recognize that political decisions are increasingly made in the executive branch rather than in the legislative branch and want not only a share of bureaucratic authority, but also permanent recognition of their claim to bureaucratic authority. They obtain that authority by seeing to it that agencies are organized in such a way that interest-group demands are institutionally preserved."[38]

So noted, interest groups appear to be highly selective in choosing their engagement in organizational structure. There is no doubt, for example, that they play a role in cabinet making, having pushed most recently for establishment of the Departments of Education and VA. It is not clear, though, that interest groups care much about the internal structure or wiring diagrams of the new departments.

This is not to say that interest groups have no structural preferences at all. The veterans' and education groups made it clear that they wanted certain bases covered in the organization charts and they certainly knew

TABLE 4-11. *Interest Group Involvement in the Creation of New Government Positions*

	High	Low	Not Discernible
Statutory vehicle			
Cabinet bills	53	0	0
Noncabinet bills	4	20	64
Decade position created			
1960–68	16	0	11
1969–80	26	6	22
1980–91	15	14	31
Statutory origin			
President	39	0	28
Congress	18	14	16
Not discernible	0	0	26
Legislative visibility			
Visible	54	14	25
Buried	3	0	45
Specificity of change[a]			
Specific	24	14	36
Nonspecific	33	0	34

SOURCES: Legislative histories of statutory changes.
a. Specificity refers to whether the duties of a new position are clearly specified.

something about executive pecking order. However, neither set seemed to care much whether the given department had eight assistant secretaries or six, one under secretary or two. In short, interest groups may establish a favorable environment for thickening but may not be much involved in the specifics. They may press for a given position here and there to represent their interests—an assistant secretary for X in the new department of Y—but rarely seem to care about nomenclature.

Once past cabinet bills, interest groups appear to play an even lesser role (see table 4-11). They simply do not express opinions on most new positions. Of the eighty-eight noncabinet posts created between 1961 and 1992, interest groups were highly involved in just four, weakly involved in twenty more, and not visible at all in sixty-four more. They reserve their visibility, it seems, for cabinet bills, where the potential for claiming credit among their members is the highest.

Their role as hidden sources of thickening may be more difficult to prove but is well suspected nonetheless. Terry Moe argues, for example, that interest groups have at least two motives for sabotaging organizations through unwieldy hierarchy. Interest groups that are currently advantaged, for example, tend to think about the long term, when their side will be out of power, and act to protect their agents by writing detailed legislation, imposing specific deadlines for action, placing a high emphasis on professionalism and credentials among agency employees, opposing strong external oversight, sheltering favored units in friendly departments and away from political appointees, and favoring "judicialization" of agency decisions as a way of insulating those decisions from outside influence. "The driving force of political uncertainty, then," writes Moe, "causes the winning group to favor structural designs it would never favor on technical grounds alone: designs that place detailed formal restrictions on bureaucratic discretion, impose complex procedures for agency decision making, minimize opportunities for oversight, and otherwise insulate the agency from politics."[39]

In contrast, groups that are currently disadvantaged tend to think about the immediate and act to protect their interests by doing exactly the opposite, favoring structures that "work against effective performance," resisting deadlines and professionalism, favoring stronger oversight, seeking more political appointees and more open, objective decisionmaking procedures. "Opposing groups are dedicated to crippling the bureaucracy and gaining control over its decisions," Moe concludes, "and they will pressure for fragmented authority, labyrinthine procedures, mechanisms of political intervention, and other structures that subvert the bureaucracy's performance and open it up to attack."[40]

Moe is only presenting a theory, of course, and has yet to prove that groups in power think far into the future, while groups out of power think in the present. However, the motives ring true, suggesting that interest groups hardly need to care about internal wiring diagrams to have an impact on thickening. Groups in power and out have ample cause for thickening as a strategy for effectiveness—those in power use it to set their agendas in stone, while those out of power use thickening to freeze those agendas from action. The aims may be different, but the outcome is the same. Interest groups are key hidden roots in the thickening process, enabling, permitting, even encouraging Congress and the president to keep adding to the hierarchy.

Conclusion

As Parkinson's mythical botanist might argue, the thickening of government is rooted in a very complex garden indeed. At the middle level, for example, OMB and OPM both constitute a substantial source of the problem. Although their weakening was not by choice, the two institutions no longer ask the tough questions about the expanding hierarchy. Federal managers are part of the drama too. Even if their behavior can be explained away by pay gaps and freezes, they are intimate players in the middle-level bulge. Yet because past Congresses and presidents allowed OMB and OPM to atrophy, and because federal managers may take their thickening cues from higher up in the hierarchy, there is plenty of blame to push upward.

Presidents need only look across the cabinet table to find the inner cabinet secretaries who launch so many of the new layers and positions, and need only step outside for a quick look up Pennsylvania Avenue to see another source of thickening. Presidents (and vice presidents) who look only to the middle-management ranks as a source of thickening are missing equal, if not more important, targets for reform. Democratic presidents, Republican presidents, cold war presidents, post-cold war presidents, Great Society makers, and new federalists all deserve a share of credit for thickening too. Even new departments are not completely guilt free. They may not be the innovators per se, but they surely generate more thickening by adopting the latest in taller, wider hierarchy.

The key question now is not "whodunit?" but "how does thickening endure year to year?" Perhaps the roots of thickening merely provide a stable supply of positions to meet some underlying demand. Lacking much resistance from OMB and OPM and little opposition on Capitol Hill or in the White House, perhaps thickening is just a natural state of organizational affairs.

5

How Does Thickening Endure?

One of the great mysteries of thickening is how it endures under hostile conditions. Reagan campaigned hard against government growth, yet the thickening continued. Federal employment fell in all but three departments during his administration, yet the thickening continued. The number of pages in the *Federal Register* dropped from a little more than 87,000 in 1980 to roughly 53,000 in 1988, yet the thickening continued.

This chapter asks how thickening endures year after year. It is naive to assume that the federal government can halt thickening just by putting itself on a fad diet—that is, by squeezing federal jobs, increasing contracting or mandating out, or reducing workload whatever the mission (for example, by reducing the number of shuttle launches, or integrating the food stamp program and aid to families with dependent children). The number of veterans eligible for VA benefits, for example, continues to decline as the World War II generation passes on, yet the agency remains as thick as ever.

Thickening does not occur by accident. At the top, for example, there is one way, and one way only, to reach Title 5 of the *U.S. Code*, where all executive level presidential appointments reside: A bill must become a law. Likewise, there is one way, and one way only, to leave Title 5: A position must be repealed. Lesser constraints apply at lower levels, where positions are created and voided by presidential and secretarial orders. Regardless of level, though, thinning requires action.

Thickening does not occur invisibly. Bills get introduced, debated, and passed; orders get explained and promulgated. Although much of the thickening of government is buried in procedures so arcane or minute as to be mostly invisible to outsiders, there is enough evidence on the creation of new Title 5 positions to suggest that thickening endures through a simple two-step process.

At step one, the new positions and layers are established, often for perfectly logical reasons. A new program gets created, a priority gets set, a new agency comes on line. The new position may widen an existing layer or may represent an entirely new rank within the department. Regardless, presidents and Congress pay a remarkably low price for each new position—the salary cost is minimal in the grand scheme of things, and the potential cost of the new layer of review is never discussed.

At step two, the new position may spread ever outward as departments try to keep up with each other. Department executives do not, of course, sit around all day waiting to hear of the latest new title. Instead, what Kaufman called a "built-in thrust" seems to lead departments to pay attention to other organizations in their environment.

Unfortunately, it may never be clear which comes first—the position or the underlying thrust. Congress and the president often establish new positions based on the prevailing image of what a department should look like, not understanding that merely creating the new position may create a ripple effect upward through the span-of-control principle. Once established, the new post may force adjustments throughout the executive establishment. Professional societies may decide that their allies in government need the same level of pay and prestige; interest groups may be offended that their pet department is not keeping pace; presidents may conclude that every department needs some new lever of power; Congress may expand an experiment, such as the creation of the inspector general position, to every corner of the executive establishment.

Thus the first reason thickening endures is that the many separate events in the process are well rationalized. To thin government requires repealing statutes and orders that may have been exceptionally well argued at some time in the past. The second reason thickening endures is that each new position becomes part of a prevailing vision of what government should look like. Part of that vision can still be found in Luther Gulick's principles of administration. To understand how thickening can be stopped, therefore, reformers must first understand how thickening endures. This chapter considers the two steps of thickening in order, by looking at changes in the most senior ranks of government, where legislative histories are clearer.

How New Positions Are Created

Because all new executive posts must be created by statute, the first step in thickening is often revealed in the legislative record. That record, in turn, may reveal some of the ways the president and Congress package new posts. Unfortunately, the amount and quality of explanation can vary greatly across the three primary legislative vehicles used to amend Title 5: cabinet, single authorization, and annual department-wide authorization bills.

Cabinet bills are always the most clearly justified. Congress takes cabinet making seriously and subjects most bills to at least some legislative scrutiny. All department bills carry at least some justification, are almost always subject to debate, and always carry a legislative record. Even bills that will never see the light of day carry at least some justification. Thus the 100 or so cabinet bills introduced over the past decade carry virtually all of the possible rationales for thickening. This is not to argue that the justifications vary much from bill to bill, however. As a simple test, match the following justifications to the department, Energy or Education.

—By establishing a Department of _____, effective management and coordination of Federal programs can be substantially improved. The relatively low bureaucratic status of _____ means that _____ receives less attention from the Cabinet and the President. The large number of existing Federal _____ has created management problems at the Federal, State, local, and institutional levels. The scattering of programs across Federal agencies has resulted in poor coordination in addition to multiple, duplicated, and conflicting regulations. Fragmentation at the Federal level has led to piecemeal approaches to _____ and _____-related problems.

—The creation of a Department of _____ will have wide-ranging benefits for both the executive branch and the American people. It will provide a comprehensive overview of and national perspective on _____ matters. It will insure a more stabilized _____ policy framework with a single Cabinet-level _____ spokesperson. It will provide a clear focus within the executive branch on _____ policy and programs and the necessary central staff capability to analyze a wide range of _____ issues. The Department of _____ will, in this integrated organizational structure, provide for the reduction of overlap and unnecessary duplication, leading to more effective policy formulation, data collection and analysis.

They are virtually interchangeable and in fact owe footnotes to the Transportation and HUD justifications a decade earlier, which in turn owe a debt to HEW, and so on back through history.[1] The justifications are so similar because Congress and its staff often borrow heavily from the past in drafting new legislation. The quickest way to explain the need for an education department is to reread the report on the Energy Department; the quickest way to write a bill for a veterans affairs department is to pull the old statute on the Department of Education.

The single authorization bills that created one or two positions at a time are almost as clearly argued as cabinet bills, though rarely debated as closely. Authorizing committees often take the time to justify new posts in the departments they oversee and may go to some lengths to make the case for a particular innovation. New positions do get buried in omnibus bills—for example, in the Omnibus Diplomatic Security and Antiterrorism Act of 1986, which created an assistant secretary of state to head the new Bureau of Diplomatic Security. Even here, however, authorizing committees still take care to provide a justification. In this case, the bureau was created to "reverse the historic trend in the department which resulted in too many offices with overlapping responsibilities and competing interests."[2] An assistant secretary was merely a way to give the effort additional status.

Of all single authorization bills, none are as well articulated as those that come from the House and Senate Government Operations committees. Because these committees almost always create positions that apply to more than one department, they are often in the unenviable position of invading the turf of other authorizing committees. As a protection perhaps, the bills often carry detailed rationalizations. The 1990 Chief Financial Officer Act created twenty-two positions across government, some of which were new; others were merely relabeling of existing positions. Although the issue was hardly controversial, the bill nonetheless made a long list of findings, not the least of which was that the billions of dollars lost each year to fraud, waste, abuse, and mismanagement "could be significantly decreased by improved management."[3] Similar detail accompanied the Inspector General Act of 1978, which expanded the IG concept first established at HEW to a dozen agencies, and the Inspector General Act Amendments of 1988, which expanded the concept again to over forty departments and smaller agencies.

Alas, the third and final vehicle for new positions all too often leaves a murky trail at best. Annual department-wide authorizations are designed to do many things—create new programs, raise spending ceilings, tighten old programs, change rules, even create new executive level positions—but are often so long and deep that some of the explanations get left behind. The 1993 National Defense Authorization Act for fiscal years 1992 and 1993, for example, created a deputy under secretary for policy with no explanation at all. Besides the formal text of provision—that the deputy "shall assist the Under Secretary of Defense for Policy in the performance of his duties" and "shall act for, and exercise the powers of, the Under Secretary when the Under Secretary is absent or disabled"—the new occupant had little to go on.[4] That the post would be lost in the bill is not surprising, however. The table of contents alone runs more than four pages.

Thus even the hardest search for explanations can come up empty. Of the 199 statutory changes discussed in chapter 4, almost half had no legislative record to help explain their origins. Nevertheless, there is enough legislative history from the rest of the changes to suggest eight competing justifications for thickening at the very top of the federal hierarchy: (1) to aid in the recruitment of a prized appointee, (2) to boost the morale of a specific unit, (3) to smooth the transfer of a unit out of one department into another, (4) to ease the workload of beleaguered executives, (5) to improve accountability, (6) to expand advice to the secretary, (7) to make a symbolic statement about a national priority, and (8) to provide status equal to other similar positions in government. Although these justifications are drawn from the record surrounding the most senior positions in government, they yield at least some lessons about what might be happening below.

Recruitment Thickening

A new position is sometimes created to recruit a prized assistant who might not otherwise consider joining the government. This recruitment thickening is usually done with an informal position such as chief of staff, largely because informal posts can be put on the chart fairly quickly.

However, sometimes nothing less than executive rank will suffice. In 1985, for example, Secretary of Transportation Elizabeth Dole apparently asked Congress to establish an associate deputy secretary post as a way to recruit a preferred candidate. Although the position had existed since 1979 under administrative order, Dole felt a statutory mandate would make it more attractive.[5] Some secretaries have authority to assign assistant secretary billets at their discretion. In 1981, for example,

Defense Secretary Caspar Weinberger is said to have used his reorganization authority to create an assistant secretary for international security policy for recruiting Richard Perle, who reportedly would not take anything less than a level IV post.[6] What is clear is that positions created for special recruitment efforts do not disappear once its creator or the prized catch leaves. The associate deputy secretary position at Transportation was alive and filled in 1993, long after Dole had left. The assistant secretary for international security fared less well, having been merged into a single assistant secretary for policy under Clinton. Still, it survived Perle's departure for a time, and would be there in the 1984, 1988, and 1992 Plum Books for future appointees to find and possibly renew.

Morale Thickening

Raising morale is the rarest of justifications for adding a new position to government, but it exists nonetheless. In theory, bumping a unit up to, say, assistant secretary status might make the employees feel better about their jobs. Elevation also raises the salary of the unit head, allowing some limited movement upward in the overall pay structure.

The most telling example of morale thickening involves the 1978 Foreign Relations Authorization Act, which elevated the State Department's human rights coordinator for human rights and the administrator of consular affairs to assistant secretary rank.[7] The first was justified on status grounds—that is, because other comparable units were at the higher level. Note how the ranking Republican on the House International Operations Subcommittee, John Buchanan of Alabama, walked Patricia Derian, then human rights coordinator, through the case for elevation:

> Mr. Buchanan. I want to ask you now this question. Chairman Fascell and I have been talking about your position. It just seems to me that your job ought to be Assistant Secretary given the emphasis that the new administration is putting on human rights. Are you not at that level now?
>
> Ms. Derian. Yes; when the Congress made this job I suppose about 18 months ago it was designated as an Assistant Secretary-level position but it has a different name. I am not sure how that came to be. Some people say it was in the legislation, some people say it was in the State Department.

Mr. Buchanan. I believe the Department would have the authority. I am not sure that it would not; perhaps this committee would. Speaking for myself it just seems to me given the level of responsibility involved here and emphasis of this administration on that area and the things that are taking place . . . and so forth that there are a lot of reasons why.

Ms. Derian. It would be, I think, a very significant outward and visible sign of the new standing of the office with the new administration and heaven knows we need the extra people. We have two people working on human rights and they share a secretary.[8]

The case for elevation of consular affairs was made on entirely different grounds. Subcommittee chairman Dante Fascell, Democrat of Florida, mentioned the bump only once in the hearings, never on the floor, and made his case as follows: "The upgrading of the title of the Administrator of Security and Consular Affairs costs no money; it is just a change in title. But a change in that title in the Department hierarchy is a very important thing, and besides that, all of us are concerned with doing something to help morale in the Bureau of Consular Affairs. This is one small way of doing it."[9] Once the change arrived in the Senate, it was justified on competitive grounds—that is, the need for offices of equivalent responsibility to have equal weight in title and pay. As Senator Claiborne Pell, Democrat of Rhode Island, explained the proposal, the administrator title was "an anomaly in the Department of State as well as in the Government as a whole. Positions in the Department having equivalent or lesser responsibilities typically are titled Assistant Secretary and have direct access to seventh floor principals without going through an intervening organizational layer."[10]

There is no indication of any concern about increasing spans of control on the seventh floor, where the secretary and deputy secretary reside. Each bump was taken on its own out of the broader organizational context. There is no doubt that humanitarian affairs deserved greater status and no question that consular affairs needed higher morale. But there also was no concern about the ultimate consequences of action on either position. As for a sequential referral to the House Post Office and Civil Service Committee, which technically had jurisdiction over changes in pay under Title 5, there was simply no time.[11]

Transfer Thickening

Elevation of an existing agency to cabinet status inevitably increases the grade and titles of its senior officers. Changing an administrator to a secretary exerts a pull on all lower offices. If there is any standing rule in cabinet making 101, it is that there should be no gaps in grade between titles—a secretary at level I should supervise a deputy at II, under secretaries at III, and so on down the line. Bumping one means bumping all. Because the costs of bumping are minimal—of the $33 million five-year cost of the elevation of VA to cabinet status, less than $50,000 went toward higher salaries for appointees; the rest was for new signs—there is no financial barrier to elevation.

In the same vein, transfer of a unit from one department to another invariably requires a bump in status. The 1977 transfer of the Mine Enforcement and Safety Administration from Interior to Labor is a case in point. Justified by a detailed analysis of underenforcement of the key statutes protecting America's mine workers, the move made eminent sense from a policy perspective but increased the rank nonetheless. After summarizing a long list of mining disasters, the Senate Human Resources Committee concluded, "Years after enactment of these mine safety laws, miners can still go into the mines without even rudimentary training in safety. Mine operators still find it cheaper to pay minimal civil penalties than to make the capital investments necessary to adequately abate unsafe or unhealthy conditions, and there is still no means by which the government can bring habitual and chronic violators of the law into compliance." [12]

Part of the problem was a historical weakness in the mine safety statutes themselves—fines were too low, incentives for safety investment almost nonexistent. But part of the problem was in organizational placement. Although the Senate justified the transfer to Labor by briefly noting that "enforcement of safety and health laws should be the responsibility of agencies which are generally responsible for the needs of workers," some members worried that the Department of the Interior was predisposed to support the mining industry, even if that meant the death of mine workers. In contrast, Senator Orrin Hatch, Republican of Utah, saw "nothing more than a disguised effort to improve mine safety enforcement by organized labor leaders who really want to put the program in that part of the bureaucracy where they have the greatest influence." [13]

As for justifying the higher rank, the Senate provided the main text, arguing that a new assistant secretary would "provide specialized treatment and enforcement" of the enhanced mine safety and health statutes: "A separate enforcement structure with separate attention to mine safety and health problems is mandated by the very high fatality and injury rates for the industry. At the same time, issues which have arisen in the past because of overlapping jurisdiction between Interior and Labor, particularly in the area of milling of minerals, will be easier to resolve with the establishment of this new Assistant Secretary."[14]

Workload Thickening

Creating a new position to deal with increasing workload is one of the most common paths to thickening. New programs, broader mandates, additional staff, and larger budgets can all contribute to a sense that there is too much to do. Hence the need for more positions. There is no better example of this pressure than the Health Research Facility Amendments of 1965, which explained the need for three new assistant secretaries as follows:

> In the 12 years since the Department of Health, Education, and Welfare was created, it has been the fastest growing Department of the U.S. Government. . . . This growth has been accompanied by the creation of a large number of interrelated programs. The 88th Congress added 20 major new programs to the Department. During the 83d, 84th, 85th, 86th, and 87th Congresses there were more than 100 public laws enacted that added to the responsibilities of the Department and increased its needs for personnel at top levels.[15]

The argument was not without controversy, however. The House debated the issue at some length when the final bill reached the floor in May 1965. Some members argued that there was no need for the posts. "There has been some tendency in this particular Department, however," one representative argued, "to use Assistant Secretaries as dumping grounds for assorted programs. There is a definite need for better compartmentalization and unification of related activities. We are willing to go along with the request, but we are watching with interest the way these new positions are used."[16]

In response, supporters created a secondary set of justifications, including accountability and equal status for equal work. "The Secretary can delegate the responsibility to those who represent him, and not have to depend on the Civil Service employee who does not have the same responsibility to the Secretary," Representative Oren Harris, Democrat of Pennsylvania, argued. "All we are trying to do here is get the organization set up in HEW where the Secretary can have someone that he can hold responsible and that we in the Congress can hold responsible." [17]

The problem, of course, is that workload that goes up does not necessary come down with staff or budget cuts. Even the best laid plans for downsizing can go awry. Consider, for example, the 1977 Defense reorganization, which abolished one of two deputy secretaries. [18] The second deputy had been created in 1972 to alleviate what Secretary of Defense Melvin Laird called "excessive workload," but had never caught on. [19] As the new secretary of defense, Harold Brown, explained in his letter requesting the change, abolishing the second deputy would not only halve the number of executive level II slots in the department, it would "eliminate confusion regarding the distribution of executive authorities immediately below the Secretarial level. It will clarify the role of the remaining Deputy Secretary as the single principal assistant and alter ego to the Secretary in all areas of Defense management." [20] Brown's 1977 hierarchy involved a four-layer chain—one secretary, one deputy secretary, two under secretaries, and two principal deputy under secretaries or assistant secretaries—and a total of six occupants.

The problem was that the deputy was not being abolished so much as demoted. In place of the old executive level II post would be a new executive level III position with the title under secretary of defense for policy. To prevent layering in this new compartment, Brown proposed that the assistant secretary for international security affairs be designated as the principal deputy to the under secretary. At the same time, the assistant secretary for communications, command, control, and intelligence was to serve as the principal deputy under secretary for research and engineering. Finally, as part of a more general reorganization, the assistant secretary for health would report upward through the assistant secretary for manpower and reserve affairs.

In theory, having assistant secretaries pull double duty as principal deputy under secretaries would prevent layering, especially if both under secretaries kept their compartments small and did not worry about their relative status in the Washington pecking order. In reality, the novel reporting chain collapsed with the change of administrations. By 1984 the under secretary for policy had created his own deputy. By 1992 Brown's chain had grown to six layers—one secretary, one deputy secretary, two under secretaries, two principal deputy under secretaries, six assistant deputy under secretaries, and five assistant secretaries—and a total of seventeen occupants.

Accountability Thickening

Congress and the president also create new positions in the search for accountability, giving rise to what political scientist William Gormley calls "counter-bureaucracy."[21] Inspectors general are the most visible counterbureaucrats. After first establishing the IG prototype in HEW in 1976, Congress expanded the concept thirteen times over the next thirteen years. By 1989 the total number of presidential IGs appointed by the president and subject to Senate confirmation stood at twenty-seven, while the number of small-entity IGs appointed by agency heads without presidential or Senate approval was thirty-four.

The IG expansion involved more than a simple thirst for accountability, however. Congress could have just as easily addressed the public discontent by investing in modern financial management systems, higher entry-level pay, or better program design. The fact that it chose the IGs reflected a need for information. "The IG Act [of 1978] basically moved Congress from retail into wholesale," as one legislative participant described the history. "One of the basic reasons for adopting the idea was that we had been busting our butts to cover even a fraction of our agencies. It wasn't that we couldn't get information, but it was always like pulling teeth. The IGs gave us a middleman in the system, someone who would give us regular input through the semiannual reports and irregular access through the development of good working relationships."[22]

In a similar vein, Congress could have answered the defense procurement scandals of the early 1980s by requiring less-sophisticated weapons systems or changing overall defense strategy. Instead it opted for an under secretary for acquisitions and upped its status by assigning it a level II pay grade.[23]

The idea came from Reagan's Blue Ribbon Commission on Defense Management, chaired by former deputy defense secretary and industrialist David Packard. The commission made streamlining its top priority and a new under secretary its top recommendation when it issued its report in 1986. Noting first that "federal law governing acquisition has become steadily more complex, the acquisition system more bureaucratic, and acquisition management more encumbered and unproductive," the commission called for a new position with "full-time responsibility for managing the defense acquisition system." Although the commission also recommended simplification of the procurement regulation, it placed much more faith in that new position, making its justification as follows:

In the absence of a single, senior DoD official working full time to supervise the overall acquisition system, policy responsibility has become fragmented. As a result, the Services have tended to assume policy responsibilities and to exercise them at times without necessary coordination or uniformity. Worse still, authority for executing acquisition programs—and accountability for their results—has become vastly diluted.

For these reasons, it is fundamental that we establish unambiguous authority for overall acquisition policy, clear accountability for acquisition execution, and plain lines of command for those with program management responsibilities.[24]

Endorsed during passage of a sweeping Defense Department reorganization in 1986, it became law shortly after, along with a deputy under secretary at executive level III.[25] Because the new acquisitions under secretary replaced the old under secretary for research and engineering, the change had no net impact on the hierarchy other than raising the old posts a level in pay.

Ultimately, the IGs and the under secretary for acquisition reflect the prominence of a compliance-based approach to improving government performance. Unlike capacity-based accountability, which rests on workforce training and improved technologies, or performance-based accountability, which relies on individual or group incentives, compliance-based accountability places its faith in rules and enforcement. It tends to focus on catching wrongdoing after it occurs and relies on negative sanctions as a basis for future deterrence. As I have argued, the three types of accountability have very different implications for the role of managers: "Capacity building views the role of management as one of advocacy and stewardship. Managers are responsible for both securing and maintaining the tools and resources to achieve effectiveness. By comparison, performance accountability requires goal setting and reinforcement, while compliance accountability requires tight supervision and needed discipline."[26] When in doubt, add more rules and enforcers.

Compliance accountability, and the infinite number of command-and-control systems that go with it, is not only more familiar to most government managers, it is plain good politics.[27] Those who do the compliance monitoring—IGs—tend to produce the kinds of stories that are more visible on Capitol Hill and in the media, which in turn yield much greater opportunities for credit claiming by members of Congress and the president. More important, compliance accountability yields recommendations that are cheaper to implement and generate greater political consensus—Democrats and Republicans alike can agree that cheaters should be punished. "But when the issue is one of paying employees for successful performance or recruiting the best and brightest to government, those agreements quickly break down. Why pay for something government workers should produce automatically? Why hire the most capable when the less capable (and less expensive) will do?"[28]

Advice Thickening

The past twenty years have also witnessed a proliferation in the number of positions created to help secretaries manage their departments. Secretaries have never had so many advisers, particularly within the assistant secretary compartment. (Recall table 1-8, which suggests that staff units rise in equilibrium with line delivery units.)

Part of this growth reflects the rising number of positions accountable to outside interest groups. The Senate Governmental Affairs Committee was unusually candid in explaining the role of interest groups in the Energy Department Act in 1977. "Most of these concerns were expressed by suggesting additional designations at the assistant secretary level. . . . By statutorily designating such officers as responsible, witnesses testified, they were assured consideration of the particular issue involved."[29]

Among the petitioners, the Public Interest Research Group (PIRG) and the Energy Action Committee petitioned for an assistant secretary for competition to preserve competition in the power industry; the Sierra Club and PIRG asked for an assistant secretary for solar energy; the National Governors Association and the National Association of State Legislators asked for an assistant secretary for intergovernmental relations; the National Rural Electric Cooperatives Association and the American Public Power Association advocated an assistant secretary for power marketing; and the American Physical Society called for an assistant secretary for research. In the end, Congress created eight assistant secretaries and left the assignment of a long list of duties up to the secretary. Within the list, however, were solar energy, environmental responsibilities, intergovernmental relations, competition, power market-ing, and energy conservation.[30]

Part of the growth involves the conversion of units once located in the secretary's office into full-scale assistant secretaryships far down the hierarchy. The Commerce Department's Office of Congressional Affairs was converted in 1977, for example, as Congress endorsed the notion that performance of the liaison function "requires a top official who has the confidence of the Secretary and the administration, and who has been appointed by the President by and with the advice and consent of the Senate." As if that were not enough, there was always the call for equal status: "A further indication of the importance of this position is the fact that of the 10 other Cabinet Departments, 8 currently have an Assistant Secretary for Congressional Affairs or an equivalent official."[31]

The Commerce conversion was merely one in a long list of new staff assistant secretaries, some created to lead the call for new programs (such as evaluation and policy analysis), others to monitor existing activities (budget, logistics), still others to strengthen liaison of one kind or another (congressional relations, intergovernmental relations). Secretaries were getting more advice, not so much because they were splitting the old assistant secretaries for administration (ASAs) but because they were adding new functions that had not existed before (see table 5-1).

No longer was the ASA the only staff assistant secretary. Each successive president brought his own innovation to the staff side—Kennedy and Johnson spurred the evaluation movement, Nixon the intergovernmental affairs function, Carter the IGs, Reagan public affairs, Bush the chief financial officers. Each function seemed to merit its own assistant secretary. Each new function seemed to call for a political appointee. Of the roughly seventy staff assistant secretaries in 1992, only three— the assistant secretary of HHS for personnel, the assistant secretary of labor for administration and management, and the assistant secretary of transportation for administration—were career civil servants.

Priority Thickening

The call for greater visibility and national priority is one of the most frequent justifications for new positions and bumps. It is also the most common case made for new cabinet departments. Perhaps lacking the budget or personnel to do something more, Congress and the president often explain the creation of new units in highly symbolic terms. Even when substantive reform is involved, Congress may opt for special rank as a way of reinforcing its commitment.

The under secretary of commerce for travel and tourism remains the defining case in point. The idea actually started out in the Carter years as a proposal for an independent U.S. travel and recreation agency, coupled with a national travel and recreation policy council to monitor

TABLE 5-1 *New Under and Assistant Secretary Titles, Selected Years, 1960–92*

Title	1960	1964	1968	1972	1976	1980	1984	1988	1992
Policy; evaluation; planning; research & development	3	4	6	9	10	13	14	12	14
Budget; controller; chief financial officer	5	5	6	6	6	9	10	8	17
Administration; management; logistics; manpower; personnel[a]	20	18	21	19	19	20	22	24	23
Legislation; public affairs; intergovernmental relations	4	4	4	5	11	14	19	19	20
Inspector general	3	4	4	4	3	10[b]	11[b]	11[b]	14

sources: See appendix.
a. Includes assistant secretary of defense for health affairs.
b. Includes inspectors general at executive level V and nonstatutory inspectors general at Justice and Treasury.

and coordinate federal policy on tourism. Proposed by Senators Daniel Inouye, Democrat of Hawaii, and Larry Pressler, Republican of South Dakota, both with obvious and substantial interest in promoting tourism, the proposal passed Congress only to be pocket vetoed by Carter at the very end of his presidency. As Carter explained, "The establishment of independent agencies to promote individual aspects of international trade would only impede the efficient management and coordination of important related functions. Furthermore, the bill would create an agency not only independent of a Cabinet department but also virtually independent of Presidential direction." [32]

Notwithstanding its new Republican majority, the Senate was not to be deterred. Inouye and Pressler reintroduced the proposal and won easy Senate passage on January 27, 1981, only days after Reagan's inauguration. A less enthusiastic House countered with the under secretary idea that spring, bringing its bill to a vote July 28, just days after Reagan's massive budget and tax cut victories. In a decision that would presage its stand on VA cabinet status, the Reagan White House supported the under secretary as a "reasonable middle-of-the-road position" between what it saw as an "unnecessary and counterproductive" Senate bill and the president's own preference for abolishing, not creating, new bureaucracy. [33]

Given its strong Republican support, the under secretary proposal gave Democrats a rare and delicious opportunity to portray themselves as anti-big government. "If you believe in more government, in government interfering with the private sector by subsidizing a thriving industry, vote for . . . the National Tourism Policy Act," Representative Patricia Schroeder, Democrat of Colorado, argued. "If, however, you believe, as I do, that competition and free enterprise, without government interference, will produce the most good for our people, oppose this boondoggle. . . . If you believe in free enterprise, if you want to cut the budget, if you care to stop the cancer-like growth of the Federal government, vote against this silly bill." [34]

After damning the bill with the faint praise that it was "a little less awful than last year's version," Jack Brooks, Democrat of Texas, then chairman of the Government Operations Committee, made a similar case:

> For the past 6 months, this congress has been working toward drastic cuts in funding for programs that have served essential needs of our citizens. We have cut programs in health, education, and other social

services. At the same time, the new administration has been working mightily to curtail Government regulatory control and involvement with private industry. This is exactly the wrong time for us to be setting up a new bureaucracy to promote a private industry that seems to be doing a perfectly adequate job of promoting itself.[35]

Not all of the House Republicans were in favor, however. James Collins, Republican of Texas, argued that someone with such an "awful high position . . . will get busy to develop many forms and reports to justify this position. . . . For instance, they will ask for a report on all the travel agencies in America. They will say, 'How many people from France went to Mantolooking, N.J., last summer?' Or they will ask, 'How many people from Spain had children between the ages of 10 and 14 that ate hot dogs when they visited Kansas City?'"[36] Earlier, a group of seven Republicans on the House Energy and Commerce Committee, whence the bill had come, objected on more traditional organizational grounds.

The Department of Commerce now has one Under Secretary, whose responsibilities cover many economic sectors, with a commitment of 2,200 employees and a budget of $175,000,000. If an agency with 75 employees, a budget of under $8 million, and responsibility for a single, albeit extremely important economic sector, should have an Under Secretary, why not the Patent and Trademark office, the Bureau of the Census, the Minority Business Development Administration, or the National Bureau of Standards?[37]

Why not indeed? Commerce would get an under secretary for economic affairs and three years later an under secretary for export administration. Three years after that, it had an under secretary for technology. The Patents and Trademarks Administration and the Census Bureau, both then at level V, never quite made it to level III but did move up to assistant secretary rank. This is not to argue that creation of the travel and tourism post sucked up a host of lesser offices. Much of the activity surrounded efforts to rebuild American competitiveness in an era of escalating trade deficits. Yet there was a certain precedent in creating a mighty under secretaryship around such a small entity.

Competitive Thickening

Competition for status appears to be the most frequent justification for bumping positions upward. Even when the primary case is national priority, morale, or accountability, it is a safe bet that status will be mentioned somewhere in the legislative record. It is an insurance justification of sorts.

The assistant secretary of HHS for family support is a prime example.[38] Passed as part of the 1988 Family Support Act, the new assistant secretary was clearly warranted by the scope of the massive welfare reform. Yet after first noting that the Family Support Administration was the only one of the department's five operating divisions not then headed by an assistant secretary, the Senate Finance Committee made its case for the post on status grounds, with a familiar call for accountability thrown in for good measure:

> The Committee believes that this program addresses a major priority of the Nation and deserves to be headed by an individual of a stature equal to that of the administrators of other major governmental programs. Moreover, the Committee feels that vigorous oversight of the implementation and operation of this reformed welfare program would appropriately begin by giving careful consideration through the Senate confirmation process to the individual nominated to administer it.[39]

As such, the new assistant secretary for family support reflected a search for *internal* parity—if position X in the department is at executive level II, position Y should be too. Sometimes this search is couched in consistency terms, as in the case made for the Department of Education. In explaining its altogether logical choice to put all the assistant secretaries, the IG, and the GC at level IV, the Senate Governmental Affairs Committee argued for balance: "No one interest will be able to dominate over another because their principal officers will all be equal in stature, and all will report to the single, top official—the Secretary of Education."[40]

At other times the call is for equity, as in the case for converting all of the career-reserved level V ASAs into presidential appointments at level IV. The ASAs resisted the conversion, but it was almost always made on the basis of internal equity. Secretary of the Interior Rogers Morton penned the typical request for an ASA conversion in 1971:

> The Assistant Secretary for Administration is responsible for a variety of functions, including offices of Budget, Management Operations and Survey and Review. These functions cut across the department and involve substantive policy as well as more routine administrative

matters. Placing the new Assistant Secretary for Administration on the same level as the other Assistant Secretaries will, we feel, substantially enhance his effectiveness in dealing with the other Assistant Secretaries and in carrying out his functions.[41]

Only two career-reserved ASAs remained by 1976, in Agriculture and Transportation. Agriculture's was converted in 1982.[42]

At still other times the case is made on priority, as in the creation of a new under secretary of commerce for economic affairs in late 1981: "The Department currently has an Under Secretary for International Trade, and needs an equal focal point for domestic economic policy."[43] Because the proposal was to bump an existing assistant secretary for policy up to level III, the absolute number of executive level positions did not change and cost only $3,000 in higher pay. "The proposal is simple," testified Deputy Commerce Secretary Joe Wright for good measure. "It involves the reorganization within the Department of Commerce to improve our planning, coordination, and management, to take advantage of the resources we have in the economic areas to be of greater use in making Federal Government policy decisions and to improve our services to American business."[44]

Positions are also created or raised in the search for external parity—if department X has a given post at executive level II, so should department Y. Sometimes the case is made in international terms, as in the elevation of the patents and trademarks commissioner to level IV. "It is the intent of the conferees to upgrade this office at this time because the Commissioner of Patents and Trademarks is the chief governmental spokesman for the delegation representing the United States at the third Session of the Diplomatic Conference on the protection of industrial property, which will take place in Geneva, Switzerland, in October 1982," the House-Senate conferees rationalized. "The session is of critical importance to the United States and the representatives from our government to this conference should come from the highest levels of our government." Moreover, whatever the outcome of the negotiations, "This will provide the President and the Secretary of Commerce with an authoritative advisor on a wide variety of intellectual property issues confronting the nation."[45]

Why Positions Spread

Ultimately, these eight rationales for thickening can be reduced to one basic impulse: keeping up with the prevailing image of department structure. Even the purest rationale almost always carries some reference to equal status for equal work. Despite the occasional effort to pare down the hierarchy, such as Brown's Defense Department reorganization, the justifications lead upward.

Students of organization have long debated whether there is some built-in thrust that might explain this nearly inexorable rise, some mechanism akin to Senator Daniel Patrick Moynihan's "Iron Law of Emulation" that may have led the congressional staff structure to resemble the executive branch. This is not the book either to explore the history of the debate or to resolve it once and for all.[46] Suffice it to say that there is some agreement that organizations generally prefer to rise, but great disagreement about why. Some, like Anthony Downs, see social complexity as one underlying cause of bureaucratization. Others, like sociologists Michael Hannan and John Freeman, find natural selection at work, a survival of the fittest that favors bigger, more complex structures within a given population of organizations.[47] Still others, notably Terry Moe, see a political hand at work.

Moe's work is noteworthy in the field because it concerns itself with why government organizations are so often designed to fail. "Bureaucratic structure emerges as a jerry-built fusion of congressional and presidential forms, their relative roles and particular features determined by the powers, priorities, and strategies of the various designers," Moe writes of federal agencies. "The result is that each agency, whatever the technical requirements of effective organization might seem to be, cannot help but begin life as a unique structural reflection of its own policies."[48]

Although there is much to admire in Moe's theory of public bureaucracy, not the least of which is his effort to escape the confines of narrow economic theories of how organizations work, the portrait of uniqueness appears overdrawn. Not only is there a good deal of mimicry in cabinet making, Congress and the president constantly compare departments with each other as an excuse for making agencies look more alike. If interest groups are conspiring to fix organizational structure to fail, they are acting in unprecedented concert.

Indeed, the thickening of government reflects a rather staggering lack of creativity across agencies. Although individual positions are often justified on extraordinarily narrow, even unique grounds—such as the Geneva talks on industrial property—almost all appear to be linked by some common pressure to make each department as much like other departments as possible. As sociologist Howard Aldrich argues, "the major factors that organizations must take account of in their environments are other organizations."[49]

His colleagues Paul DiMaggio and Walter Powell label this institutional isomorphism—that is, the tendency of organizations in the same environment to become like each other. "Organizations are still becoming more homogeneous, and bureaucracy remains the common organizational form," they write. "Today, however, structural change in organizations seems less and less driven by competition or by the need for efficiency. Instead, we contend, bureaucratization and other forms of organizational change occur as the result of processes that make organizations more similar without necessarily making them more efficient." Building on the work of new institutional sociologists, as they call themselves, DiMaggio and Powell argue that there are at least three mechanisms undergirding institutional isomorphism: "(1) *coercive* isomorphism that stems from political influence and the problem of legitimacy, (2) *mimetic* isomorphism resulting from standard responses to uncertainty, and (3) *normative* isomorphism, associated with professionalization."[50]

The past fifty years of thickening seem to show isomorphism at work. The IGs, for example, can be seen as the product of coercive isomorphism—Congress mandated a specific structure for ferreting out fraud, waste, and abuse, no matter the uniform resistance of the departments about to be covered. The deputy secretaries at Treasury, Labor, and elsewhere, can be seen as the result of mimetic isomorphism—those departments copied others so that they would look the way departments are supposed to look. Finally, the elevation of the career assistant secretaries for administration from level V to IV can be viewed as a result of normative isomorphism—Nixon decided that all assistant secretaries should look the same, albeit for political purposes.

This is not to argue that organizations in the same environment will come to resemble one another perfectly. "Some organizations respond to external pressures quickly;" write DiMaggio and Powell, "others change only after a long period of resistance." So noted, individual departments score high on all six of the conditions that seem to foster efforts to become more like their peers:

1. The greater the dependence of an organization on another organization, the more similar it will become to that organization in structure, climate, and behavioral focus.
2. The greater the centralization of organization A's resource supply, the greater the extent to which organization A will change

isomorphically to resemble the organizations on which it depends for resources.

3. The more uncertain the relationship between means and ends, the greater the extent to which an organization will model itself after organizations it perceives as successful.

4. The more ambiguous the goals of an organization, the greater the extent to which the organization will model itself after organizations that it perceives as successful.

5. The greater the reliance on academic credentials in choosing managerial and staff personnel, the greater the extent to which an organization will become like other organizations in its field.

6. The greater the participation of organizational managers in trade and professional associations, the more likely the organization will be, or will become, like other organizations in its field.[51]

Numbers one and two reflect coercion—organizations become like one another because they are forced to by circumstance. Numbers three and four represent mimicry—organizations become more like one another to cope with uncertainty. Numbers five and six mirror normative pressure—organizations resemble one another because of a prevailing image of what organizations should look like, an image that is socialized through academic training and professional interaction.

Translated to the federal government, departments would resemble one another if the organizations on which they depend for resources, Congress and the White House, also thickened over decades; if the organizations that are perceived as most successful thickened too; and if some common principles of organizational management defined common wisdom.

All appear to hold for government. Earlier chapters have already examined the continued influence of Gulick's span-of-control principle, a principle still taught in many graduate programs. The rest of this chapter examines the parallel thickening of Congress and the White House and the ways in which particularly successful departments (measured by budget and size) might be teaching the rest of the executive branch about the value of thickening.

DiMaggio and Powell also offer six conditions that determine the speed that organizations become like one another. Federal departments score high on five:

1. The greater the extent to which a field of organizations is dependent upon a single (or several similar) source of support for vital resources, the higher the level of isomorphism.

2. The fewer the visible alternative organizational models in a field, the faster the rate of isomorphism.

3. The greater the extent to which technologies are uncertain or goals are ambiguous within a field, the greater the rate of isomorphic change.

4. The greater the extent of professionalization in a field, the greater the amount of institutional isomorphic change.

5. The greater the extent of "structuration" in a field—that is, the degree to which a field has stable and broadly acknowledged centers, peripheries, and pecking orders—the greater the degree of isomorphism.[52]

Translated again, federal departments would come to resemble one another more quickly if almost all depended on one or two sources— Congress and the White House—for basic resources; if there were few credible alternatives to the prevailing structure of departments; if goals were ambiguous; if professionals moved up through similar paths; and if the field itself had strong central principles of organization. All appear to hold for federal departments.[53]

Consider, for one example, the professionalization of the Senior Executive Service. SESers not only share a common pay system, they also are socialized through a similar recruitment process, often belong to professional groups such as the Senior Executives Association, and most certainly share a common set of titles. If there is an innovation in the titling of one, all 8,000 will soon know.

Consider, for a second example, the shortage of credible models of how "normal" departments should look. There are few alternatives to the traditional image of government organization first articulated by Hoover. Although there has been a slight increase in the number of quasi-government corporations over the past two decades—the most notable being the U.S. Postal Service—the model is not applicable to most departments. When members of Congress and their staff sit down to design a new department, they still go back to the existing statutes; when presidents propose a new public enterprise such as national health care, they still think in terms of traditional hierarchy, whether called health alliances or something else. And, as Gore discovered in 1993, when presidents propose converting traditional federal activities such as air traffic control into quasi-public corporations, they quickly find that Congress still prefers the old approaches.

Ultimately, this book is less concerned with the speed at which departments come to resemble one another than with the simple fact that the resemblance exists. It appears that the resemblance can be traced to two main sources: the thickening of Congress and the White House, and the lessons learned from thicker, faster-growing departments.

Parallel Thickening

As federal departments look outward to an uncertain world, or merely up and down Pennsylvania Avenue, they receive signals about how to play the organizational game. Thickening does not occur in a political or social vacuum.[54] Indeed, it parallels the thickening of America's corporations, universities, churches, labor unions, and even schools of public policy and management. "I see it in universities, for example," writes political scientist James Q. Wilson. "The Kennedy School of Government at Harvard is training people for administrative service, and the hierarchy of that school has become as complex as the hierarchy of the Department of State. Perhaps a process of emulation is at work: in order to train people for being deputy assistant secretaries, the school has created deputy assistant deans."[55]

Thus, the first reason thickening spreads across departments may be that it occurs elsewhere in their environments. The same orthodoxy that shapes departments shapes other institutions. "Bureaucratic growth is an outcome of modern concepts of administration that have become deeply embedded in Western societies, as much or more so in the U.S. as elsewhere," write sociologists Marshall Meyer, William Stevenson, and Stephen Webster. "Problems are confronted by constructing organizations; new problems are confronted by adding more organization to existing structures. Our culture views this problem-organization-problem-more organization cycle as for the most part reasonable and rational."[56]

Consider, for example, parallel thickening in the Executive Office of the President and Congress. Although Roosevelt's Brownlow committee would likely argue that the expanding departments started it all, prompting the White House countercentralization, both ends of Pennsylvania Avenue have made impressive strides in expanding the hierarchy. American government has never had so many overseers.

Start with the White House, where virtually every unit in the Executive Office of the President has thickened. By 1974, as Stephen Hess argues, the White House had been bureaucratized:

> By the time Richard Nixon left office, the number of people employed by the White House and the Executive Office was nearly twice that

under Johnson, just as Johnson's was nearly twice that of Roosevelt's. In fifty years the White House staff had grown from 37 to more than 900, the Executive Office staff, from zero to many thousands. With the bureaucratizing of the presidency, it is hardly surprising that the White House fell heir to all the problems of a bureaucracy, including the distortion of information as it passes up the chain of command and frustrating delays in decisionmaking.[57]

In the years since, the number of odd, often personalized titles once used to attract or label friends of the president—special consultants, special assistants in the White House, and senior counselors of one kind or another—has declined as a set of standard titles has taken hold (see table 5-2).

Looking just at the names and titles listed in the *U.S. Government Manual*, and recognizing therefore that this is but a superficial count, the White House core staff goes from five layers and twenty-nine key assistants in 1960 to five much more fully established layers and eighty-one occupants in 1992.[58] Although the lack of West Wing office space may create an absolute limit on the size of the inner circle, it has yet to be reached.

The patterns are more pronounced at the Office of Management and Budget, which started relatively flat in 1960 and grew both taller and wider over the ensuing decades. Rising from three layers and but ten occupants in 1960, the agency ends up three-plus decades later with eight layers and thirty-two occupants. Part of the expansion is attributable to the politicization of the agency in Nixon's second term. Led by a new OMB director, Roy Ash, and his deputy director and expert in bypass layering, Fred Malek, the once proud career-led agency was converted into a political arm of the president. Once Watergate hit and the White House staff dissolved, Ash later argued, "OMB clearly and undisputably became a presidential right hand. It was absolutely a myth to say that the government was not managed in the last few months of the Nixon administration. It was probably better managed in terms of government function than it has been in any other time in American history, except not by the President. We had that place humming."[59]

Nixon was not the first to order noncareer officers into the budget trenches, however. The practice began, perhaps again not surprisingly, with Eisenhower, who created four noncareer assistant directorships in the early 1950s. Those four slots expanded slowly but steadily over the next two decades until Nixon created the new title of program associate

TABLE 5-2. *Thickening in Presidential Agencies, Selected Years, 1960–92*

White House	Bureau of the Budget	Office of the Vice President
1960		
1 assistant (chief of staff)	1 director	No formal office
1 principal deputy assistant	1 deputy director	
6 deputy assistants	8 assistant directors/counsels	
20 special assistants		
1 deputy special assistant		
1972		
2 counselors	1 director	1 administrative assistant
9 assistants	1 deputy director	11 staff assistants
10 deputy assistants	2 associate directors/counsels	
24 special assistants	9 assistant directors	
1980		
1 assistant (chief of staff)	1 director	1 chief of staff
12 assistants to the president	1 deputy director	1 deputy chief of staff
22 deputy assistants	3 executive associate directors[a]	5 assistants
19 special assistants	6 associate directors/counsels	2 deputy assistants
	13 deputy associate directors	4 special assistants
	7 assistant directors	
1992		
1 chief of staff	1 director	1 chief of staff
1 deputy chief of staff	1 principal deputy director	1 deputy chief of staff
16 assistants	1 deputy director for management	8 assistants
29 deputy assistants/associate counsels	2 executive associate directors[a]	2 deputy assistants
34 special assistants	8 associate directors/counsels	2 special assistants
	12 deputy associate directors	
	4 assistant directors	
	3 deputy assistant directors	

SOURCES: *The United States Government Manual*, respective years.
a. Includes administrators of the Offices of Federal Procurement Policy and Information and Regulatory Affairs.

director in his second term. This in turn prompted a backlash on Capitol Hill, which for the first time required Senate confirmation of the OMB director and deputy director.[60] Congress continued the practice at several points, most recently when it created a new deputy director for management in 1990.[61]

The parallel layering is most visible in the Office of the Vice President, an office that simply did not exist in the formal White House hierarchies of the 1950s and 1960s. Its rising pyramid reflects the emergence of a "new vice presidency" under Nelson Rockefeller and Walter Mondale. Before these two occupants, the office was little more than an afterthought. With no formal responsibilities but to break tie votes in the Senate, and the only one true function to replace the president in the event of some mishap, the office eventually emerged as a force in its own right. "The Vice-President's office is now a replica of the President's office, with a national security adviser, press secretary, domestic issues staff, scheduling team, advance, appointments, administration, chief of staff, and counsel's office," I have argued. "And, in 1972, the Vice-President's office finally was listed as a distinct unit in the *U.S. Government Organization Manual*, a major sign of institutional identity."[62]

The office structure itself appears to be the product of parallel layering in other White House units. As Mondale took on a much more influential role in the Carter White House, he designed a hierarchy that mirrored presidential reality just across the street from his Old Executive Office Building suite—he would have a national security adviser to connect with the president's; he would have a press secretary because that is what the president had. In turn, his success generated resources that led to further growth: "Because Vice-Presidents had more money for staff, they were able to recruit more policy specialists. Moreover, as the staff grew, Vice Presidents were able to build an administrative and political core in the office. No longer did the Vice-President's top policy staff have to double as campaign workers or administrators."[63]

As for presidential promises to start the thinning of government with their own White House staffs, the record has been dismal. Presidents may have shown some skill at using accounting gimmicks to disguise White House staff as something else but have mostly failed to keep the staffs thin and the hierarchy flat. That appears to be the fate of Clinton's early promise to cut his White House staff by 25 percent and 350 jobs. By the end of his first year in office, he had more senior staff than Reagan had ten years earlier. Along the way he also created a second deputy chief of staff to add to table 5-2.

Turn next to Capitol Hill, where a panoply of support and leadership hierarchies have come to resemble the executive branch (see table 5-3). The reasons for the mirroring can be quite rational—the growing legislative agenda, increasing policy complexity, growing budgets, post-Watergate efforts to curb the imperial presidency. Indeed, congressional and presidential thickening might be compared to a nuclear arms race in which both sidestep up their armaments in pace with each other. It may not matter who started it, just that it is hot.[64]

The growth of the House and Senate whip hierarchies is one case in point. Part of the deepening of titles reflects the growing ambition of individual members of Congress. As former Senate leader Everett McKinley Dirksen, Republican of Illinois, once said: "There are 100 diverse personalities in the U.S. Senate. O Great God, what an amazing and dissonant 100 personalities they are! What an amazing thing it is to harmonize them. What a job it is."[65] If they were amazing under Dirksen, who died in office in 1969, they are nothing short of extraordinary today.

The fact that members of both chambers have become more entrepreneurial over the past three decades means that the job of coordinating floor debate has become more complicated.[66] As Congressional Research Service senior specialist Walter Oleszek shows, the Senate whip structure evolved in four distinct steps: (1) creation of the Senate policy committees in the 1940s, which gave each whip access to needed legislative information, (2) creation of the first assistant whips in 1966, which reflected an effort to further strengthen the flow of information on an increasingly complex calendar, (3) expansion of the Republican whip title in 1969 to include "assistant majority leader," which gave the occupant greater internal power as a senior party officer, and (4) the invention, again under the Republicans, of regional whips in 1970, which further extended the office outward.[67]

With these precedents set, the whip hierarchy continued to spread as an institutional monitoring mechanism. There was simply more and more happening on the floor. According to political scientist Steven S. Smith, "A wide range of mutually reinforcing developments enhanced the role of the House and Senate floors as arenas for policymaking. More complex and controversial issues, growing constituencies, an expanding community of interest groups and lobbyists in Washington, intensifying campaign pressures, and personal policy interests motivated members to pursue issues more frequently on the chamber floors."[68] In context, expanding whip hierarchies makes perfect sense.

TABLE 5-3 *Thickening in Congressional Agencies, Selected Years, 1960–92*

General Accounting Office	Senate majority leadership	Senate minority leadership	House majority leadership	House minority leadership	Congressional Research Service
1960			**1960**[a]		
1 comptroller	1 president pro tempore	1 leader	1 speaker	1 leader	1 librarian
2 assistant comptrollers/ counsels	1 leader	1 whip	1 leader	1 whip	1 chief assistant librarian
	1 whip		1 whip		1 deputy chief assistant librarian
					1 assistant librarian
1972			**1972**[a]		
1 comptroller	1 president pro tempore	1 leader	1 speaker	1 leader	1 librarian
1 deputy comptroller	1 leader	1 whip	1 leader	1 whip	1 deputy librarian
1 special assistant	1 whip	5 regional whips	1 whip		1 assistant librarian
4 assistant comptrollers/ counsels	4 assistant whips				1 counsel
1980			**1980**[a]		
1 comptroller	1 president pro tempore	1 leader	1 speaker	1 leader	1 librarian
1 deputy comptroller	1 leader	1 whip	1 leader	1 whip	1 deputy librarian
1 special assistant	1 whip	16 assistant whips	1 whip		1 principal associate librarian
5 assistant comptrollers/ counsels	1 chief deputy whip				2 associate librarians
	9–11 deputy whips				2 assistant librarians
					1 counsel
1992			**1992**		
1 comptroller	1 president pro tempore	1 leader	1 speaker	1 leader	1 librarian
1 deputy comptroller	1 leader	1 whip	1 leader	1 whip	1 deputy librarian
1 special assistant	1 whip	13 deputy whips	1 whip	2 chief deputy whips	1 principal associate librarian
12 assistant comptrollers/ counsels	1 chief deputy whip		3 chief deputy whips	6 deputy whips	6 associate librarians
	4 deputy whips		1 floor whip	3 assistant deputy whips	2 assistant librarians
	4 assistant deputy whips		13 assistant whips	4 regional whips	1 counsel
			62 at-large whips		
			14 zone whips		

SOURCES: *The United States Government Manual*, respective years; additional information from *Congressional Yellow Book* (Monitor Leadership Directories), respective years.
a. Incomplete information for both sides of the House.

TABLE 5-4. *Thickening among Congressional Full Committee Staffs, 1961 and 1993*[a]

Committee 1961	1993
	Senate

Appropriations

1 chief clerk	1 staff director
1 assistant chief clerk	1 deputy staff director
1 assistant clerk	1 chief clerk
15 professional staff	4 professional staff
	2 staff assistants

Appropriations subcommittees

1 chief clerk	13 clerks
1 assistant clerk	19 professional staff
17 professional staff	13 staff assistants

Armed Services

1 chief counsel	1 staff director
2 counsels	1 general counsel
	13 professional staff
	11 staff assistants
	1 chief clerk
	1 assistant chief clerk

Banking and Currency

1 chief of staff	1 staff director/chief counsel
9 professional staff	3 staff director
	1 deputy staff director
	12 professional staff/counsels
	9 staff assistants
	1 chief clerk
	1 assistant chief clerk

Finance

1 chief clerk	1 staff director
1 assistant chief clerk	1 deputy staff director
1 professional staff	3 chief counselors
	1 senior counselor
	11 professional staff/counsels
	3 research assistants

Foreign Relations

1 chief of staff	1 staff director
5 consultants	1 deputy staff director
4 staff assistants	1 chief counsel
1 chief clerk	29 professional staff
1 assistant chief clerk	1 chief clerk
11 assistant clerks	

(continued)

TABLE 5-4. *(Continued)*

Committee 1961	1993
	House of Representatives
Appropriations	
1 clerk	1 clerk/staff director
1 assistant clerk	7 staff assistants
14 staff assistants	1 administrative assistant
	3 administrative aides
Appropriations subcommittees	
18 staff assistants	10 staff assistants
	32 staff assistants
	10 administrative aides
Armed Services	
1 chief counsel	1 staff director
2 counsel	1 general counsel
	42 professional staff
	1 chief clerk
	1 assistant chief clerk
Banking and Currency	
1 clerk/general counsel	1 clerk/staff director
1 counsel	1 general counsel
1 deputy counsel	1 deputy general counsel
1 assistant	11 professsional staff/counsels
Ways and Means	
1 chief clerk	1 staff director
1 assistant chief clerk	1 assistant director
4 professional staff	1 chief tax counsel
8 staff assistants	18 professional assistants
	28 staff assistants
Foreign Affairs	
1 staff administrator and clerk	1 chief of staff
1 senior staff consultant	1 deputy chief of staff
3 staff consultants	1 chief counsel
4 senior staff assistants	2 senior staff consultants
6 staff assistants	16 staff consultants
	5 staff associates
	1 senior staff assistant
	4 staff assistants
	6 directors/coordinators
Government Operations	
1 staff director	1 staff director
1 general counsel	1 deputy general counsel
1 associate general counsel	1 senior policy adviser
5 staff members	8 professional staff/associate Counsel
	5 staff assistants/assistant counsels
	1 chief clerk

SOURCES: *Congressional Directory* (U.S. Congress, Joint Committee on Printing, 1961 and 1993); *Congressional Staff Directory* (Staff Directories, Ltd., 1961 and 1993); *Congressional Yellow Book* (Monitor Publishing, Winer 1993).
   a. Table does not include subcommittee, clerical, and other support staff.

The thickening is also evident among the standing committees of Congress, where the rising number of staffers has increased both the width and the height of the hierarchy. As the number of committee staff members increased from just over 900 in 1960 to roughly 3,000 today, the number of supervisory layers increased as well.[69] Even though the growth of committee staffs is flatter than that of the executive branch, they have grown taller over time (see table 5-4).[70]

This thickening of congressional staffs has provoked a range of complaints, not the least of which is from Morris Fiorina, who argues that large staffs may diffuse the accountability of decisionmakers to the electorate. According to Fiorina, "discretion inevitably accompanies delegation. The staff act as gatekeepers, affecting the flow of information to and from members. They make judgments about what to pass on and how to present it. And while they must keep members' political interests primary as a condition of their employment, they have interests of their own as well."[71] Thus may the thickening of Congress also contribute to the diffusion of accountability within the executive branch, for as agencies read the rising hierarchy on Capitol Hill, they may find solace for their expanding hierarchies.

Ultimately, the assortment of parallel thickening described here makes perfect sense in isolation—the vice president needs a national security adviser to prepare for succession; the Senate needs a chief deputy whip to coordinate the assistant deputy whips; the House needs three chief deputy whips to coordinate thirteen assistants, sixty-two at-large whips, and fourteen zone whips; the House Foreign Affairs Committee needs a vast infusion of layers to keep track of a complicated world; the Congressional Research Service needs a principal associate librarian to coordinate the work of the associate and assistant librarians; and so forth. Yet this parallel thickening may have a double cost nonetheless: first, by subjecting Congress and the White House to the same diffusion of accountability that affects the departments; and second, by confirming thickening as the prevailing model of how to organize.

Models of Success

Just as departments look to Congress and the White House for signals, so do they look to each other. They note the latest innovations in thickening at the inner cabinet; they pay attention to the budget process—who is winning, who is getting cut. They look at how given organizations do in individual years and how they do over time. The

TABLE 5-5. *The Volume of Government Departments, 1980 and 1992*

	1980			1992		
Department	Layers[a]	Division directors	Volume[b]	Layers[a]	Division directors	Volume[b]
Agriculture	25	317	3,963	26	286	3,718
Commerce	22	381	4,191	24	569	6,828
Defense	25	212	2,650	28	430	6,020
Education	16	149	1,192	18	76	684
Energy	16	316	2,528	24	398	4,776
HHS	24	633	7,596	26	593	7,709
HUD	12	172	1,032	12	126	756
Interior	18	203	1,827	24	221	2,652
Justice	21	105	1,103	20	191	1,910
Labor	18	219	1,971	22	148	1,628
State	16	161	1,288	18	328	2,952
Transportation	18	471	4,239	23	605	6,958
Treasury	20	216	2,160	25	382	4,775
VA	. . .	. . .	. . .	17	141	1,199

a. All layers, no matter how broadly filled, are counted in the total.
b. Volume = layers ÷ half the number of division directors.

thickness of successful departments should have some bearing on the degree to which other departments struggle to keep up.

There is no question that the fourteen departments of government come in different thicknesses, which can be measured as the simple number of layers between top and bottom (see table 3-3 for the comparison). Thickness can also be measured more elegantly as the total volume of a triangle at the top of each department—the number of layers multiplied by half the number of occupants. Using division directors to anchor the bottom of this triangle, departments vary rather significantly in total volume, from Education and HUD at one end to Commerce, Defense, HHS, and State at the other (see table 5-5).[72]

That four departments lost volume during the 1980s—Agriculture, Education, HUD, and Labor—speaks to Reagan's impact in cutting domestic government. His ideology and budget clearly shaped the size of the four departments, which in turn reduced the total volume of their hierarchies. Of some interest in determining his ultimate success, however, is the fact that none of the departments lost height. Reagan may have been successful in scaling back total girth, but he left in place many of the layers that have served in the past as a plate for weight gain. This is perhaps a key lesson in how to stop future thickening—the diet must apply to height as well as width. Shortening agencies may be as important as shrinking the number of occupants at any given layer.

TABLE 5-6. *Explaining Differences in the Volume of Government Departments, 1992*

	Thick	*Thicker*	*Thickest*
	(Education, HUD, Justice, Labor, VA)	*(Agriculture, Energy, Interior, State, Treasury)*	*(Commerce, Defense, HHS, Transportation)*
Average volume	**1,236**	**3,776**	**6,879**
Size			
Outlays	$28,280,000	$75,396,000	$222,231,000
Civilian employment	78,887	85,932	311,186
Work-force demographics			
Average grade	9.59	9.60	9.76
Work-force age	42.5	42.2	42.2[a]
Percentage of GS 11–15 managers	11.2	9.1	10.2
Percentage eligible for retirement	7.1	7.2	7.7[a]
Political history			
Department age (years)	49	139	87
Inner-cabinet members	1	2	1
Leadership			
Number of political appointees	99	129	166
Percentage drawn from business	10.6	27.0	53.7
Percentage drawn from government	37.2	44.0	22.2
Percentage drawn from law	43.6	25.2	13.0
Percentage drawn from education	8.5	3.8	11.1

SOURCES: See endnote number 73 in the text.
a. Department of Defense data are for the Office of the Secretary of Defense only.

There are several potential explanations for differences in volume between the fourteen departments at any point in time (see table 5-6).[73] Budget and civilian employment seem to be the most powerful predictors, with most demographic indicators rather unimpressive in explaining differences. At least in the federal government, the larger the agency, the greater the volume of the executive hierarchy, a possible confirmation of Peter Blau's notion that size matters to organizational structure.[74]

Among the leadership indicators, there is more effect than cause. The number of political appointees is likely more a consequence of budget and size than a cause of volume, as is the tendency of business executives to be found in the thickest departments. Presidents may explicitly search for business leaders to run the larger departments.

TABLE 5-7. *Changes in the Volume of Departments, 1980–92*
Percentage

	Negative (Agriculture, Education, HHS, HUD, Labor)	Fast (Commerce, Energy, Interior, Justice, Transportation)	Faster (Defense, State, Treasury)
Average change in volume	−18.2	66.9	126.2
Outlays (in 1992 dollars)	11.9	16.2	66.1
Outlays (excluding HHS)	−0.3	. . .	. . .
Political appointees	23.2	16.8	66.8
Civilian employment	−14.4	11.8	15.8
Average grade[a]	3.7	3.7	11.3
Work-force age	7.0	2.0	0.5[c]
GS 11–15 managers[a]	−11.6	−7.1	4.3
Eligible for Retirement[b]	−1.2	−1.0	−3.1[c]

SOURCES: See endnote 73 in the text.
a. 1983–92 data only.
b. 1976–90, does not include Education or Energy.
c. Department of Defense data are for the Office of the Secretary of Defense only.

The same general patterns hold for changes in volume over time, here between 1980 and 1992 (see table 5-7). Cutting budgets and civilian personnel is the quickest way to reduce the overall volume of a department's hierarchy, although as suggested above, most of the 1980–92 shrinkage involved width, not height. Note in particular the budget figures when HHS is not included. Much of the HHS budget grows automatically as social security and medicare rise. Table 5-7 also shows a modest impact of average grade on overall change in volume, as well as reductions in the number of grade 11–15 managers. However, as with the number of political appointees, these relationships could be consequences, not causes, of shrinking.

It is impossible to untangle the impact of budget and personnel in using these numbers. However, because personnel costs are such a small part of the overall federal budget—accounting for less than $1 in every $10 of spending—it is unlikely that personnel cuts alone will knock back the hierarchy. There is some evidence, admittedly thin, that organizations ratchet up symmetrically, with staff and line positions rising in roughly equal proportions, but decline asymmetrically, with line units dropping faster than staff.[75] This problem may be particularly acute for monitoring units such as the Offices of Inspector General. As Downs argues:

First, once a monitoring agency has assembled the minimum necessary staff, genuine economies of scale may enable it to greatly expand output without adding many more staff members. Conversely, when it contracts output drastically, it may still need to retain that minimum-sized group. Second, most top-level officials seek to increase control over their subordinates rather than to reduce it. Hence they may deliberately retain the same sized staff to monitor a smaller operating section, knowing this will intensify control. Third, members of the monitoring agency are sometimes organizationally closer to the bureau's top-most officials than members of the operating bureau. Hence topmost officials may retain large control staffs in order to maintain their own power, income, and prestige, or those of their bureau.[76]

In this way, personnel cuts can stimulate even more middle- and upper-level layering. New staff get hired to write streamlining plans, new monitors to ensure that those plans are followed, new advocates to provide career counseling for those on their way out.

Just because the tables do not show much impact from organizational demographics does not mean they have no play in the upward thrust of the hierarchy. As chapter 1 argued, the best available evidence suggests that the aging of the government work force (and the promotional desires that might go with it) is much less important in explaining grade increases than the changing nature of work.

Ultimately, middle- and upper-level thickening may be mostly unrelated to each other. Those who expect Gore's middle-level flattening to somehow reduce the upper-level bulge are imagining a link that simply may not exist. The top of government appears to rise on its own—sparked by highly individualized innovations, spread by isomorphism—while the middle level rises on the basis of perhaps more predictable explanations—such as pay, contracting out, and changing jobs. Even if reduction of the middle-level bulge eliminates the workload and span-of-control justification for higher-ups, there are plenty of other justifications available.

The question is what the "losers" might learn from the "winners." One answer is that smaller agencies cannot help but see lessons in the thicker superstructures of their larger, more successful peers. Obviously, the Department of Education will never be as large as HHS. It does not have the agenda. But that did not prevent Education from trying to resemble HHS, at least at the top. Having that superstructure did not protect Education from cuts during the 1980s, but the department did emerge with its higher-level posts intact, with all that may mean for future thickening under more favorable administrations.

Conclusion

This chapter offers sobering advice to those who hope to reverse the thickening of government. If all organizations within a given population are not thinned together, the thinning may not hold for long on those that are thinned. More important perhaps, if the leading organizations are left untouched—whether they provide the central resources or are recognized as successful in dealing with an uncertain environment—the thickening may return even faster.

Will government continue to thicken in coming years? The answer appears to be yes. This book has already questioned the Gore decision to exempt political executives from the thinning now under way at the middle and lower levels of government. Now it must also ask whether leaving Congress and the Executive Office of the President mostly untouched is equally risky. Certainly, this chapter argues for involving Congress much more in cutting the top level of government. And, if political realities prevent Congress and White House from being thinned, perhaps they can at least be kept from thickening further.

Even at the middle, thickening will likely continue with the changing nature of work and pay freezes. Indeed, it is no small irony that the Gore effort was launched at roughly the same time that a pay freeze took effect under Clinton's first-year budget. If backdoor pay increases are one source of middle-level thickening, a pay freeze would be just about the worst strategy to support the Gore reform. Moreover, nothing has happened to reduce the number of interest groups and their calls for representation at the upper reaches of government.

This does not mean that a more comprehensive effort would fail. Changing work itself does not mean there need to be more managers, for example. Increasing grade levels does not require more supervisors per se. Even if middle- and upper-level thickening appear to be unrelated, the two can be part of a broad solution to the ladders of control that get in the way of front-line workers. It may not matter much to air traffic controllers and social security claims representatives whether the layer comes from Hoover's first commission or Reagan's last pay freeze, from cabinet status or from the thirst for accountability. For them, the issue is cutting layers, regardless of origin.

6

Can Thickening Be Stopped?

American presidents have never had so much help, their department secretaries never so much staff. There are more presidential appointees, senior executives, and middle managers than ever before, a legacy both of repeated efforts over the past half century to gain control of an unwieldy bureaucracy and of the enduring impact of Luther Gulick's span-of-control principle. Each new administration adds its innovations without clearing out the old. Accountability is steadily diffused as the sediment thickens. Bypass layering begets bypass layering ad infinitum.

Ironically, the new positions may fit perfectly with the prevailing incentives facing both ends of Pennsylvania Avenue. The workload may be too heavy, the call for a symbolic gesture on a national priority too great, the need for a level playing field in an international negotiation obvious. Nonetheless, each new position adds to the diffusion of accountability. As much as they think that adding a new layer or occupant to an already thick hierarchy will help, presidents and Congress may end up with even less control and responsiveness. As Hugh Heclo wrote in 1977, when there were twenty-two, not thirty-two, layers in the top compartments of government:

> More layers of technocratic political appointees may well reduce rather than increase bureaucratic responsiveness to broader political leadership by the President and department heads: this in turn increases incentives for the White House to politicize the civil service by trying to build an executive team of loyalists throughout the political and higher career levels. Protectors of the civil service can react by well-tried techniques—more emphasis on functional specialties in the bureaucracy, closer ties with clienteles, more

166

extensive civil service coverage, rules and regulations—but this will probably only remove self-interested bureaucracies further from the reach of political leadership.[1]

Thus thickening may be rational only in the narrowest terms and may well leave a legacy of an even more impenetrable bureaucracy in the future. More important, it is not clear that thickening causes government to perform better. If the burden of proof is on the defenders of thickening, they have a very heavy burden indeed. The costs of thickening appear high—information distortion, inertia, disunity of command, a gap between responsibility and authority, lost innovation and involvement, even problems recruiting the best and brightest into government service. The gains, however, seem minimal. Supervisors may be able to track what their subordinates do, but to what end?

A Brief Review

The problem with the increasing corps of presidential "helpers" is not in the absolute numbers. Simply put, the numbers do not matter nearly as much as how they are distributed throughout the hierarchy. The top of the hierarchy has grown from a seventeen-layer pyramid in 1960 to thirty-two layers today, while the number of occupants has increased almost sixfold. The number of layers has also grown at the middle level, rising from seven in 1980 to eight in 1992, and increasing by roughly 2,000 occupants.

Although approximately four in ten of those occupants are presidential appointees of one kind or another, the majority are now career executives. Indeed, one of the great ironies of politicization is that it has thickened the career executive ranks too. No longer do presidents control almost all of the top jobs in government. Presidents are fooling themselves if they believe that more senior helpers will improve their command. Exactly the opposite seems to be true: more helpers clutter the message.

Whether the top jobs are occupied by careerists or presidential appointees may not matter at all. Rather, the lead story here is that government is much taller and wider today than it was thirty years ago. Every layer has widened—there are more secretaries, more deputy secretaries, and more under secretaries. However, the growth has been particularly impressive in the assistant secretary compartment, which has grown from just forty-three occupants and two layers under FDR to nearly 1,500 occupants and eight layers a half century later.

Much of this thickening was created by amendments to existing titles. No matter how much presidents and Congress promise that a new position will not take up more space, rare is the new position that does not bring a collection of title-riders. A new assistant secretary gets created, followed by a deputy assistant secretary, an associate deputy assistant secretary, a principal deputy assistant secretary, and a chief of staff to the assistant secretary. The title is extended downward and outward to its extreme, at which point the entire unit becomes eligible for elevation to an even higher executive level. So too for the other growth industries in thickening: chiefs of staff, general counsels, and inspectors general. The span-of-control principle remains alive and well today.

Thickening has hardly been accidental. It reflects an administrative state in chaos, a beleaguered president in desperate need of help, and a government in desperate need of scientific leadership. Starting with Gulick's contribution to *Papers on the Science of Administration* in 1937, the search for tighter and tighter control has been extended by virtually every commission, task force, and blue-ribbon panel since.

No one was more important to the implementation of the scientific design than Herbert Hoover. In his search for administrative order, Hoover's 1949 commission created the blueprint for the future thickening of government. Whether that blueprint could have worked will never be known, for it was almost instantly reworked by politics. His carefully drafted organization charts were amended by individual departments in the search for more control or status; his rationalization for greater secretarial leadership was soon converted by Eisenhower into a political job system. Thus did the rationale for thickening change. Whereas narrow spans of control had once been justified by the inherent limits of leaders, they eventually came to reflect distrust of the career civil service. Presidents and secretaries needed more help because the career service might sabotage their plans.

The key question is whether the thickening matters. Again, the answer is best made not in raw numbers but in the changing shape of the hierarchy. Although senior executives make obvious and positive contributions to government, not the least of which are administrative due process and rule-bound consistency, they also increase the overall distance between the top and bottom of government. That distance, in turn, may undermine the president's best efforts to lead the government. What may have suffered along the way to Gulick's tightly managed government is unity of command. The number of managers, whether at the top or in the middle, may simply mean that no one is ultimately accountable for anything that government does.

This diffusion of accountability permeates much of what happens in the federal government today. The information distortion that comes from the growing distance between top and bottom may mean that no one unit or individual can be held accountable for the poor analysis or misinformation that creates mistakes; the administrative inertia that comes with multiple internal checks and detours may mean that no one can be held responsible for a lack of action; the disunity of command that comes with high vacancy rates among political appointees—who stay an average of eighteen months—may mean that no appointee can be blamed for decisions made on someone else's watch. The list of costs associated with the diffusion of accountability goes on, but the point is simple: thickening denies presidents and Congress the opportunity to hold anyone accountable for what government does.

There are, of course, several methods for measuring the thickness of government. Span of control is by far the most common approach, yet it carries great risk in the aggregate. An average span across government is practically meaningless, the numbers are easily manipulated, and they fail to accommodate differences in either the mission of the agency or its internal compartments. As a result, spans are difficult to use as a methodology for thinning. How can government possibly mandate a single span of 1:15 as a goal, when agencies vary so much in what they do and who does it?

A more promising approach is to measure the decision chain between the front line at the bottom of a department and the most senior executive. As a diagnostic tool, the chain estimates true distance, thereby illustrating the potential costs of multiple policy- and budget-making detours up and down the "trunk" of the department. More important, the chain focuses attention on what government does, forcing questions about what the middle-and senior-level jobs contribute by way of value added to the final "product."

The first step in efforts to stop thickening is to find out where it starts. It is always tempting to blame middle-level bureaucrats, who have few defenders on Capitol Hill and no visible interest groups. However, there are deeper roots for the thickening. Just about the only weak roots are in new departments, which are almost never a source of innovations in thickening. New departments do contribute to the thickening of government, of course. By definition, they widen the secretarial compartment and are often wider than the departments they join. Moreover, even if they are not the first to adopt an innovation, they are frequently the second or third, legitimizing a new position or layer in the eyes of other departments.

Once past the new departments, the roots are harder to untangle. The inner cabinet, for example, is the source of much of the innovation in layering. Congress plays a role too. At least in the formal thickening that occurs through statute, Congress has become increasingly active in changing the shape of government. During the 1970s and 1980s, Congress not only claimed a growing share of authorship in adding new positions to the formal structure, it also became increasingly specific about what it wanted. Gone are the days when Congress gives the president or department secretary the discretion to decide how to task a new assistant secretary.

As for Democrats and Republicans, there is simply no party of flatness. Adjusted for years in office, Democrats and Republicans have added almost the same number of assistant secretaries and new occupants. Where they appear to differ most is in where they make the additions. Republican presidents have invested more heavily in adding thickness in the top four executive compartments—secretary through assistant secretary—while Democrats have put more energy into the fifth compartment, administrator. Democrats appear to favor thickening the delivery units of government, Republicans the control and policymaking units. Democrats have also been more likely to support the creation of new cabinet departments.

Despite the multiple roots on new positions and layers, the past decade seems to have been more hostile than favorable toward thickening. Still, the hierarchy has continued to grow. The question, therefore, is how thickening endures. The simple answer is that it has enormous momentum behind it. Society as a whole has thickened over the past half century, as have Congress and the White House. The departments are merely one part of what appears to be a larger engine that supports thickening.

Again, just as each new position can be justified in its own right—whether as a recruiting tool, a morale booster, a way to sweeten or smooth a transfer of units between departments, a call for narrower spans of control or accountability, a source of needed advice for the secretary, a way to show national priority, or a path to needed status—all may be propelled forward by the simple desire of departments to look like one another. Although departments differ in the total number of layers and occupants—differences largely driven by size and budget—

the central tendency is toward thickening. Even departments that have lost volume over the past decade have lost it in girth, not height, suggesting that the potential for quick weight gain is still present.

What to Do about Thickening

Given this momentum, thickening will be hard to stop. But there are at least two causes for hope. First, past attacks on hierarchy have produced at least some short-term thinning, particularly through middle-level cutbacks. Whatever the ultimate cost of these past "battles of the bulge" in employee morale and lost productivity, there is evidence that government can be thinned, albeit through an exceedingly blunt instrument that has done little to shorten the chains of command.

Second, other nations have already shown the way. The British bureaucracy, for example, runs with but a handful of political appointees, roughly one-tenth as many career executives, and barely five layers between the minister and the British equivalent of the deputy assistant secretary (compared to more than sixteen here). There is no tradition of politicization to note.

The secret is in the British Treasury (which is analogous to the president's Office of Management and Budget), where senior civil servants have succeeded in raising the price of new positions to a nearly prohibitive rate. The informal price is set by the Treasury's expenditure divisions, which establish and monitor agency budgets. The Treasury approves new positions and conducts periodic reviews of the top structure. OMB could do the same in the United States, embargoing any new positions without central clearance.[2]

Thus the question is not so much whether thickening can be stopped but whether the president and Congress are willing to abandon their prevailing image of what organizations should look like. Raising the price for new positions would also force the president and Congress to forswear some of their time-honored justifications for thickening— creating new positions as a symbolic or status gesture would be out, as would most of the list provided in chapter 5. There are real political costs to thinning government, not the least of which is having to explain to constituents the lack of even symbolic action on pressing national priorities.

Nevertheless, assume for a moment that presidents and Congress do want to stop thickening. Two basic questions must be answered. First, how can the current level of thickness be reduced? Second, how can future rethickening be prevented? It hardly makes sense for government to invest the political capital to cut layers and widen spans of control if they only grow back once the fervor is lost.

Losing the Weight

The options for reducing thickness are relatively straightforward. The quickest way to thin government is to cut personnel at the middle and upper levels. This is precisely what the Gore report recommended and the Clinton administration adopted in pledging a cut of 252,000 jobs. The result will surely be a reduction in the total volume of hierarchy across government.

Yet focusing just on width may leave the government vulnerable to rapid growth once the scrutiny and freezes are off. The temptation is always to attack width first. It is more easily targeted, if only because departments know exactly how many people they employ, and is more quickly implemented, if only because there is more than enough attrition each year to create opportunities for downsizing. Nevertheless, at the risk of stretching the analogy, departments can lose a great deal of weight in a short time but can still retain the appetite and metabolism of a larger entity. The trick, therefore, is not just taking the weight off, but keeping it off. And that means attacking layers too.

Unfortunately, layers are extremely difficult to cut, in part because they are often based in statute, in part because most departments would rather thin themselves to a rail than risk the status or pay reduction that comes with layers. Presidents and Congress have relatively few options, therefore. I offer the following four possibilities:

1. *Collapse the field structure.* Given the current debate about information highways, the federal field structure remains an anachronism. Supervisors no longer need to see their employees to supervise—Gulick's complaint about information overload is vastly overstated. "The vast nationwide network of 30,000 federal government offices," the Gore report notes, "reflects an era when America was a rural country and the word 'telecommunications' was not yet in the dictionary. While circumstances have changed, the government hasn't. As a result, workloads are unevenly distributed—some field offices are underworked, others are overworked, some are located too far from their customers to serve them well, and few are connected to customers through modern communications systems."[3] So noted, field offices have strong

constituents, not the least of which are the members of Congress who cut the ribbons to create them.

2. *Eliminate alter-ego deputies.* One of the easiest ways to de-layer is to target 1:1 spans of control. In theory, only two 1:1 spans of control can be justified in the federal system. The first is between the president and the vice president, a 1:1 span rooted in the constitution. The second is between secretaries and deputy secretaries, a 1:1 span rooted in the Hoover Commission's call for at least one alter-ego deputy to fill in when the secretary is out. The rest of the government's 1:1 spans appear superfluous. It would be relatively easy to mandate that all alter-ego chiefs of staff, principal deputies, senior deputies, and the like be forced downward into the layer from which they came, thereby reducing the total height of government quickly and rather painlessly. The problem, of course, is that the principals to whom these alter-ego deputies report would find it hard to give up the buffering and status that comes with a single subordinate. Moreover, these alter-ego deputies fill in for the principal during vacancies caused by high turnover in political posts and are sometimes required under statutes that require backups on backups for meeting congressional deadlines.

3. *Cap title-riding.* Another deceptively quick way to reduce layering is to limit the number of amendments to existing titles to some absolute number, say two. Thus an assistant secretary title might be extended downward to a deputy assistant secretary and associate deputy assistant secretary, but no further. Departments would have to decide just how to allocate titles, paying more attention to layering as a result. The problem here is that departments have shown enormous creativity in inventing new titles. Title-riding is a relatively cheap way to extend existing hierarchy downward but is hardly the only way to increase layers. Thus one can imagine the need for some kind of title czar in OMB or the Office of Personnel Management to monitor titles, process applications, and define once and for all what is an entirely new title and what is an extension of an old label. Departments, in turn, might need to create whole new title units to comply with policy guidance from above. In addition, Congress could drastically reduce or eliminate past specifications of titles, thereby giving presidents more discretion to downsize the executive compartments of government.

4. *Create a height and width limit.* Like Gore's call for a uniform span of control across government, a maximum height could be crafted for each department based on some analysis of what the department does, who it serves, and how risky the venture. The problem, of course,

is twofold. First, government would have to figure out what the current heights are. Such data are not currently kept anywhere in OMB or OPM and have not ordinarily been of much interest to departments. A whole new industry would have to be invented merely to take the measure of departments and their subunits. Second, once current heights had been calculated, Congress and the president would likely bargain over ideal heights. Just as there is no way to establish an ideal span of control, so too is there no way to create a perfect height. Much as one suspects that government is too tall, particularly in comparison with flatter organizations in the private and not-for-profit sectors, setting a maximum height would be impossible to do and ultimately might create more layering than it would prevent. Knowing the height of Justice or State might just push other departments to grow.

The problem with these four options is that layers and particular positions have strong constituents, not the least of whom are the occupants themselves. Positions are often so well justified that the cost of de-layering is prohibitive. Moreover, the federal government is not some monolith. Just as there can be no ideal span of control across government, neither can there be a uniform height limit, a ban on alter-ego deputies, or an end to title riding. The alternative way to flatten government is to figure out the true distance between the top and bottom, ask which positions add value, winnow out excess girth, and occasionally redistribute resources downward as needed.

The politics suggests the need for some device to wrap reductions into an unassailable package—that is, some way to give Congress and the president the needed protection to inflict the kind of sweeping change required for de-layering. The legislative vehicle may already exist in the Executive Organization Reform Act of 1993 introduced by Senators John Glenn, Democrat of Ohio, and William Roth, Republican of Delaware, which would create a national reform commission to examine govern-ment structure and operation.[4]

What makes this bill different is an implementation mechanism giving the president fifteen days to approve or disapprove the commission's final recommendations and, assuming approval, calling for action by Congress ten days thereafter. It is a device modeled on the military base closure commission, which was created in 1988 to help Congress identify hundreds of obsolete facilities.[5] Unable to close bases one at a time, Congress decided to take an all-or-nothing approach. In its first round of cuts, the commission recommended closing eighty-six bases and shrinking fifty-nine more, for a total cut of nearly 21,000 jobs and $5.5

billion over twenty years. By focusing congressional attention on the overall good of budget reduction rather than the individual pain of base closures, the commission was able to muster far more than the majority needed to pass the plan.

A similar approach, albeit without an automatic legislative trigger, was used by the 1983 National Commission on Social Security Reform, chaired by former Council of Economic Advisers chairman Alan Greenspan.[6] By treating reform as a "house of cards," in which no one piece can be removed without toppling the fragile package, Congress and the president appear able to reach beyond the parochial interests underpinning any single military base, social security constituency, or, in theory, any layer, unit, or department of government.[7]

The Glenn-Roth proposal was set aside to give the Gore National Performance Review ample running room. OMB Director Leon Panetta politely told Congress, "We have asked that the Senate defer action on any of the commission bills currently introduced . . . based on a belief that the better course would be to use the recommendations of the Gore National Performance Review to help define the nature and content of any legislation in this area."[8] Nevertheless, without some action-forcing device, government reform is simply more than any single Congress or president, no matter how mightily committed, can handle.

Thus it may be time to put the Glenn-Roth bill back on the calendar. Reform is hard enough to accomplish in its own right, let alone in a piecemeal process. With a more limited charge—perhaps restricted to issues of layering and broad departmental organization—the base-closure device offers a reasonable opportunity to actually flatten government. Moreover, such a commission could generate the needed research to separate the good layers and positions from the bad. Without such research, flattening will remain a very blunt exercise indeed, with high potential for hollowing out key units across government.

Keeping the Weight Off

Once flattened, the key question is how to prevent government from thickening again. If government has a general tendency to thicken, a one-time flattening will not suffice. It may even be a waste of precious political capital. The key to a successful diet is knowing how to lose weight and keep it off. Here, presidents face four broad options.

1. *Create an orthodoxy of thinning.* The first step in preventing future thickening is to create a strong rationale for thinning, a rationale

that currently does not exist. Although organizational gurus call for wider spans of control, there is simply not enough research to demonstrate either the positive effects of flat, thin organizations or the negative costs of their tall, thick counterparts. The place to begin is with a thorough evaluation of what each position in the chain of command contributes in value added to what government does.

Whatever the method—from job audits to detailed case studies—it is essential to learn what each level of hierarchy contributes to the bottom line. The thinning of government will require enormous trade-offs. Reformers imagine information technology filling some of the gap, but broader spans of control will put new stresses on consistency and fairness. Pushing authority downward commensurate with responsibility will demand new, perhaps unheard-of levels of trust from senior appointees and Congress, dictating a diminution of the micromanagement that has driven so many successful campaigns for office. Knowing what each level does is the first step toward deciding which one should be thinned.

2. *Raise the price of thickening.* Thickening is almost cost-free today. Cabinet bills appear less "expensive" than they used to be, and new positions are routinely created through less visible vehicles. Departments pay no tax for recommending new positions, and the president has almost no way of knowing when new positions are coming on line. This situation suggests that changes are necessary at both ends of Pennsylvania Avenue.

On Capitol Hill, Congress could set a higher price for new positions first by strengthening the oversight capacity of the House and Senate government operations committees, and second by referring all position-creating legislation to those committees. Currently, the two committees have jurisdiction only over cabinet bills, inspectors general, and chief financial officers. Requiring automatic sequential referral on any bill, or portion thereof, containing a new post would raise the potential cost of thickening to the authorizing and appropriations committees. The threat of additional scrutiny and the delay that goes with it would deter some of the new positions and might force the authors to at least explain their rationales. Recall that most new positions do not carry any legislative record at all.

Congress could also set a higher price by requiring the Congressional Budget Office (CBO) to broaden its analysis of the cost of new positions. Currently, CBO estimates such costs only in terms of salaries, which in many cases constitute only a few thousand dollars. Congress could easily require CBO to track the impact of new positions on the overall structure of government—that is, to report on how proposed positions affect the height and width of a given department's hierarchy. In turn, CBO and the General Accounting Office could both be encouraged to think more broadly about the hidden costs of thickening. By simultaneously making new positions more visible through sequential referral and elevating the consideration of cost, Congress could create enough resistance to deter many of those posts.

A similar strategy might work at the White House. Future presidents could set a much higher price for thickening by requiring that all new executive level positions be reviewed by OMB and the Office of Presidential Personnel (OPP). This would require, of course, a new commitment to management at OMB and a resurrection of the old organizational studies unit, which was abolished under Reagan. Currently, neither OMB nor OPP has the institutional capacity to review new positions, let alone to ask which ones have merit. As for OMB, the spring 1994 merger of management and budget may make such oversight even more difficult, although the British Treasury experience suggests that budget analysts can play a significant role in simply monitoring new posts. All it may take is an executive order requiring that all new posts be cleared in a revitalized spring budget review, which focuses more on implementation of the budget to begin with.

As for OPP, it continues to resist Senate pressure for an annual report on political appointee positions, qualifications, and job descriptions, arguing that Congress should not meddle in presidential appointments.[9] Such an inventory could, however, send an important message to departments that proposed new executive positions must carry some minimum statement of need and could create more visibility for what remains an ad hoc process of ever-rising hierarchy across the departments. Again, a presidential order would suffice.

As for middle-level thickening, OPM could raise the cost of thickening by strengthening its government-wide oversight process. Currently slated for its own reorganization and downsizing according to the Gore proposals, OPM may be tempted to delegate all position management to the departments. There is no doubt that OPM needs to give agencies greater freedom to govern personnel management. There are simply too many rules, too much confusion, and too much time spent processing paper. At the same time, departments must accept some policy guidance, particularly when it comes to creating new layers of management. Someone near the president needs to strengthen oversight, particularly as departments begin to experiment with the new "broad-banded" classification system proposed by the Gore task force. Experience suggests that departments have abused classification freedom when they had it.

3. *Lower the cost of thinning.* Any current presidential proposal for consolidation or flattening must go through the normal legislative process. The president's reorganization authority first established in 1939 expired in 1988 and has never been reauthorized. Under the authority that existed from 1939 to 1981, presidents were allowed to submit reorganization proposals to Congress that would take effect provided that neither house did not enact a simple resolution of disapproval.[10] After the Supreme Court declared such legislative vetoes unconstitutional, Congress amended the act to require a joint resolution of approval, making reorganizations much more similar to normal legislation.[11]

The question is whether renewing the act again is worth the political cost. As a general tool of management, the authority has an uneven past. Although Truman used the reorganization authority thirty-five times in implementing the first Hoover commission report, political scientists Louis Fisher and Ronald Moe report that, "Aside from this one burst of systematic and philosophically cohesive reorganization activity, there has been little in the way of coherence among the proposals. Each plan appears to be justified on an ad hoc basis."[12]

The value of the reorganization authority for flattening government resides more in its symbolic impact. As congressional scholar Harvey Mansfield argued:

The particular utility of the plan method is not to displace previous methods of securing a reorganization, but to capitalize on the advantages of its unique characteristics. The statute is not to be had for the asking. Each President must negotiate for it anew. What he gets, that he could not otherwise secure, is an opportunity from time to time to present the Congress, the country, and the entrenched interests with a reorganization package of his own devising, as a *fait accompli*, barring a veto; and if a protest is raised, an opportunity to appeal directly to the full membership of either house for support in a floor vote within a stipulated time on the package as he put it together, bypassing both the leadership and the legislative committee seniors if they are unsympathetic. This is an opportunity our constitutional system otherwise seldom affords.[13]

Fisher and Moe may be on target in responding that the reorganization authority assumes the worst about Congress: "It assumes that members of Congress are irresponsible and will not support sensible legislative proposals submitted by the executive branch." They may also be quite right in their analysis of its use over the past half century: "Little of value has been accomplished by a reorganization plan that could not have been done through the regular legislative process."[14]

Nevertheless, reorganization authority gives the president a particularly useful tool to use in the flattening of government. First, reorganization authority would allow the bundling into a unified package of the many small statutory revisions that would otherwise get lost in the ordinary legislative process. Second, reorganization plans are automatically referred to the two government operations committees, which are clearly favorable to the kinds of flattening envisioned here.

4. *Change the incentives.* The prevailing structure of incentives favors the thickening of government. Managers move up by creating new positions; nonmanagers gain higher pay by taking those positions. One way to limit these incentives is by flattening the current classification system. Much of what the Gore report recommends in this regard is long overdue. Under its suggested "broad-banding" system, government would abandon its 450-plus job classifications and the associated fifteen-grade and ten-step pay system in favor of a much simpler set of five career paths and four to six pay bands within each.

The reforms, designed by the National Academy of Public Administration, could eliminate at least some of the incentives for promoting subordinates as a way to eventually promote oneself.[15] As the Gore report notes, a broad-banding system "would give agencies greater flexibility to hire, retain, and promote the best people they find. They would help agencies flatten their hierarchies and promote high achievers without having to make them supervisors. They would eliminate much valuable time now lost to battles between managers seeking to promote or reward employees and personnel specialists administering a classification system with rigid limits. Finally, they would remove OPM from its role as 'classification police.'"[16] Again, it is not yet clear that OPM can dismantle its position management "police" or that agencies have learned how to run the new system effectively. The 5,000 full-time employees at the General Accounting Office, for example, have been operating under a broad-banding experiment since 1991 and are still working out the problems. So forewarned, classification reform would make middle-level layering less likely and is worth enacting.

Classification reform can work better in thinning government if it is accompanied by adequate entry-level and middle-level pay. This is not the book to review the bidding on federal pay—some argue that the pay gap is growing larger; others who add in the real value of rather generous federal benefit packages say the pay gap is nonexistent. The best available research suggests that the problem is most acute in certain jobs and localities and at some levels. As Reagan's Grace commission argued, the entry-level gaps put pressure on managers to advance their best workers into higher layers to catch up with lagging federal pay. Similar problems exist in high-cost localities such as Boston, Washington, Baltimore, Los Angeles, and San Francisco, where managers may advance subordinates into supervisory posts to close the local pay gap.

What is also painfully clear from both research and experience is that pay freezes exacerbate the incentives to promote subordinates to keep pace.[17] Thus just about the worst time to attempt a flattening of government is during a pay freeze, which is exactly what the Clinton administration tried to do in 1993–1994. However tempting such a freeze might be politically, it works its own magic in pushing government upward. So too do decisions to delay the location-based cost-of-living adjustments that are already part of the law. Promotions in Los Angeles due to hidden cost-of-living pay increases quickly spread to Kansas City, Denver, and Atlanta. The tendency of departments and their units to seek parity is not restricted to high-cost field offices. The short-term savings from a pay freeze may be more than lost in the long-term layering that results.

Classification and pay reforms will likely have much less impact on upper-level thickening, where political appointees and senior executives appear to be less sensitive to economic incentives.[18] Parallel thickening in Congress and the White House is far more important in forcing departments upward, as is the thickening of the inner cabinet. Placing an embargo on the creation of new executive level posts is a viable first step toward eliminating the kind of competitive thickening described in chapter 5. Such a unilateral embargo will likely fail, however, if Congress does not change how it creates new positions and tasks executive officers. The rising tide of specification in new positions must recede if presidents are to redesign the departments.

Pay and classification reform are, however, low-powered incentives. They may not matter much in the face of higher-powered incentives that underpin the keeping-up-with-the-Joneses isomorphism that causes so much thickening. Finding these high-powered counterincentives—

for example, competition and other market forces—will be important in building a new orthodoxy of thinning.

Government currently pays a very low price indeed for each new position it creates. Although the reforms offered above will raise the price or the penalty for new layers and greater width, they may still be too weak to prevent thickening. To some, they may even resemble the diet fads that so often fail. The federal government will no doubt get thinner over the coming few years, in large part because of the 252,000-employee cut in government jobs about to be enshrined in statute. Whether it will stay thin is a different question.

The private sector worries about thickening in its own ranks because of the potential costs and productivity losses that register on the profit line. It cares about keeping customers because customers mean survival. The federal government does not appear to have the same worries. Will agencies be allowed to fail if they do not meet the performance standards created under the Government Performance and Results Act in 1993? Or will they merely be exhorted to do better next year?

That the federal government will always be thicker than the private sector seems inescapable, if only because government faces a set of fairness and due process goals that require greater consistency and oversight. Yet even if it is never able to inflict the ultimate penalty that seems to keep the private sector flatter, government can do better. Thus the case for the thinning of government should not be made on profit grounds and perhaps not even on productivity grounds, but on performance grounds. A flatter federal government would likely deliver better, faster, and more responsive services.

Conclusion

In the final analysis, thinning must involve changes in the prevailing image of effective presidential leadership. The days when leadership simply meant having more help are long over. Presidents have ample support now, ample staffs, and ample numbers of political appointees. So do secretaries and members of Congress for that matter. Adding more people to the top or middle of the hierarchy will not improve the chances that the nation will solve its pressing policy problems.

Leadership is not measured by the number of people the president brings into office or the number of helpers at the top and middle of government. It is not achieved by further tightening of the command-and-control model that evolved under Eisenhower and his successors.

Instead, a president's leadership is most likely to be judged by his clarity of vision, his articulation of cause, and the ultimate value produced by what government does. As such, it is likely to be stronger with fewer helpers, and clearer with fewer steps in the chain of command. Presidential leadership, therefore, may reside in stripping government of the barriers to doing its job effectively, not in adding more cross-checkers, auditors, investigators, and second-guessers to the fray. Thickening can be stopped, but in stopping it government will have to learn new ways of doing business, while presidents and Congress will have to find new ways to generate the political benefits that flow from adding bulk to the hierarchy. Both are serious challenges indeed.

Appendix

The Core Tables

The core data for this book come from an inventory of job titles presented in the two following tables: "Number of Layers Occupied in Government" and "Number of Occupants by Layer of Government." The tables were calculated from 126 organization charts, one each for every department of government that existed in 1935, 1952, and at the end of every four-year administration since 1960.[1] The charts focus only on the top five leadership compartments in government: secretary (level I in the Executive Schedule), deputy secretary (level II), under secretary (level III), assistant secretary (level IV), and administrator (level V).

Within each compartment, layers are defined by job titles, and occupants by the number of similar title holders. A layer is declared only when a title exists in a position subordinate to one immediately above and a position superior to one immediately below—for example, through a modifier such as "assistant," "associate," "principal," or "deputy" to an existing title, which this book calls "title-riding."[2]

The Sources

The first draft of each organization chart was drawn using a congressional title inventory affectionately known to legions of presidential job seekers as the Plum Book.[3] Published after every presidential election, the Plum Book has become the bible of appointee opportunities and lists most of the senior titles in government.[4]

The 1992 edition, for example, listed over 9,000 "leadership and support" positions and provided rank and salary data for each position. This information was particularly important for sorting out the different titles used at the five layers created by the executive pay schedule: Executive Level I, reserved for secretaries; Executive Level II, reserved for deputy secretaries or their equivalent; Executive Level III, reserved for under secretaries or their equivalent; Executive Level IV, for assistant secretaries or their equivalent; and Executive Level V, for administrators or their equivalent. Because all occupants paid at the same salary level do not necessarily have the same title, the core tables were built on a simple coding rule: all occupants *regardless of title* paid at the same executive salary level are treated as occupants of the same layer.[5]

For convenience, the core tables use the secretary, deputy secretary, under secretary, assistant secretary, and administrator labels. But readers should note that every layer except secretary actually contains a mix of titles. Most Executive Level IV positions are assistant secretaries, but some are inspectors general, others general counsels, still others administrators, directors, chiefs, and so forth.

Even though this rule probably understates the total number of layers at the top of government—particularly at the deputy secretary layer where some Level II "equivalents" may report sideways to a formal Level II deputy secretary title—it is a rule that minimizes the myriad judgment calls that would likely confuse the core tables beyond interpretation. Pay, not formal title, often determines who truly reports to whom in the federal hierarchy.

Because the quality of the Plum Books has been uneven over the years, they could be used only as a starting point for the 126 organization charts, which were verified against three additional sources.

The charts were first checked against annual *United States Government Manuals*.[6] Published by the Office of the Federal Register as "the official handbook of the Federal Government," the manual provides an office address, a central phone number, a list of top officials by title and name, and a brief history of the agency and its subunits. Built from department submissions rather than from piecemeal submissions to Capitol Hill, it is likely to be more accurate, albeit much less deep, than the Plum Book. It remains the best verifier of the very top positions of government and was the primary source for outlining the departmental hierarchies in 1935 and 1952.[7]

The post-1976 charts were also verified against *Federal Yellow Book* phone directories. Published by Monitor Leadership Directories starting in 1976, the *Yellow Book* has become one of the most reliable sources of information on the top positions in Washington, offering an invaluable device for cross-checking the 1980, 1984, 1988, and 1992 organization charts used in this book.[8] Deeper probing of the 1980 and 1992 *Yellow Books* also provided an exceptionally detailed inventory of the federal hierarchy before and after the Reagan and Bush presidencies, which can be used to investigate why thickening occurs.

Finally, the charts were checked against changes in Title 5 of the *U.S. Code*. Because all presidential appointees paid under the Executive Schedule must be listed in Title 5, the statute is an absolute check on the number of secretaries, deputy secretaries, under secretaries, assistant secretaries, and most but not all administrators. Moreover, the legislative histories attached to each Title 5 position inform the history of thickening. A careful analysis of how each position came into being, whether it was buried or visible, whether interest groups were involved, and where the idea originated helps explain why thickening occurs.

The Caveats

Even with all of this information, the 126 charts are likely incomplete. Like most information collected over time and from different sources, the numbers must be handled carefully. Three caveats are in order.

First, the numbers do not go very deep into the hierarchy. This is a book primarily about the top jobs in government. There is simply no way to calculate the exact number of layers and occupants between the very top of government and the absolute bottom. Indeed, with increasing amounts of contracting out and mandates to state and local government, the bottom often no longer resides in the federal establishment at all. The numbers used throughout this book mostly apply to the first five compartments of government—secretary, deputy secretary, under secretary, assistant secretary, and administrator. Much of the thickening of middle-level government must be inferred.

Second, the numbers are more precise at the top of each hierarchy. There should be no doubt, for example, about the fourteen cabinet secretaries in 1992. Their positions are recorded in the *U.S. Code*; their names are public record. There is much less certainty about the 507 deputy assistant secretaries and 4,494 division directors. The numbers could be slightly higher or lower. Even the most careful research, followed by the most rigorous verification, cannot pick up every title, particularly in the earlier years covered by this analysis.

Third, the numbers of political and career occupants at each layer are best seen as illustrative only. Although the Plum Book was designed to provide this most basic of information on each position, changes in the nomenclature of political appointments make the data uneven.

Creation of the Senior Executive Service (SES) in 1978 makes the 1980 Plum Book particularly unreliable.

Ultimately, therefore, the core numbers are best seen as illustrative, stronger in the more recent years and toward the top of the hierarchy, softer further back in time and toward the bottom. This is not to suggest that the conclusions and trends are weak. If anything, the cleaning, cross-checking, and verification were so conservative as to understate the true depth of government. Those who believe, for example, that chiefs of staff to secretaries do not belong in the inventory because they may not always be in a subordinate-superior chain may redo the tabulations as desired. The central trends, however, will likely be undisturbed. The federal government has gotten much thicker over the past decades, plus or minus a layer here and there.

TABLE A-1 *Number of Layers Occupied in Government, Executive Levels I–V, 1935–92*

Layer (Primary title)	Number of departments where layer exists										
	1935	1952	1960	1964	1968	1972	1976	1980	1984	1988	1992
Secretary	10	9	10	10	12	11	11	13	13	13	14
Chief of staff	..	..	..	..	..	..	..	..	4	6	11
Deputy chief of staff	..	..	..	..	..	..	..	..	1	1	2
Deputy secretary	..	3	3	3	4	4	5	8	8	9	14
Chief of staff	..	..	..	..	..	..	..	..	..	1	2
Associate deputy secretary	..	..	1	1	2	2	1	2	5	3	6
Under secretary	3	7	8	9	11	11	11	13	13	12	9
Principal deputy under secretary	..	..	1	1	2	2	2	2	3	3	2
Deputy under secretary	..	1	4	8	9	11	10	12	12	11	11
Principal associate deputy under secretary	..	..	..	..	..	..	..	..	..	..	1
Associate deputy under secretary	..	..	..	..	..	2	3	3	4	3	6
Assistant deputy under secretary	..	..	..	..	1	..	1	1	1	1	1
Associate under secretary	..	..	..	..	..	..	..	..	..	1	1
Assistant secretary[a]	7	9	10	10	12	11	11	13	13	13	14
Chief of staff to assistant secretary	..	..	..	..	..	..	..	..	..	1	4
Principal deputy assistant secretary	..	..	1	1	2	1	4	6	9	8	8

TABLE A-1 (*Continued*)

Layer (Primary title)	1935	1952	1960	1964	1968	1972	1976	1980	1984	1988	1992
					Number of departments where layer exists						
Deputy assistant secretary[b]	...	2	7	10	12	11	11	13	13	13	14
Associate deputy assistant secretary[c]	2	1	5	6	7	7	7	12	13	13	14
Deputy associate deputy assistant secretary[d]	...	...	1	...	1	1	3	2	7	7	7
Assistant general counsel/inspector general	...	...	3	5	6	6	9	12	13	12	14
Deputy assistant general counsel/ inspector general	...	...	...	...	...	...	1	5	8	9	11
Administrator	...	...	9	9	11	11	11	13	13	11	11
Chief of staff	...	...	...	1	1	1	1	1	1	2	2
Principal deputy administrator	...	...	...	1	5	6	4	4	3	2	3
Deputy administrator	...	...	8	9	9	10	11	10	12	10	10
Associate deputy administrator	...	...	...	...	...	...	...	2	...	1	1
Assistant deputy administrator	...	...	1	...	1	2	3	1	2	2	4
Associate administrator	...	...	2	4	4	6	2	10	8	9	9
Deputy associate administrator	...	...	...	1	1	1	...	5	4	5	6

Assistant administrator	...	7	8	9	8	8	9	9	8	8
Deputy assistant administrator	...	...	1	2	...	...	6	7	6	8
Associate assistant administrator	...	...	...	...	...	...	...	...	...	1
Layers invented I–IV	3	5	−1	2	0	2	0	2	3	1
Layers invented V	...	...	3	1	−1	−1	3	−1	1	1
Layers open I–V	...	17	19	22	21	22	25	26	30	32
Departments adopting new layers, I–IV	10	22	10	17	−1	10	27	23	0	26
Departments adopting new layers, V only	...	...	7	9	2	−5	21	−2	−3	7
Total departments adopting new layers	10	22	17	26	1	5	48	21	−3	33

SOURCES: See appendix text.

Ellipses indicate that position does not yet exist or has been abolished.

a. Includes general counsel and inspector general, including those at executive level V.

b. Includes deputy inspector general and deputy general counsel.

c. Includes associate assistant secretary, associate inspector general, associate general counsel.

d. Includes deputy associate general counsel.

TABLE A-2 *Number of Occupants by Layer of Government, Executive Levels I–V, 1935–92*

						Number of occupants in each layer					
Layer	1935	1952	1960	1964	1968	1972	1976	1980	1984	1988	1992
Secretary	10	9	10	10	12	11	11	13	13	13	14
Chief of staff	…	…	…	…	…	…	…	…	4	6	11
Deputy chief of staff	…	…	…	…	…	…	…	…	1	1	2
Deputy secretary	…	3	6	6	7	9	13	14	14	15	21
Chief of staff										1	2
Associate deputy secretary	…	…	2	2	3	4	2	4	13	10	21
Under secretary	3	7	15	17	21	24	24	28	33	32	32
Principal deputy under secretary	…	…	1	1	2	2	3	7	7	6	8
Deputy under secretary	…	1	9	19	24	33	37	38	55	53	52
Principal associate deputy under secretary											1
Associate deputy under secretary					…	4	5	7	10	5	11
Assistant deputy under secretary					2	…	1	2	16	15	11
Associate under secretary	…	…			…	…	…	…	…	1	1
Assistant secretary[a]	38	45	87	86	103	105	121	159	168	181	212
Chief of staff to assistant secretary									…	1	5
Principal deputy assistant secretary	…	…	1	1	4	10	18	33	46	55	76

Position										
Deputy assistant secretary[b]	507	412	401	364	248	159	152	135	78	12	…
Associate deputy assistant secretary[c]	258	145	159	89	55	50	30	23	20	4	5
Deputy associate deputy assistant secretary[d]	121	51	39	20	14	5	5	…	4	…	…
Assistant general counsel/inspector general	203	158	117	125	98	59	43	35	16	…	…
Deputy assistant general counsel/inspector general	57	60	47	25	8	…	…	…	…	…	…
Administrator	128	125	114	115	118	105	107	102	90	…	…
Chief of staff	7	4	3	3	3	3	2	1	…	…	…
Principal deputy administrator	9	5	7	7	7	13	6	2	…	…	…
Deputy administrator	190	129	143	148	81	102	86	72	52	…	…
Associate deputy administrator	15	1	…	24	…	…	…	…	…	…	…
Assistant deputy administrator	48	18	25	28	7	4	1	…	2	…	…
Associate administrator	105	69	85	70	39	40	23	11	3	…	…
Deputy associate administrator	28	18	14	40	…	4	9	2	…	…	…
Assistant administrator	159	130	115	144	66	99	65	71	55	…	…
Deputy assistant administrator	66	32	44	72	…	…	12	4	…	…	…

TABLE A-2 (Continued)

Layer		1935	1952	1960	1964	1968	1972	1976	1980	1984	1988	1992
							Number of occupants in each layer					
Associate assistant administrator		...	...	...	...	...	...	...	...	...	...	12
Total, I–IV		56	81	249	335	408	475	658	928	1,143	1,221	1,626
Absolute increase		...	25	168	86	73	67	183	270	215	78	405
Percentage increase		...	47	207	35	22	16	39	41	23	7	33
Total, V only		...	...	202	265	311	370	321	651	550	531	767
Absolute increase		...	...	...	63	46	59	−49	330	−101	−19	236
Percentage increase		...	...	...	31	17	19	−13	103	−16	−3	44
Total, I–V		...	...	451	600	719	845	979	1,579	1,693	1,752	2,393

SOURCES: See appendix text.

Ellipses indicate that position does not yet exist or has been abolished.

a. Includes general counsel and inspector general, including those at executive level V.

b. Includes deputy inspector general and deputy general counsel.

c. Includes associate assistant secretary, associate inspector general, associate general counsel.

d. Includes deputy associate general counsel.

Notes

Chapter 1

1. Luther Gulick and L. Urwick, eds., *Papers on the Science of Administration* (New York: Institute of Public Administration, 1937), p. 13.

2. For a quick review of the principles, see Herbert Kaufman, "Reflections on Administrative Reorganization," in Joseph A. Pechman, ed., *Setting National Priorities: The 1978 Budget* (Brookings, 1977), pp. 391–418.

3. Gulick and Urwick, eds., *Papers*, p. 9.

4. Ibid., p. 14.

5. Ibid., p. 7.

6. Ibid., pp. 7–8.

7. V. A. Graicunas, "Relationship in Organization," in Gulick and Urwick, eds., *Papers*, p. 184.

8. Herbert A. Simon, *Administrative Behavior: A Study of Decision-Making Processes in Administrative Organization*, 3d ed. (Free Press, 1976), p. 20.

9. Ibid., p. 28.

10. Gulick and Urwick, eds., *Papers*, p. 44.

11. Herbert Kaufman, *Are Government Organizations Immortal?* (Brookings, 1976), pp. 9–10.

12. Ibid., p. 34.

13. Ibid., p. 70.

14. See Herbert Kaufman, *Time, Chance, and Organizations: Natural Selection in a Perilous Environment* (Chatham House, 1985).

15. Kaufman, *Government Organizations*, pp. 67–68.

16. Marshall E. Dimock, *Administrative Vitality: The Conflict with Bureaucracy* (Harper & Brothers, 1959), p. 116.

17. Kaufman, "Reflections," p. 395.

18. Dwight Waldo, "Organization Theory: An Elephantine Problem," *Public Administration Review*, vol. 21 (Autumn 1961), p. 220.

19. Al Gore, *From Red Tape to Results: Creating a Government That Works Better and Costs Less*, report of the National Performance Review (GPO, 1993), p. 70.

20. Patricia W. Ingraham, Elliot F. Eisenberg, and James R. Thompson, "Political Management Strategies and Political/Career Relationships: Where Are We Now in the Federal Government?," paper prepared for delivery at the annual meeting of the American Political Science Association, September 1993, p. 16.

21. Kaufman, *Government Organizations*, p. 67.

22. Hugh Heclo, *A Government of Strangers: Executive Politics in Washington* (Brookings, 1977), p. 56.

23. The average structure is determined by taking all "institutionalized" layers (those that exist in at least half the departments) and dividing the total number of occupants by the total number of departments then existing.

24. Unfortunately, a detailed chronological history of the rise and fall of each position created over the past thirty years was impossible to undertake given the time and budgetary constraints governing this project—the total number of positions in the 1960–92 time frame was 11,004.

25. One explanation for the linkage is to be found in William Bailey, "Restructuring the Federal Establishment," *Public Personnel Management*, vol. 14 (Summer 1985), pp. 105–29.

26. Congressional Budget Office, "Reducing Grades of the General Schedule Work Force" (GPO, 1984), pp. 9–10.

27. James Hayes and others, "A Preliminary Analysis of the Increase in the Average Grade of General Schedule Federal Employees," Report R-2329-MRAL (Rand Corporation, November 1978).

28. Robert S. Hatfield, Donald R. Keough, and John A. Puelicher, "Report of the Task Force on Personnel Management," (President's Private Sector Survey on Cost Control, April 15, 1983).

29. National Performance Review, "Reinventing Human Resource Management" (September 1993).

30. Bureau of Programs and Standards, *The Nature and Meaning of Grade Escalation under the Classification Act* (United States Civil Service Commission, March 1963), p. 11.

31. Samantha L. Durst, Patricia M. Patterson, and John J. Ramsden, "Impacts of Traditional Explanatory Factors on Average Grade Increases in U.S. Cabinet-Level Departments," *Public Administration Review*, vol. 49 (July/August 1989), p. 368.

32. See Frederick C. Mosher, "The Changing Responsibilities and Tactics of the Federal Government," *Public Administration Review*, vol. 40 (November/December, 1980), pp. 541–48; see also H. Brinton Milward, Keith G. Provan, and Barbara A. Else, "What Does the 'Hollow State' Look Like?," in Barry Bozeman, ed., *Public Management: The State of the Art* (Jossey-Bass, 1993), pp. 309–22; see also Donald Kettl, *Sharing Power: Public Governance and Private Markets* (Brookings, 1993).

33. These figures are drawn from a National Performance Review memorandum summarized in "The Ayers Memorandum: Managers First to Go," *Government Executive*, vol. 56 (January 1994), p. 13.

34. These figures are drawn from Mosher, "Changing Responsibilities," updated for fiscal year 1990 through *Special Analyses, Budget of the United States Government, Fiscal Year 1991* (GPO, 1991), p. B-8.

35. H. Brinton Milward and Jennifer L. Boyd raise many of these questions in their paper "Contracting for the Hollow State," prepared for delivery at the Conference on Rethinking Public Personnel Systems, sponsored by Syracuse University, Washington, D.C., March 4–6, 1993.

36. Kaufman, *Government Organizations*, p. 66.

37. Ibid.

38. Author interview, March 1992. All respondents were assured complete confidentiality in return for their candor.

39. For a history of the two Hoover commissions, the first in 1947–49, the second in 1953–55, see Ronald C. Moe, *The Hoover Commissions Revisited* (Westview, 1982); see also Peri Arnold's broader work on presidential efforts to reform government, *Making the Managerial Presidency: Comprehensive Reorganization Planning, 1905–1980* (Princeton University Press, 1986).

40. H. Struve Hensel and John D. Millet, *Departmental Management in Federal Administration: A Report with Recommendations*, prepared for the Commission on the Organization of the Executive Branch of Government (GPO, 1949), p. 11.

41. Ibid.

42. Moe is not the only scholar who appears to favor short-term politicization as a perfectly rational response to prevailing incentives; see Richard P. Nathan, *The Plot That Failed: Nixon and the Administrative Presidency* (New York: John Wiley, 1975).

43. Position description DHES-0172, Chief of Staff, Department of Health and Human Services, revised January 22, 1986, p. 1.

44. Ibid., pp. 1–2.

45. General Accounting Office, *Management of HHS: Using the Office of the Secretary to Enhance Departmental Effectiveness*, GAO/HRD-90-54 (February 1990), p. 57.

46. Ibid., p. 56.

47. *Department of Veterans Affairs Act of 1988*, S. Rept. 100-342, 100 Cong. 2 sess. (GPO, May 12, 1988).

48. These figures are drawn from Harold W. Stanley and Richard G. Niemi, *Vital Statistics on American Politics*, 4th ed. (CQ Press, 1994), p. 273.

49. This discussion is based largely on Paul Light, *Monitoring Government: Inspectors General and the Search for Accountability* (Brookings, 1993).

50. The 1978 Inspector General Act did not require an Office of Inspector General to have a deputy IG.

51. Light, *Monitoring Government*, p. 185.

52. Kaufman found a similar distribution in his data—line units accounted for 58 percent of the units in 1973, down from 64 percent in 1923. See Kaufman, *Government Organizations*, p. 38.

Chapter 2

1. Letter to the president of the United States conveying the report of the National Performance Review, September 7, 1993.

2. Al Gore, *From Red Tape to Results: Creating a Government That Works Better and Costs Less*, Report of the National Performance Review (GPO, 1993), p. 3.

3. Ibid., p. 70. Emphasis in original.

4. Robert Stone, quoted in Tom Shoop, "Targeting Middle Managers," *Government Executive*, vol. 26 (January 1994), pp. 11–12.

5. House Committee on Government Operations, "Summary of the Objectives, Operations and Results of the Commissions on Organization of the Executive

Branch of the Government (First and Second Hoover Commissions)," Committee Print, 88 Cong. 1st sess. (GPO 1963), p. 30.

6. These streams form the basis of my current project for the Governance Institute, *Fixing Government: Paths to Improvement in the 1990s*.

7. Anthony Downs, *Inside Bureaucracy* (Little, Brown, 1967), p. 19.

8. Ibid., p. 20. Emphasis in original.

9. Luther Gulick and L. Urwick, eds., *Papers on the Science of Administration* (Institute of Public Administration, 1937), p. 7.

10. MacMahon and John D. Millett, *Federal Administrators: A Biographical Approach to the Problem of Departmental Management* (Columbia University Press, 1939) appendix A, p. 481.

11. These and other pieces of history can be found in Paul P. Van Riper, *History of the United States Civil Service* (Row Petersen, 1958); it is still the best single source on the history of the civil service available.

12. This history is drawn largely from Peri E. Arnold, *Making the Managerial Presidency: Comprehensive Reorganization Planning, 1905–1980*, (Princeton University Press, 1986).

13. President's Committee on Administrative Management, *Report of the Committee with Studies of Administrative Management in the Federal Government* (GPO, 1937), p. 5.

14. See G. Calvin Mackenzie, "Radical Makeover: The Post-War Transformation of the American Presidency," paper prepared for the annual meeting of the American Political Science Association, September 3, 1993, p. 6.

15. Memo from Louis Brownlow to the president, November 5, 1936, cited in Arnold, *Making the Managerial Presidency*, p. 103.

16. James A. Morone, *The Democratic Wish: Popular Participation and the Limits of American Government* (Basic Books, 1990), pp. 138–39.

17. See Stephen Hess, *Organizing the Presidency*, 2d ed. (Brookings, 1988), chapter 2, for an analysis of Roosevelt's impact on the White House organization.

18. Harold Seidman and Robert Gilmour, *Politics, Position, and Power: From the Positive to the Regulatory State*, 4th ed. (New York: Oxford University Press, 1986), p. 5.

19. Commission on Organization of the Executive Branch of Government, *General Management of the Executive Branch* (GPO, February 1949), pp. 3–5.

20. Seidman and Gilmour, *Politics, Position, and Power*, p. 9.

21. Commission on the Executive Branch, *General Management*, pp. 31, 34–35.

22. Ibid., pp. 36, 30; the congressional liaison officer is noted in the text at p. 38 but not in the organization chart at p. 30; no explanation for the disparity is given.

23. H. Struve Hensel and John D. Millett, *Departmental Management in Federal Administration: A Report with Recommendations*, report prepared for the Commission on Organization of the Executive Branch of the Government (GPO 1949), p. 44.

24. Commission on the Executive Branch, *General Management*, p. 37.

25. Alan Dean, "Enhancing Management in the Executive Department: The Role and Status of the Assistant Secretary for Administration," unpublished paper, April 1990, pp. 5–6.

26. The commission produced charts for the Departments of State, Defense, Commerce, Agriculture, and Interior; a united medical administration built from the Veterans Administration; the Public Health Service; the armed services medical system; the Department of Labor; and a new department of social security and education. I am grateful to Lisa Zellmer, my research assistant on this part of the project, for her careful tracking of the implementation of these reports.

27. These breaches are summarized in Lisa Zellmer, "Breaches in the Hoover Model for Executive Department Reorganization," July 15, 1993, pp. 1–2.

28. Seidman and Gilmour, *Politics, Position, and Power*, p. 335.

29. Lisa Zellmer, "Hoover Commission Recommendations," memo to Paul Light, July 15, 1993, p. 2.

30. John Hart, "Eisenhower and the Swelling of the Presidency," paper prepared for the annual meeting of the American Political Science Association, August 31–September 2, 1990, pp. 14–15.

31. Fred I. Greenstein, *The Hidden-Hand Presidency: Eisenhower as Leader* (Basic Books, 1982), p. 101.

32. Ibid., p. 238.

33. According to his chief of staff, Sherman Adams, "Eisenhower gave each cabinet member and agency director complete responsibility for his department and almost never intervened in the selection of their assistants and other key personnel," quoted in Dean E. Mann with Jameson W. Doig, *The Assistant Secretaries: Problems and Processes of Appointment* (Brookings, 1965), p. 69.

34. Van Riper, *History of the Civil Service*, p. 496.

35. See ibid., p. 496, for the specific figures; see also Patricia W. Ingraham, "Building Bridges or Burning Them? The President, the Appointees, and the Bureaucracy," *Public Administration Review*, vol. 47 (September/October 1987), pp. 425–35, for analysis of the changing roles of political appointees.

36. Van Riper, *History of the Civil Service*, pp. 489–90, 493.

37. "Enhancing Management in the Executive Department," pp. 7–8; see also Thomas McFee, "Excellence in Human Resources Management," unpublished mimeo.

38. P. L. 1310, Section 1310, *Third Supplemental Appropriation Act, 1952*, approved June 5, 1952.

39. Van Riper, *History of the Civil Service*, p. 503.

40. Task Force on Government Reorganization, in an unpublished document cited by Richard J. Stillman, ed., *Basic Documents of American Public Administration since 1950* (Holmes & Meir, 1982), p. 20.

41. Ibid., p. 64.

42. Ibid., pp. 64–65; emphasis in the original.

43. Arnold, *Making the Managerial Presidency*, pp. 297–98.

44. From the Office of Management and Budget, *Papers Relating to the President's Departmental Reorganization Program* (GPO, 1971), p. 19.

45. Ibid., pp. 19–20.

46. *Presidential Campaign Activities of 1972: Senate Resolution 60*, Hearings before the Senate Select Committee on Presidential Campaign Activities, 93 Cong. 2 sess., vol. 19 (GPO, 1974), pp. 8907, 8911.

47. Ibid., p. 9006–7.

48. Ibid., pp. 9009–11.

49. Ibid., p. 9011.

50. Ibid., p. 9012.

51. Ibid., p. 9013–14.

52. This conclusion is based on my interviews with presidential transition advisers during my work as a Senate Governmental Affairs Committee staffer on revisions in the Presidential Transitions Act in 1988. This admittedly cursory review suggested that the so-called Malek manual had been read by senior members of the Carter and Reagan transitions in 1976 and 1980 respectively.

53. See Dean, "Enhancing Management in the Executive Department."

54. Quoted in Arnold, *Making the Managerial Presidency*, p. 313.

55. Ibid.

56. G. Calvin Mackenzie, "The Paradox of Presidential Personnel Management," in Hugh Heclo and Lester M. Salamon, eds., *The Illusion of Presidential Government* (Westview, 1981), p. 130.

57. Ibid., p. 129.

58. For the figures, see Patricia W. Ingraham, Elliot F. Eisenberg, and James R. Thompson, "Political Management Strategies and Political/Career Relationships: Where Are We Now in the Federal Government?," paper prepared for delivery at the annual meeting of the American Political Science Association, September 2–5, 1993.

59. Toni Marzotto, "Wither the Generalist Manager: Reinventing the Senior Executive Service," paper prepared for the annual meeting of the American Political Science Association, September 2–5, 1993, p. 8.

60. Ibid., p. 19.

61. Peter M. Benda and Charles H. Levine, "Reagan and the Bureaucracy: The Bequest, the Promise, and the Legacy," in Charles O. Jones, ed., *The Reagan Legacy: Promise and Performance* (Chatham, N.J.: Chatham House, 1988), p. 106.

62. For a summary of the VA elevation, see Paul C. Light, *Forging Legislation* (New York: W. W. Norton, 1992).

63. Becky Norton Dunlop, "The Role of the White House Office of Presidential Personnel," in Robert Rector and Michael Sanera, *Steering the Elephant: How Washington Works* (New York: Universe, 1987), p. 149.

64. These data from earlier research by Joel Aberbach and Bert Rockman are cited in Joel D. Aberbach, "The President and the Executive Branch," in Colin Campbell and Bert A. Rockman, eds., *The Bush Presidency: First Appraisals* (Chatham, N.J.: Chatham House, 1991), p. 230.

65. General Accounting Office, *Federal Employees: Trends in Career and Noncareer Employee Appointments in the Executive Branch*, GAO/GGD-87-96FS (July 1987), pp. 52–53.

66. Ibid..

67. Aberbach, "The President and the Executive Branch," p. 225.

68. Author interview, March 1992. All respondents were assured complete confidentiality in return for their candor.

69. S. 533, *Department of Veterans Affairs Act*, S. Rept. 100-342, 100 Cong. 2 sess. (GPO, 1988).

70. Arnold, *Making the Managerial Presidency*, p. 361–2.

Chapter 3

1. See Max Weber, *The Theory of Social and Economic Organization*, trans., Talcott Parsons (Oxford 1947).

2. Tom Peters, *Thriving on Chaos: Handbook for a Management Revolution* (New York: Harper-Perennial edition, 1991), p. 426.

3. Peters, *Thriving on Chaos*, p. 430. Peters's emphasis.

4. Peters was a celebrated consultant to the National Performance Review.

5. Dwight Waldo, "Organization Theory: An Elephantine Problem," *Public Administration Review*, vol. 21 (Autumn 1961), p. 220.

6. Letter from John Sturdivant to the National Performance Review, quoted in "Reinventing Human Resource Management," unpublished National Performance Review report, September 1993, p. 29.

7. Al Gore, *From Red Tape to Results: Creating a Government That Works Better and Costs Less*, report of the National Performance Review (GPO, 1993), pp. 13–14.

8. Moreover, the Congressional Budget Office (CBO) has been reluctant to "score," or validate, much of the promised savings, accepting only $305 million of the promised $6 billion in first-year savings, in part because CBO projected a much lower sale price of federally owned apartment buildings and much lower savings from Agriculture Department field-office closings and medicare streamlining; see Steven Greenhouse, "Savings Vastly Overestimated in Streamlining Plan, Agency Reports," *New York Times*, November 17, 1993, p. A-22.

9. John J. DiIulio, Jr., Gerald Garvey, and Don F. Kettl, *Improving Government Performance: An Owner's Manual* (Brookings, 1993), pp. 10–11.

10. See, for example, Laurence E. Lynn, Jr., "Policy Achievement as a Collective Good: A Strategic Perspective on Managing Social Programs," in Barry Bozeman, ed., *Public Management: The State of the Art* (Jossey-Bass, 1993), pp. 108–33; and Barbara Koremenos and Laurence E. Lynn, Jr., "Leadership of a State Agency: An Analysis Using Game Theory," paper prepared for the National Public Management Research Conference, Madison, Wisconsin, 1993.

11. James E. Swiss calculates that an organization of 11,000 employees and a span of control of ten would yield just five organizational layers, while a span of control of four would generate eight layers; see *Public Management Systems: Monitoring and Managing Government Performance* (Prentice-Hall, 1991), p. 285.

12. Anthony Downs, *Inside Bureaucracy* (Little, Brown, 1967), pp. 77–78.

13. Ibid., p. 118.

14. Theodore L. Reed, "Organizational Change in the American Foreign Service, 1925–1965: The Utility of Cohort Analysis," *American Sociological Review*, vol. 43 (June 1978), pp. 404–21.

15. See Toni Marzotto, "Whither the Generalist Manager: Reinventing the Senior Executive Service," paper prepared for the annual meeting of the American Political Science Association, Washington, D.C., September 2–5, 1993.

16 G. Calvin Mackenzie, "The Presidential Appointment Process: Historical Development, Contemporary Operations, Current Issues," background paper for the Twentieth Century Fund Panel on Presidential Appointments, March 1, 1994, p. 1.

17. My interviews were hardly comprehensive; I spoke with E. Pendleton James, who directed the Reagan Office of Presidential Personnel, and Philip Lader, who led the Clinton personnel search as Clinton's second director just before he became deputy chief of staff.

18. Mackenzie, "The Presidential Appointment Process," p. 5.

19. Paul Light, "When Worlds Collide: The Political-Career Nexus," in G. Calvin Mackenzie, ed., *The In-and-Outers: Presidential Appointees and Transient Government in Washington* (Johns Hopkins University Press, 1987), p. 157.

20. Gore, *From Red Tape to Results*, p. 44.

21. Jane Fountain, Linda Kabolian, and Steven Kelman, "Service to the Citizen: The Use of 800 Numbers in Government," paper prepared for delivery at the annual meeting of the Association for Public Policy and Management, October 29–31, 1993, pp. 21–22. The research compared the success of 800 numbers at the Internal Revenue Service, Social Security Administration, and Immigration and Naturalization Service against that of American Express, General Electric, and L. L. Bean.

22. Gore, *From Red Tape to Results*, p. 69.

23. See John R. Kimberly and Michael T. Evanisko, "Organizational Innovation: The Influence of Individual, Organizational, and Contextual Factors on Hospital Adoption of Technological and Administrative Innovations," *Academy of Management Journal*, vol. 24 (December 1981), pp. 689–713; see also Zoltan J. Acs and David B. Audretsch, "Innovation in Large and Small Firms: An Empirical Analysis," *American Economic Review*, vol. 78 (September 1988), pp. 678–90, and Richard L. Gooding and John A. Wagner III, "A Meta-Analytic Review of the Relationship between Size and Performance: The Productivity and Efficiency of Organizations and Their Subunits," *Administrative Science Quarterly*, vol. 30 (December 1985), pp. 462–81.

24. Michael Tushman and David Nadler, "Organizing for Innovation," *California Management Review*, vol. 28 (Spring 1986), p. 83.

25. Gore, *From Red Tape to Results*, p. 7.

26. David I. Levine and Laura D'Andrea Tyson, "Participation, Productivity, and the Firm's Environment," in Alan Blinder, ed., *Paying for Productivity: A Look at the Evidence* (Brookings, 1990), pp. 203–4; emphasis in original.

27. See Alan Blinder, Introduction, in ibid.; p. 13, emphasis in original.

28. See Michael R. Dulworth, Delmar L. Landen, and Brian L. Usilaner, "Employee Involvement Systems in U.S. Corporations: Right Objectives, Wrong Strategies," *National Productivity Review*, vol. 9 (Spring 1990), pp. 141–56.

29. I was senior adviser to the commission and wrote the draft final report.

30. National Commission on the Public Service, *Leadership for America: Rebuilding the Public Service: the Report of the National Commission on the Public Service* (Washington, D.C., 1989), p. 26.

31. Ibid.

32. Charles T. Goodsell, *The Case for Bureaucracy: A Public Administration Polemic*, 2d ed. (Chatham, N.J.: Chatham House, 1985), p. 37.

33. Gore, *From Red Tape to Results*, p. 70.

34. This research assumed, for example, that each headquarters office had at least two layers below the branch chief: (1) another supervisor, and (2) a layer of staff (for example, budget analysts and policy analysts). Given the patterns found higher up the hierarchy, it is an exceedingly conservative assumption.

It is important to add, however, that the decision chains are not exact. Much as I tried to confirm the upward structure of each chain, some of the construction was guess work based on my reading of the *Federal Yellow Book*. The chains are most accurate at the bottom, in large measure because they were confirmed through face-to-face interviews and phone calls with the various front-line units. Like the rest of the data in this book, the chains are best viewed as an illustration of the general trend toward thickening than absolute proof of a specific number of layers top to bottom.

The one Minnesota job where top-to-bottom distance may be overstated is forest ranger. Even though the number of Forest Service layers in Washington remains substantial, the Eastern Regional Office in Milwaukee has tried hard to limit the consequences of layering through a total-quality-management effort labeled Project Spirit. Working in teams rather than traditional layered units, the regional office has trimmed its work force from 220 to 170, a 35 percent cut, thereby reducing its administrative overhead to just 7 percent of the total budget; the average is almost 13 percent in other regions.

I am indebted to Shannon Swangstue, my research assistant on this part of the project, for her work in scheduling and participating in all of the interiews. This piece of the project could not have been completed without her dedication.

35. In all, nine of the thirteen district directors heading the federal offices containing the front-line jobs were interviewed in the summer of 1993; all respondents were assured complete confidentiality in return for their candor.

36. For a discussion of compliance-based accountability, see Paul Light, *Monitoring Government: Inspectors General and the Search for Accountability* (Brookings, 1993).

37. Richard P. Nathan, *The Plot That Failed: Nixon and the Administrative Presidency* (New York: Wiley, 1975).

38. Ibid., p. 62.

39. Terry M. Moe, "The Politicized Presidency," in John E. Chubb and Paul E. Peterson, eds., *The New Direction in American Politics* (Brookings, 1985), p. 245.

40. National Commission on the Public Service, *Leadership for America*, p. 17.

41. I have been one of those most loudly complaining; see ibid.

42. General Accounting Office, *Federal Employees: Trends in Career and Noncareer Employee Appointments in the Executive Branch*, GAO/GGD-87-96FS (July 1987), pp. 20, 22, 24, 32, 34, 36, 40, 58, 60.

43. General Accounting Office, *Federal Employees: Trends in Career and Noncareer Appointments in Selected Departments*, GAO/GGD-87-103FS (August 1987), pp. 13 and 23.

44. See the core tables in the appendix. It is useful to note again that these tables do not include numbers on Schedule C appointees, who make up the vast majority of personal and confidential assistants, special aides, and executive assistants. This research did not ask, and cannot tell, just where they go, although some do show up in the core tables in the assistant secretary compartment on some of the lower layers.

45. B. Dan Wood and Richard W. Waterman, "The Dynamics of Political Control of the Bureaucracy," *American Political Science Review*, vol. 85 (September 1991), p. 822.

Chapter 4

1. C. Northcote Parkinson, *Parkinson's Law and Other Studies in Administration* (Houghton-Mifflin, 1957), pp. 1, 4, 7, 12, 13.

2. Ibid., p. 13.

3. James G. March and Johan P. Olson, "Organizing Political Life: What Administrative Reorganization Tells Us about Government," *American Political Science Review*, vol. 77 (June 1983), pp. 284, 285.

4. I am grateful to Pamela Mincy Jackson, my research assistant on this piece of the project, for her work in tracing the origins of the Departments of Transportation, HUD, Energy, and Education.

5. See Alan L. Dean, "The Organization and Management of the Department of Transportation," background paper prepared for the National Academy of Public Administration, March 1991.

6. Beryl A. Radin and Willis Hawley, *The Politics of Federal Reorganization: Creating the U.S. Department of Education* (Pergamon, 1988), p. 189.

7. *Department of Veterans Affairs Act*, S. Rept. 100-342, 100 Cong. 2 sess. (GPO, May 12, 1988), pp. 19–20.

8. One of the most notable early references is in Richard F. Fenno, *The President's Cabinet: An Analysis in the Period from Wilson to Eisenhower* (Harvard University Press, 1959).

9. Thomas E. Cronin, *State of the Presidency* (Little, Brown, 1975), pp. 191, 197.

10. Jeffrey E. Cohen, *The Politics of the U.S. Cabinet: Representation in the Executive Branch, 1789–1984* (University of Pittsburgh Press, 1985), pp. 144–45.

11. Cronin, *State of the Presidency*, p. 194.

12. For a quick history of tensions in this process of control, see Anna Kasten Nelson, "National Security I: Inventing a Process (1945–1960)," and I. M. Destler, "National Security II: The Rise of the Assistant (1961–1981)," in Hugh Heclo and Lester M. Salamon, eds., *The Illusion of Presidential Government* (Westview, 1981).

13. Donald P. Warwick, *A Theory of Public Bureaucracy: Politics, Personality, and Organization in the State Department* (Harvard University Press, 1975), p. 123.

14. Francis E. Rourke, "Whose Bureaucracy Is This, Anyway? Congress, the President and Public Administration," *PS: Political Science & Politics*, vol. 26 (December 1993), p. 690.

15. For a history of the elevation of the Veterans Administration to cabinet status, see Paul C. Light, *Forging Legislation* (W. W. Norton, 1992).

16. I am grateful to two research associates for helping me collect this data: Deborah Lesser, who prepared a detailed history of cabinet bills in the 95th to 100th Congress as an associate of mine at the U.S. Senate Governmental Affairs Committee in 1987; and Kirk Johnson, who updated the information while a student at the Humphrey Institute in 1993.

17. Morris P. Fiorina, *Congress: Keystone of the Washington Establishment* (Yale University Press, 1977), p. 48.

18. Ibid., p. 49; emphasis in original.

19. See, for example, Lawrence C. Dodd and Richard L. Schott, *Congress and the Administrative State* (Wiley, 1979), pp. 277–78, for a discussion of why Congress delegates "sublegislation" to agencies.

20. James L. Sundquist, *The Decline and Resurgence of Congress* (Brookings, 1981).

21. The three administrators slipped in as level IV positions downgraded to level V. Cross-checked against the core tables in the appendix, the inventory is not quite complete. The number of secretaries and under secretaries fits exactly with the core tables, but four deputy secretaries and twenty assistant secretaries are missing. Because of recodification of the *U.S. Code* and a new indexing system introduced in the 1970s, some positions simply could not be tracked. Thus the following analysis can only provide clues about who is to blame for thickening, not definitive evidence one way or another. If there is a historical bias in the missing data, it is toward the earlier years. The 1980–92 data are very solid. I am grateful to my research assistant Rick Christofferson for his work on this portion of the project.

22. As Robert A. Katzmann shows, Congress has been equally interested in judicial structure; see *Judges and Legislators: Toward Institutional Comity* (Brookings, 1988).

23. P.L. 97-63, National Tourism Policy Act.

24. David R. Mayhew, *Divided We Govern: Party Control, Lawmaking, and Investigations, 1946-1990* (Yale University Press, 1991).

25. This reflects a bitter fight during the VA cabinet debate to get the restriction loosened somewhat.

26. See, for example, Frederick C. Mosher, *A Tale of Two Agencies: A Comparative Analysis of the General Accounting Office and the Office of Management and Budget* (Louisiana State University Press, 1984).

27. Richard J. Stillman, II, ed., *Basic Documents of Public Administration since 1950,* (Holmes & Meir, 1982), p. 57.

28. Ronald C. Moe, "Traditional Organizational Principles and the Managerial Presidency: From Phoenix to Ashes," *Public Administration Review*, vol. 50 (March/April 1990), p. 134.

29. Leon Panetta, quoted in "Executive Memo: OMB Management Merger, vol. 26," *Government Executive* (April 1994), p. 8.

30. U.S. Civil Service Commission, *The Nature and Meaning of Grade Escalation under the Classification Act*, March 1963, p. 24.

31. General Accounting Office, *Classification of Federal White-Collar Jobs Should Be Better Controlled*, FPCD-75-173 (December 4, 1975), pp. 8–9.

32. Ibid., p. 29.

33. Ibid., pp. 11–12.

34. President's Private Sector Survey on Cost Control, *War on Waste* (Macmillan, 1984), pp. 234–35.

35. President's Private Sector Survey on Cost Control, *Report of the Task Force on Personnel Management*, April 1983, p. 85.

36. See, for example, William Bailey, "Restructuring the Federal Establishment," *Public Personnel Management*, vol. 14 (Summer 1985), pp. 110–11.

37. President's Private Sector Survey, *Report of the Task Force on Personnel Management*, p. 86.

38. James Q. Wilson, "On Predicting the Bureaucratization of American Government," in Larry B. Hill, ed., *The State of Public Bureaucracy* (M. E. Sharpe, 1992), p. 214.

39. Terry M. Moe, "The Politics of Structural Choice: Toward a Theory of Public Bureaucracy," in Oliver E. Williamson, ed., *Organization Theory: From Chester Barnard to the Present and Beyond* (New York: Oxford University Press, 1990), p. 137.

40. Ibid., p. 138.

Chapter 5

1. The first statement was used to justify the Education Department, the second the Energy Department.

2. *Omnibus Diplomatic Security and Antiterrorism Act of 1986*, H. Rept. 99-494, 99 Cong. 2 sess. (GPO), March 12, 1986, p. 8.

3. P.L. 101–576, *Chief Financial Officer Act of 1990*.

4. P.L. 102-190, Section 901 (b) A National Defense Authorization Act for Fiscal Years 1992 and 1993.

5. P.L. 98-557; Alan Dean related the history in "The Organization and Management of the Department of Transportation," background paper prepared for the National Academy of Public Administration, March 1991, p. 29.

6. This story emerged in a not-for-attribution interview with a senior Defense Department official.

7. P.L. 95-105, Foreign Relations Authorization Act, Fiscal Year 1978; this search for explanation was supported by two research assistants, Rick Christofferson and Lisa Zellmer, both of whom enriched the following pages immeasurably.

8. *Foreign Relations Authorization for Fiscal Year 1978*, Hearings before the Subcommittee on International Operations of the House International Relations Committee, 95 Cong. 1 sess. (GPO, 1977), p. 171.

9. Ibid., p. 265.

10. *Congressional Record*, June 16, 1977, p. 19473.

11. See *Foreign Relations Authorization Act, Fiscal Year 1978*, H. Rept. 95-231, 95 Cong. 1 sess. (GPO, 1977), pp. 18–19, for the exchange of letters between the International Relations and Post Office committees asking for release from sequential referral.

12. *Federal Mine Safety and Health Act of 1977*, S. Rept. 95-181, 95 Cong. 1 sess. (GPO, May 16, 1977), p. 4.

13. Ibid., pp. 8, 190.

14. Ibid., p. 47.

15. *Health Research Facilities Amendments of 1965*, S. Rept. 367, 89 Cong. 1 sess. (GPO, June 24, 1965), p. 7.

16. Rep. William Springer (R-Ill), *Congressional Record*, May 10, 1965, p. 9962.

17. Rep. Oren Harris (D-Ark.), *Congressional Record*, May 10, 1965, pp. 9958–60.

18. P.L. 95-140, Defense Department, Deputy and Under Secretaries of Defense, Position Changes.

19. P.L. 92-596.

20. H. Rept. 95-519, 95 Cong. 1 sess. (GPO, 1977), p. 4; Department of Defense Executive Reorganization.

21. William Gormley, "Counter-Bureaucracies in Theory and Practice," unpublished paper.

22. Quoted in Paul C. Light, *Monitoring Government: Inspectors General and the Search for Accountability* (Brookings, 1993) p. 56.

23. Nevertheless, it is counted at the under secretary level in the core tables in the appendix.

24. The President's Blue Ribbon Commission on Defense Management, *A Formula for Action: A Report to the President on Defense Acquisition* (GPO, 1986), pp. 15–16.

25. P.L. 99-500.

26. Light, *Monitoring Government*, p. 15.

27. For a discussion of the bureaucratic paradigm within which compliance accountability most comfortably resides, see Michael Barzelay with Babek J. Armajani, *Breaking through Bureaucracy: A New Vision for Managing in Government* (University of California Press, 1992).

28. Light, *Monitoring Government*, p. 20.

29. *Department of Energy Organization Act*, S. Rep. 95-164, 95 Cong. 1 sess. (GPO, 1977), p. 15.

30. P.L. 95-91; Department of Energy Organization Act.

31. *Maritime Appropriation Authorization Act for Fiscal Year 1978*, S. Rept. 95-160, 95 Cong. 1 sess. (GPO, 1977), p. 7.

32. *Weekly Compilation of Presidential Documents*, vol. 16 (December 24, 1980), p. 2838.

33. Stockman's letter to Representative Jim Santini (D-NV) appears in the *Congressional Record*, July 28, 1981, p. 17695.

34. Ibid., p. 17702.

35. Ibid., p. 17705.

36. Ibid., p. 17700.

37. *National Tourism Policy Act*, H. Rept. 97-107, 97 Cong. 1 sess. (GPO, May 19, 1981), pp. 27–28.

38. P.L. 100-485; Family Support Act of 1988.

39. *Family Support Act*, S. Rept. 100-377, 100 Cong. 2 sess. (GPO, 1988), p. 60.

40. *Department of Education Organization Act of 1979*, S. Rept. 96-49, 96 Cong. 1 sess. (GPO, 1979), p. 17.

41. *Establishing within the Department of the Interior the Position of an Additional Assistant Secretary of the Interior*, H. Rept. 92-166, 92 Cong. 1 sess. (GPO, 1971), p. 3.

42. P.L. 97-325; International Carriage of Perishable Foodstuffs.

43. *Authorization for an Under Secretary of Commerce for Economic Affairs*, H. Rept. 97-391, 97 Cong. 1 sess. (GPO, 1982), p. 3.

44. *Under Secretary of Commerce for Economic Affairs*, Hearings before the Subcommittee on Human Resources of the House Committee on Post Office and Civil Service, 97 Cong. 1 sess. (GPO, 1981), p. 2.

45. *Copyright Office—Fees*, H. Conf. Rept. 97-930, 97 Cong. 2 sess. (GPO, October 1, 1982), pp. 3–4.

46. For two recent compilations of research on the issue, see Oliver E. Williamson, ed., *Organization Theory: From Chester Barnard to the Present and Beyond* (Oxford University Press, 1990), and Walter W. Powell and Paul J. DiMaggio, eds., *The New Institutionalism in Organizational Analysis* (University of Chicago Press, 1991).

47. Michael T. Hannan and John Freeman, "The Population Ecology of Organizations," *American Journal of Sociology*, vol. 82 (March 1977), pp. 929–64.

48. Terry M. Moe, "The Politics of Structural Choice: Toward a Theory of Public Bureaucracy," in Williamson, ed., *Organization Theory*, p. 143.

49. Howard E. Aldrich, *Organizations and Environments* (Prentice-Hall, 1979), p. 265.

50. Paul J. DiMaggio and Walter W. Powell, "The Iron Cage Revisited: Institutional Isomorphism and Collective Rationality in Organizational Fields," in Powell and DiMaggio, eds., *New Institutionalism*, pp. 63–64, 67.

51. Ibid., pp. 74–76.

52. Ibid., pp. 76–77.

53. The only condition federal departments fail to meet involves the degree to which a given organization interacts with the state, a condition that is plainly not relevant to federal thickening since the departments are, in fact, the state.

54. See Jeffrey Pfeffer and Gerald R. Salancik, *The External Control of Organizations: A Resource Dependence Perspective* (Harper and Row, 1978).

55. James Q. Wilson, "On Predicting the Bureaucratization of American Government," in Larry B. Hill, ed., *The State of Public Bureaucracy* (M. E. Sharpe, 1992), p. 213.; to be fair, bureaucratization has occurred at other schools of public affairs too, including the Humphrey Institute at the University of Minnesota, where I reside.

56. Marshall W. Meyer, William Stevenson, and Stephen Webster, *Limits to Bureaucratic Growth* (Hawthorne, N.Y.: Walter de Gruyter, 1985), pp. v–vi; I am grateful to Linda Kaboolian for giving me this citation.

57. Stephen Hess, *Organizing the Presidency*, 2d ed. (Brookings, 1988) p. 5.

58. The deputy assistant layer includes press secretaries, the White House counsel, special advisers, senior consultants, and others; the special assistant layer includes the special counsel.

59. Larry Berman, *The Office of Management and Budget and the Presidency, 1921–1979* (Princeton University Press, 1979), p. 122.

60. For histories of these transitions, see Mosher, *A Tale of Two Agencies*, and Berman, *The Office of Management and Budget and the Presidency*.

61. Although the deputy director for management is paid at executive level II, the position is ranked lower than that on the organization chart.

62. Paul C. Light, *Vice-Presidential Power: Advice and Influence in the White House* (Johns Hopkins University Press, 1984), p. 63.

63. Ibid., p. 9.

64. See G. Calvin Mackenzie, "Radical Makeover: The Post-War Transformation of the American Presidency," paper prepared for delivery at the annual meeting of the American Political Science Association, September 2–5, 1993.

65. Quoted in Walter T. Oleszek, *Majority and Minority Whips of the Senate: History and Development of the Party Whip System in the U.S. Senate*, Sen. doc. 98-45, 98 Cong. 2 sess. (GPO, 1985), p. 28.

66. See Steven S. Smith, *Call to Order: Floor Politics in the House and Senate* (Brookings, 1989), and Burdette Loomis, *The New American Politician: Ambition, Entrepreneurship, and the Changing Face of Political Life* (Basic, 1988).

67. Oleszek, *Majority and Minority Whips*, pp. 6–14.

68. Smith, *Call to Order*, p. 233.

69. For a history of the staff growth, see Steven S. Smith and Christopher J. Deering, *Committees in Congress*, 2d ed. (CQ Press, 1990).

70. The structures listed in the table reflect an amalgam of sources: the *Congressional Directory*, published by the U.S. Congress Joint Committee on Printing, the *Congressional Staff Directory*, published by Staff Directories, Ltd., and the *Congressional Yellow Book*, published by Monitor Publishing. The three sources are rarely in accord—titles are sometimes just slightly different, sometimes dramatically so. As with all the material in this book, therefore, the charts are best taken as broad indicators of trends, not absolutes.

71. Morris P. Fiorina, *Congress: Keystone of the Washington Establishment* 2nd ed. (Yale University Press, 1989), pp. 120–21.

72. The division director layer was chosen as the bottom of the pyramid because it appears to be more consistent across the departments in the 1980 and 1992 *Yellow Books*.

73. The budget and personnel data are drawn from the *Budget of the United States Government, Fiscal Years 1980 and 1992* (GPO, 1990 and 1992); data on work-force demographics from General Accounting Office, *The Changing Workforce: Demographic Issues Facing the Federal Government*, GAO/GGD-92-38 (March 1992), or from the OPM central personnel data file materials presented earlier; data on leadership from Jeffrey E. Cohen, *The Politics of the U.S. Cabinet: Representation in the Executive Branch, 1789–1984* (University of Pittsburgh Press, 1988).

74. Peter Blau, "A Formal Theory of Differentiation in Organizations," *American Sociological Review*, vol. 35 (April 1970), pp. 201–18.

75. See William McKinley, "Decreasing Organizational Size: To Untangle or Not to Untangle," *Academy of Management Review*, vol. 17 (January 1992), pp. 112–23; see also Jeffrey D. Ford, "The Administrative Component in Growing and Declining Organizations: A Longitudinal Analysis," *Academy of Management Journal*, vol. 23 (December 1980), pp. 615–30, who examines changes in twenty-four school districts over a ten-year period.

76. Anthony Downs, *Inside Bureaucracy* (Little, Brown, 1967), p. 163.

Chapter 6

1. Hugh Heclo, *A Government of Strangers: Executive Politics in Washington* (Brookings, 1977), p. 82.

2. I am grateful to Martin Wheatley, a British Treasury employee who spent 1993–94 as a United Kingdom Fellow at the Humphrey Institute, for his thoughtful insights on these issues.

3. Al Gore, *From Red Tape to Results: Creating a Government That Works Better and Costs Less*, report of the National Performance Review (Government Printing Office, 1993), p. 95.

4. S. 101, *Executive Organization Reform Act of 1993*, 103 Cong. 1 sess.

5. The *Base Closure and Realignment Act of 1988* can be found at P.L. 100-536.

6. See Paul C. Light, *Still Artful Work: The Continuing Politics of Social Security Reform*, 2d ed. (McGraw-Hill, 1995), for the story of the commission.

7. For a quick history of the base-closure and other recent commissions, see Natalie Hanlon, "Military Base Closings: A Study of Government by Commision," *University of Colorado Law Review*, vol. 62 (Spring 1991), pp. 331–64.

8. Quoted in David S. Broder, "Bruised Egos Shouldn't Block Progress on Redesigning Government at Last," *St. Paul Pioneer Press*, March 29, 1993, p. A-14.

9. See, for example, Senator John Glenn's *Excellence in Presidential Appointments Act of 1992*, which was originally proposed as an amendment to S. 20, the *Chief Financial Officers Act of 1990*.

10. For a history of the reorganization authority, see Louis Fisher and Ronald C. Moe, "Presidential Reorganization Authority: Is It Worth the Cost?" *Political Science Quarterly*, vol. 96 (Summer 1981), pp. 301–18.

11. Congress ratified all of the reorganizations under the old process in P.L. 98-532. I am grateful to my research assistant Kirk Johnson for his work pulling together the more recent history.

12. Fisher and Moe, "Presidential Reorganization Authority," p. 315.

13. Harvey C. Mansfield, "Federal Executive Reorganization: Thirty Years of Experience," *Public Administration Review*, vol. 29 (July–August 1969), p. 341.

14. Fisher and Moe, "Presidential Reorganization Authority," pp. 317–18.

15. National Academy of Public Administration, *Modernizing Federal Classification: An Opportunity for Excellence* (July 1991).

16. Gore, *From Red Tape to Results*, p. 24.

17. See Samantha Durst, Patricia Patterson, and John Ramsden, "Impacts of Traditional Explanatory Factors on Average Grade Increases in U.S. Cabinet-Level Departments," *Public Administration Review*, vol. 49 (July–August 1989), p. 368.

18. See, for example, G. Calvin Mackenzie, ed., *The In-and-Outers: Presidential Appointees and Transient Government in Washington* (Johns Hopkins University Press, 1987), which shows what political and career executives value most in their jobs.

Chapter 7

1. I am grateful to my three research assistants on this task, Shannon Swangstue, Kirk Johnson, and Leslie Bruvold, for their work in collecting the basic information and then repeatedly cleaning it against other sources.

2. The core tables do not include the legions of special assistants, confidential aides, and personal attendants who orbit around senior presidential appointees and sometimes act as if they are "in line" between their bosses and the rest of the department.

3. Committee on Governmental Affairs, U.S. Senate, or Committee on Post Office and Civil Service, U.S. House of Representatives, *United States Government Policy and Supporting Positions* (GPO, 1960, 1964, 1968, 1973, 1980, 1984, 1988, and 1992). Hereafter referred to as the Plum Book.

4. The first Plum Book was actually published in 1893, U.S. Senate, *Civil List: Method of Appointment and Term and Tenure of Office*, 52 Cong. 2 sess., Senate Misc. Doc. 61 (GPO, 1893), and has been updated in one form or another ever since.

5. Only five times in the core tables does a title outrank its salary level. The decisions to elevate the title were based on the notion that title is the more important indicator of status when pay and title do not match. Two instances involve two under secretary positions paid at the deputy secretary II rank—the first in State from 1960 to 1968, the second in Transportation from 1968 to 1972. Both were kept in the under secretary layer in the core tables until the titles caught up with the pay. The third is the deputy attorney general, paid at the under secretary III rank until 1972 but placed in the deputy secretary layer until pay caught up with its title. The fourth involves all general counsels (GCs) and inspectors general (IGs), who were placed at the assistant secretary level regardless of pay. Even though a handful of both were once paid at executive level V, the title was assumed to be equivalent for all. The fifth instance involves the under secretaries of the army, navy, and air force. From 1960 through 1992, all were at executive level IV. Because assistant secretaries were also paid at level IV, the under secretaries at the higher layer to draw a clear distinction in the hierarchy.

6. Office of the Federal Register, National Archives and Records Administration, *United States Government Manual* (GPO, selected years); the first editions were published under sponsorship of the National Emergency Council through the United States Information Service and are quite elegant, complete with fold-out organization charts for every department and agency of government.

7. The Plum Book has been published in its modern form since 1960. The 1935 and 1952 numbers are for the assistant secretary compartment and above. All of the 1935 data were confirmed against Arthur W. MacMahon and John D. Millett, *Federal Administrators: A Biographical Approach to the Problem of Departmental Management* (Columbia University Press, 1939).

8. The regional office hierarchy outside Washington is still a mystery, although the Yellow Book publishers launched a regional directory in the mid-1980s that has gained increasing stature.

Index

Aberbach, Joel, 56, 57–58
Accountability: capacity-based, 140; compliance-based, 86–87, 140–41; creating new positions for, 139–41; diffusion of, 62–64, 86–87, 166, 169; performance-based, 140
Adams, Sherman, 46
Age, institutional, 35–36, 106–08
Agencies: creation of, 11–12, 18, 142–45; elevation to cabinet, 11, 135–36; Hoover commission proposals, 38, 40; longevity of, 4–5
Agriculture, Department of: inspectors general in, 24; upper management growth, 11
Aldrich, Howard, 148–49
Alter-ego deputies, 20, 173
Appointment/confirmation process: appointee turnover, 69; chief of staff position, 21, 22; delays in, 67–69; Hoover commission recommendations, 40; in National Performance Review, 36; nonmerit appointments, 45–46; political affiliation and tendencies in, 170; political control through, 88–94; presidential use of, 21; Reagan administration, 56–57; Senior Executive Service, 10; senior management, 8; as source of career executives, 167; Willis Directive on, 46
Are Government Organizations Immortal?, 6
Arnold, Peri, 49, 53–54, 59
Ash, Roy, 49, 50, 153

Blau, Peter, 162
Blinder, Alan, 72
British government, 171
Brooks, Jack, 144
Brown, Harold, 138
Brownlow, Louis, 30
Brownlow committee, 37–38, 54
Buchanan, John, 134–35
Budgeting process: control of thickening in, 162, 163; departmental hierarchy for, 80–81, 84–85

Bush administration: government reform efforts, 9–10, 34, 118; initial appointments, 67; organizational management in, 58–59; Senior Executive Service in, 10, 114

Career development, in civil service, 72–73
Carter administration: initial appointments, 67; organizational management, 53–54; under secretary of commerce for travel and tourism, 142–44; Senior Executive Service in, 54–55; thickening of government in, 29, 97
Causes of thickening, 30, 31, 97, 98, 169–70; accountability thickening, 139–41; advice thickening, 141–42; Brownlow committee in, 37–38; competition, 30, 145–47, 158–61; Congress vs. president in, 108–16; contracting practices in, 16–18; creation of cabinet departments in, 98–103; federal managers in, 122–25; implications for reform, 30, 96; inner/outer cabinet structure and, 103–08; interest groups in, 125–27; organizational tendency, 147–52, 170–71; presidential motivation in, 92; thickening of society and, 153, 170; workload thickening, 137–38
Chief financial officer, 99, 132
Chief(s) of staff: as management, 21; origins of, 21, 105; president's, 44; role of, 21–23
Civil service: distrust of, 47; grade inflation in, 122–23, 124; job classification system, 179–80; Nixon administration, 50–53; political influence in, 50–51, 56–57; presidential control of, 46; recruitment and retention, 72–73; recruitment thickening, 133–34; schedule C appointments, 45–46, 92; state to federal employee ratio, 17
Civil Service Commission, 122, 123
Civil Service Reform Act of 1978, 10, 54

211